The Deconstruction of Literature

T H E

Deconstruction of Literature

Criticism after Auschwitz

David H. Hirsch

BROWN UNIVERSITY PRESS

Published by University Press of New England
Hanover and London

BROWN UNIVERSITY PRESS

Published by University Press of New England, Hanover, NH 03755

© 1991 by Trustees of Brown University

All rights reserved

Printed in the United States of America   5 4 3 2 1

CIP data appear at the end of the book

Contents

TO JOE AND MICHÈLE,

HELENE AND GARY

Acknowledgments

I have been blessed with friends who are not only talented but generous. Although they all contributed to whatever may be of value in this book, they should not be held responsible for any intemperance in my writing, which they did their best to curb, nor for errors, which they did their best to eliminate. Gerald Rabkin read the introduction and chapters five through seven at a crucial stage. His laser-beam mind pinpointed problems, and his response encouraged me to continue. Eli Pfefferkorn shared with me both his scholarly expertise on the Holocaust and his personal experience of the death camps; in many a conversation during the summer of 1990 he helped me through a maze of uncertainties, confirming some of my hunches while rejecting others. Herman Eschenbacher, who was with the first wave of troops to land on the Normandy beachhead (but who will not like my mentioning it), listened and responded to my ideas and proved a great source of first-hand information about the European war zone. I wish to express my deep gratitude to Cleanth Brooks, a humanist in the most positive sense of the word, who journeyed to Providence to persuade me to collect my essays in a book. His caring meant a great deal to me. Claire Rosenfield read my essays and criticized them severely but always sensitively and constructively. Over coffee at Peaberry's, Laurent Ditman shared with me his knowledge of French character and the French cultural scene; I am also indebted to him for helping me to translate passages from Vladimir Jankelevitch's *L'Imprescriptible,* quoted in the text. I am thankful to Barton St. Armand for his collegiality and for keeping an eye out for information he thought would interest me. Grace Farrell gave me support and good advice. Linda Grasso and Charlie Watts read a large portion of the manuscript and favored me with some important positive feedback; Linda also suggested some helpful stylistic changes. Tom Rockmore and Joseph Margolies also provided me with positive feedback and helpful criticism. To George Core I am much in debt for sending me books to discuss, for making available to me the pages of the *Sewanee Review,* and for not hesitating to print opinions that cut against the grain of academic criticism. I would also like to thank Ernest Sosa for keeping the manuscript alive.

Two debts must be saved for last because I haven't the words to express them. George Monteiro has been my daily companion for more than thirty years, has listened to my lucubrations with great patience and understanding, and has enhanced my ideas continually. They say that when Larry Bird is on a basketball court, he makes all the other players play better. George is a Larry Bird of intellect; he makes everyone around him think more clearly. He makes you see things as you haven't seen them before. George was a part of every phase of this book.

My wife, Roslyn, has made a unique contribution to each phase of this book. When I first met her, she told not only a thousand and one tales, but more like a thousand tales a night about the experiences of a young Jewish girl in Poland under Soviet, then Nazi, occupation: the Marxist indoctrination, the expulsion from her home, the ghettos, the *aktzias,* the flight from imminent extermination, the hiding, the Poles who risked their lives to help and those who wouldn't, wanderings across the face of a disfigured post-war European landscape, displaced-persons camps—several lifetimes within a span of fifteen years. A whaling ship was Ishmael's Yale and Harvard: Roslyn gave me an education far more profound than Yale and Harvard ever could. Our son, Joe, articulated my feelings in a talk he called "The Surviving Memory" that he gave at a Holocaust memorial service; I would like to print it here because it may help readers to understand the thinking and feeling that informed this book.

I did not face the gas or the guns or the fences, but I am the son of the nightmare. When guilt addresses me from a distance and asks where I was when my mother was running from her childhood, I can only whimper in the shadow of my culture. Should I be proud of the adversity that she faced? I am lost between grudge and forgiveness . . . there is no enemy in this situation that I can face and defeat. I fabricate my wounds and pick at the scabs in the drowning of my dreams. Paranoia is a word . . . fear is a feeling.

Many of the hells in which I wander are clearly related to the confinement of American middle-class isolation, the choice or the destiny of Jews to separate their community from the at-large cultural attitude. This is a nation of masses, but where are the Jews among this crowd? Why aren't they comfortably set within the stereotype-circle, why aren't they in the dive bars, in the Midwest, why aren't they scattered in the rural dust or the railroad graveyards where the American hero-myths rest? Has the Holocaust cut our social circulation with the rusted razor of guilt, or did we settle in wide-eyed fear in the urban crowds to hide, only to resurface in the demonic eye of public opinion? This is not to condemn, not at all—I can't condemn my origins, but I am afraid of being noticed. I want to slip in and out of a crowd as a member.

My mother the survivor does not consider herself a member. She grabs onto things she loves, and fears letting go. She has not let me go. I am twenty years old and cannot let go. I feel confined to rationalizations I learned early in life. I feel unable to cope with change, and, as you have guessed, I have a tendency to generalize irresponsibly, and my awareness of this condition does not help me to defeat it. I have trouble facing the simple boundaries of satisfaction and frustration. Wealth cannot calm the tremors of insecurity. It is not good to forget, but my memory's growth has been stunted by stories of a fearful young Polish peasant girl named Rózia who was stuck in a merciful non-Jew's attic for so long that when she got out along with her mother, neither of them could walk. Her mother's iron-fisted discipline took a place in her jumbled mind and brought her an exaggerated sense of order without a key to the development of happiness. The attic I mentioned has become my brain. What in the name of the landlord of hell am I trying to remember?

Some of the material in this book appeared earlier, often in different form. In some cases, several previously published articles have been joined together to make up a single chapter. Often material was cut from the original, and in some cases I have made substantial revisions. But in all cases I have sought to preserve the spirit of the original. The Introduction, "Postmodernist Criticism and American Literary History," was first published in *Sewanee Review*, 99 (January 1991), 40–60. Chapter 1, "Penelope's Web," is made up of material from essays published in 1979, 1982, and 1983, as follows: "Signs and Wonders," *Sewanee Review*, 77 (Fall 1979), 628–638; "Penelope's Web," *Sewanee Review*, 90 (January 1982), 119–131; "The New Theoreticism I," *Sewanee Review*, 91 (Summer 1983), 417–425. Some of the material in the essay was also presented at a session on "Modern Theoretical Criticism and American Literature," at the December 1989 meeting of the Modern Language Association in Washington, D.C., chaired by Leo Lemay. Chapter 2, "Paul de Man and the Politics of Deconstruction," which was first published in *Sewanee Review*, 96 (Spring 1988), 330–338, is included here in substantially the same form as the original. Chapter 3, "Martin Heidegger and Pagan Gods," appeared essentially as it is here under the title, "After Alien Gods," in *Sewanee Review*, 96 (Fall 1988), 714–724; Chapter 8, "Marxism, Humanism, and Literature in the University," was originally published in *Imbroglio: A Journal of Misunderstandings*, ed. John Lavitt (Providence, 1989), 24–30. Chapter 10, "Metaphors and Structures," contains material from essays that appeared in 1972, 1977, 1981, as follows: "Linguistic Structure and Literary Meaning," *Journal of Literary Semantics* (December 1972); "Deep Metaphors and Shallow Structures," *Sewanee Review*, 85 (Winter 1977), 153–166; "Dwelling in Metaphor," *Sewanee Review*, 89 (Winter, 1981), 95–110. Chapter 11, "Speech Acts and the Language of Literature," was originally published as "Speech Acts and Fluid Language," in *Journal of Literary Semantics* (Winter 1976), 15–30. Chapter 12, "Postmodern or Post-Auschwitz: The Case of Poe," was originally presented at a conference on "Arthur Gordon Pym and Contemporary Criticism," Martha's Vineyard, May 19–22, 1988.

May 1991   D.H.

The Deconstruction of Literature

INTRODUCTION

Derailing American Literary History

The chapters on literary theory that comprise the bulk of this book were written in response to various literary theories and philosophies that emerged during the seventies and eighties; as a consequence, the thesis of the book developed organically. I did not start with a thesis to which "facts" later had to be accommodated, nor did I look back across a span of years, assess what had happened in the field of literary theory, and then determine to construct a narrative of these events culminating in a "present" moment leading to predictable future developments. The thread that runs through all the essays is a skeptical attitude toward what I took to be exaggerated claims of profundity in contemporary critical theories.[1]

In my detailed analyses of theoretical texts, I pursue a traditional methodology of reading that increasingly runs counter to the exotic modes of reading that go under the rubric of "deconstruction," which we may now recognize for what they are: "antihumanist."[2] I assume in my own readings that it is first necessary to get at the plain sense of a text before looking for more concealed meanings, recognizing that the contemporary tendency is to deny the very existence of "plain sense of a text."[3] In some instances I have applied traditional methods of analyzing texts to the deconstructive readings themselves, thereby deconstructing the deconstructors, so to speak. In my analyses of theoretical and critical texts, I have experimented with testing whether simpler ways of reading can be used to unlock what are presented as more powerful and complicated ways of reading, rather than falling into the current practice of using ostensibly more powerful methods of reading to interpret what are assumed to be texts that, intentionally or otherwise, resist being read or understood or refuse to yield any meaning. Above all, I have tried to be honest and true to myself and the materials being analyzed.

I started writing about literary theory at a time when Anglo-American New Criticism had about run its course. What had started as an innovative method of reading literary works creatively had, in all too many instances, declined into a robotic and repetitious exercise in counting images and demonstrating paradoxes for their own sake. A clear signal that the end was at hand for the New Criticism was the proliferation of essays whose goal seemed to be nothing more than adding up various kinds of "imagery" without regard to their importance or how the images functioned in the semantic system of the work. In a liberal society founded on an ideology of revolution and progress, change is always at hand, and one could sense that changes in the practice of literary criticism had become not only desirable but inevitable. Unfortunately, the forerunners of change that came in the form of attacks on the New Criticism were directed not against the particular essays of practical criticism but against such slogans as "the autotelic poem," "the intentional fallacy," and "the affective fallacy"—slogans derived from two theoretical essays that appeared after the innovative and most creative practical criticism had been done. In effect, the great essays of the first generation of New Critics went unchallenged and indeed remain unchallenged to this day.

In their most important work, the first generation of New Critics was not bound by the theories or the slogans that later developed around their essays. For example, in what turned out to be a seminal essay on *The Ancient Mariner*, Robert Penn Warren, far from limiting himself to an analysis of what he considered an autotelic poem, took as the starting point of his essay a historical-biographical bit of information: Mrs. Barbauld's comment, reported in *Table Talk*, to the effect that the poem had two defects—"it was improbable and it had no moral." This bit of context became the seed out of which the monograph grew, for Warren went on to state that one of the purposes of his essay was to ". . . establish that *The Ancient Mariner* does embody a statement, . . . [which is its] theme, . . . [and] that the statement which the poem does ultimately embody is thoroughly consistent with Coleridge's basic theological and philosophical views as given to us in sober prose, and that . . . the theme is therefore 'intended.' " [4] Warren's statement is clear enough to stand without comment, but the misinformation about an alleged New Critical denial of context, intention, and statement has been repeated so often that Warren's explicitly stated position may be worth summarizing. He allows that the poem makes a statement, that it is generated out of an authorial intention, and that this intention can be confirmed by recourse to Coleridge's other writings, that is by recourse to statements that Coleridge made outside the poem.

Neither is it precisely accurate to say, as has often been alleged, that the New Critics eliminated the reader. Once again I should like to cite a passage by Robert Penn Warren, often considered, along with Cleanth Brooks, the ultimate New Critic, from his essay, "The Themes of Robert Frost" (1947): "Further, and more importantly, the perfect intuitive and immediate grasp of a poem in the totality of its meaning and structure—the thing we desire—may come late rather than early—on the fiftieth reading rather than on the first. Perhaps we must be able to look forward as well as back as we move through the poem—be able to sense the complex of relationships and implications—before we can truly have that immediate grasp." [5] This assertion, describing interpretation as a "back-and-forth" process, anticipates what later became one of the fundamental tenets of both hermeneutics (the "hermeneutic circle," as it was called) and reader-response theory.

In 1967 a three-pronged attack was launched on the New Criticism; two of the attackers were American critics and the third was a European. In Anglo-American theory the attacks came from both a "reader-response" critic, and an "intentionalist" critic. The first claimed to restore the reader and the latter to restore the author to critical practice. My contention was and remains that the attacks were, for the most part, directed against straw men, since a careful reader of the work of the original New Critics would have perceived that neither reader nor author had actually been removed from the reading process. Nor were the New Critics unaware that reading was indeed a process. Moreover, it seemed that the new theories did not greatly advance our understanding of literature in particular or the ways in which we arrive at an understanding of written utterances in general. In discussing the work of Stanley Fish, who spearheaded the effort to restore the reader, I demonstrated that not only was such a restoration unnecessary, but that Fish himself had not managed to rid himself of the shackles of New Critical methods of reading, except that in his New Critical readings he adopted a slightly different rhetorical posture. That is, what Fish actually did in his criticism was to seek out image patterns, ironies, and paradoxes, just as the New Critics had instructed him, but instead of attributing "meanings" to an author or a text, he attributed meanings to the mind in the act of reading, thus institutionalizing the process described by Warren in the Frost essay.[6] As his theory of reader response evolved, Fish eventually came to the conclusion that image patterns, irony, paradoxes, and the unity of the text were all in the mind of the reader, not in the text itself, and this ultimately led him to claim that the text did not exist at all.[7] There is also a European wing of reader-responsism, represented most prominently in the United States by Wolfgang Iser and Hans Robert Jauss. Taking its impetus from Heideggerian-Gadamerian theories of hermeneutics, the European school presents some special problems that I shall touch on here in chapters 6 and 7.

The antipode of American reader response theory is intentionalist theory. As propounded by E. D. Hirsch, Jr., the theory developed the position that every text has a single fixed meaning and that this fixed meaning is the "author's intention." In the course of developing his theory, Hirsch demolished the "hermeneutic" theories of Hans Georg Gadamer, a student of Martin Heidegger. He demonstrated convincingly the many insoluble contradictions and inconsistencies in Gadamer's attempt to apply Heideggerian philosophy to methods of reading, and to establish that the meaning of a text is the reader's interpretation of that text, while affirming at the same time that there are limits to the possible number of readings.[8] The debate between reader-responsists and intentionalists was intense, but when the dust had settled it became clear that the rage for theory itself presented some serious difficulties, because the theorists were all too often inclined to paint themselves into a corner. The methods of the reader-responsists, for example, led them to the dead-end position that there was no text at all, only interpretations. Intentionalism, on the other hand, led to the position that there could be only one valid interpretation of any given text. If both these claims could be established by clever arguing, both were nevertheless counterintuitive, inconsistent with experience, and abhorrent to reason. What these extreme claims did was to raise unresolvable epistemological problems that had long been standard philosophers' dilemmas: Did meaning, if indeed there was such a thing at all, reside in the mind of the author, in the text, or in the perceiving mind? Hence, Penelope's web: what the intentionalists wove by day, reader-responsists unraveled at night.

One other aspect of the attacks on the New Criticism was surprising. One would have expected that the restoration of either author or reader to the autotelic work of art would constitute a humanizing gesture; that is, one would have expected to see the "autonomous poem" of the New Criticism replaced with a more "human" poem. One would have thought that the two positions taken together might have represented a return to the human-centered poetics of Wordsworth in his 1800 preface to *The Lyrical Ballads*: "Who is the poet? To whom does he address himself? And what language is to be expected of him?—He is a man speaking to men: a man, it is true, endowed with more lively sensibility, more enthusiasm and tenderness, . . . who rejoices more than other men in the spirit of life that is in him. . . ." But reader-response and intentionalist theories of reading, even taken together, did not return literature to a more human dimension, to a condition in which the literary work would once again become an act of passional thinking in which one human being addresses another.[9] If anything, the attacks on New Criticism were more inimical to what was "human" in literature than the New Criticism was accused of being. Hence, in an essay engaging Wimsatt and Beardsley on "the affective fallacy," Stanley Fish concluded about his own reader-oriented approach:

Becoming good at the method [of Fishian reading] means asking the question
"what does that . . . do?" with more and more awareness of the probable
(and hidden) complexity of the answer; that is, with a mind more and more
sensitized to the workings of language. In a peculiar and unsettling (to theorists) way, it is a method which processes its own user, who is also its only
instrument.[10]

Fish replaces what he takes to be a depersonalized method of reading with a robotic reader who is conceived as an "instrument . . .
processed by the method." This seems to constitute a change without
difference.

   E. D. Hirsch, presumably at the opposite end of the spectrum
from Fish, presents us with a robotized author instead of a robotized
reader:

The discipline of interpretation is founded, then, not on a methodology of
construction but on a logic of validation. . . . In the earlier chapters of this
book, I showed that only one interpretive problem can be answered with
objectivity: "What, in all probability, did the author mean to convey?" In this
final chapter, I have tried to show more particularly wherein that objectivity
lies. It lies in our capacity to say on firm principles, "Yes, that answer is valid"
or "No, it is not."[11]

As I have argued in my discussions of reader-response criticism, from
a practical standpoint it does not seem to matter greatly whether we
put the question as, "What, in all probability, did the author mean
to convey?" or "What, in all probability, does the text mean to convey?" As in reader-response criticism, we have a change without a
difference.

   Both of these attacks on "The New Criticism" were regressive,
though neither was as regressive as the third prong of the 1967 attacks,
which was more totalistic and more destructive; in order to show how
and why these particular attacks on the New Criticism were retro-
grade, I must take my narrative both forward and backward at the
same time. We must go forward from 1967 to a book by Frank Lentricchia published in 1980 that was intended to announce the passing
of the New Criticism and celebrate the development and eventual ascendancy, during the fifties and sixties, of Continental (i.e., French

and German) thinking (or, to be more precise, of French cultural criticism, a critical mode of analysis heavily influenced by the thinking of Karl Marx and Martin Heidegger—as Heidegger boasted, "When the French want to think they have to think in German."). The ascendancy of the Franco-German school was characterized by a swift series of transitions from structuralism, to semiotics, to hermeneutics, to poststructuralism, deconstruction, and postmodernism.

Lentricchia's scenario leaves no doubt who are the good guys and who are the bad. The sophisticated Continental theorists are the former; the black-hats are made up of naive Americans who do not welcome Continental developments wholeheartedly, partly because they do not understand them and partly because these American critics are hopelessly reactionary. American academics who were not thrilled by the Modern Language Association awarding the 1975 James Russell Lowell Prize to Jonathan Culler's *Structuralist Poetics* are characterized by Lentricchia as having uttered ". . . repeated cries of outrage and disbelief directed at the news of the latest French barbarism," though no evidence is ever given to support such a characterization. We are advised only that the cries could not help being overheard by "anyone working in a literary department (and particularly in an English department) in the late sixties and early seventies." [12]

As it happens, Lentricchia himself was not entirely happy with the award because, in his view, Culler's book was a betrayal of structuralism: "Culler's book has made structuralism safe for us." [13] Furthermore, according to Lentricchia, "Culler's book . . . performs the intellectually useful act of telling English-speaking critics what they need to know about formidable Continental sources of structuralist thinking, while at the same time providing the comforting reassurance that the governing conceptual framework of structuralism may be safely ignored." [14] Lentricchia is troubled because he takes Culler to be helping the forces of reaction to co-opt the revolution. I am not so much concerned with whether or not Lentricchia is right in his description of Culler's book and its presumed effects. What I want to stress is that though Lentricchia differs with Culler on certain details of the structuralist enterprise, he is, nevertheless, committed to the notion that in poststructuralism (mainly, for Lentricchia, poststructuralism of the Foucauldian, and, to some extent, of the Barthesian, variety) lies salvation. J. G. Merquior noted in 1985 that "The literature on structuralism and post-structuralism continues to grow, though there are signs (nowhere more visible than in France) of their decline as intellectual fashions. Yet most discussions are written in a vein of uncritical acceptance, the experts here tending to act as votaries."[15] While it would not be accurate to say that Lentricchia writes about poststructuralist theory "in a vein of uncritical acceptance," it is nonetheless the case that he is a votary who celebrates poststructuralism and ultimately Foucauldian "genealogical" historicism for its bitter hostility to the liberal-democratic concepts of the integrity of the individual self and the inviolability of inalienable human rights.

Lentricchia, I believe, was able to arrive at his rather distorted view of literary and cultural history by performing what the deconstructionists themselves would call a mammoth "erasure." While devoting three hefty chapters to developments of the fifties and sixties in Europe—the triumph of structuralism, poststructuralism, deconstruction, and Heideggerian and Marxist ideology—Lentricchia passes over the New Criticism in a single chapter devoted mainly to Northrop Frye's *The Anatomy of Criticism*. Perhaps he felt that the story of the eclipse of the New Criticism had already been told, but the result of the imbalance in Lentricchia's narrative is to create the impression that the New Criticism was productive only of "readings," and that the literary-cultural condition in the United States in the fifties and sixties was moribund. In fact, this was not at all the case. During the postwar years, American literature and culture experienced an efflorescence fueled by New Critical readings of nineteenth-century writers who had initially been given a new life by F. O. Matthiessen's *American Renaissance*.[16] Returning GIs, who went to college and then into Ph.D. programs on the GI Bill, participated in a rediscovery of American literature. Not surprisingly, these returning GIs brought with them a renewed sense of optimism. They believed, and not without reason, that they had contributed to saving a large part of the world not only from tyranny but from Nazism, with its culture of death and genocide implemented by means of bureaucracy and advanced technology.

In glancing backward to the post-World War II period, we can now see that American liberal humanism embarked on a decade of renewal that was to create greater opportunities for women and minorities, not only in academia but in the culture as a whole. Though it was not fully apparent at the time, in this decade a "new birth of freedom" was taking place, and the groundwork was being laid for the civil rights movement and for a wider and more meaningful participation of women in the political process and in the public life of the nation. This new birth of freedom was launched with the appearance in the mid fifties of a number of seminal New Critical books,[17] and though New Criticism was primarily a literary-critical movement that presumably advanced the cause of the autonomous poem, nevertheless the rediscovery of the literature through New Critical readings was accompanied by the introduction and development of American Studies programs intended to encourage the study of American literature in a cultural and historical context.[18] The postwar analyses of the literary works of American writers, building on Matthiessen's enabling study, tended to reaffirm enlightened values of freedom, human rights, and the sanctity of the individual human being embodied in the Declaration of Independence and the Bill of Rights, and in some instances sought to reconcile American optimism and the American belief in progress and human perfectibility with a new knowledge of "darkness" and human tragedy. These studies of the fifties, though not necessarily written by New Critics, all tended to make use of New Critical methods of textual analysis to revalue American literature. Even as broadly based and as sociologically oriented a cultural critique as Leo Marx's *The Machine in the Garden: Technology and the Pastoral Ideal in America* (1967) would not have been conceivable without the New Criticism, and indeed much of the book consists of "close" readings of the New Critical kind.

Those engaged in the study of American literature and culture responded to the limitations of the New Criticism by expanding and moving forward rather than by retrenching, as was the case with European-oriented reader responsists and intentionalists. American criticism in the sixties rediscovered a quintessentially liberating American dual source: Ralph Waldo Emerson and the poet Emerson seemed to be calling for in his essays, Walt Whitman. Emerson's contribution to the American experiment in democracy was to Americanize the aesthetics of the British Romantics and to romanticize (or perhaps spiritualize is a better word) American political theory. As an aesthetic thinker Emerson extended the Coleridgean metaphor of the organic poem. According to Coleridge, the poem was organic because, like a living thing, its unity and wholeness were both dependent on and inseparable from the perfect cohesion of its parts.[19] But for Emerson, the organic metaphor meant that a poem was the penultimate efflorescence of a tree whose roots were the "oversoul" and whose trunk was the mind of the poet: "For it is not meters but a meter-making argument that makes a poem,—a thought so passionate and alive that like the spirit of a plant or an animal it has an architecture of its own, and adorns nature with a new thing."[20] For Emerson, the poet was the conduit through whom the oversoul, or incessant inspiration, flowed.

Emerson's contribution to democratic ideology, like his contribution to aesthetics, was "expansive." He transformed the more or less precise Enlightenment juridical notions of human freedom expressed in the Declaration of Independence, the Constitution, and the Bill of Rights into the optative mode. While the Declaration stated the principles of human equality and the right to "life, liberty and the pursuit of happiness," and while the Bill of Rights was intended to restrain the state's power over the individual, Emerson proclaimed "transcendental" freedom and asserted that every individual contained within himself or herself a potential for unlimited development. For Emerson, humanity was still an ongoing experiment: "Man," he declared, "is the dwarf of himself. Once he was permeated and dissolved by spirit."[21] Emerson's governing metaphor was the medieval image of God as a circle whose center was everywhere and whose circumference was nowhere. He opened his essay "Circles" with the ringing annunciation: "The eye is the first circle; the horizon which it forms is the second; and throughout nature this primary figure is repeated without end. It is the highest emblem in the cipher of the world. . . . Every action admits of being outdone. Our life is an apprenticeship to the truth that around every circle another can be drawn; that there is no end in nature, but every end is a beginning; that there is always another dawn risen on mid-noon, and under every deep a lower deep opens."[22]

As an academic phenomenon, the revalorization of Emerson and Whitman culminated in Hyatt H. Waggoner's *American Poets* (1968), a rendering of the centrality of the Emerson-Whitman tradition of American poetry that was visionary in its own right.[23] The Emerson-Whitman revival was a cultural as well as an academic phenomenon. Allen Ginsberg's *Howl* (1956) constituted a turn away from modernist formalism and pessimism to reassert the Whitmanian "barbaric yawp."[24] Everywhere, the old "puritanism" was under attack, nowhere more trenchantly, perhaps, than in Norman O. Brown's *Life Against Death: The Psychoanalytical Meaning of History* (1959). Brown sought to transform a culture of death into a culture of love through an act of psychological liberation, converting the Western mind from an Apollonian into a Dionysian ego. Though Brown drew heavily on insights he found in Freud and Nietzsche, the book was distinctly Emersonian. As the epigraph to his chapter on "The Resurrection of the Body," Brown cited a passage from Henry Miller's *Sunday After the War* (1944):

The cultural era is past. The new civilization, which may take centuries or a few thousand years to usher in, will not be another civilization—it will be the open stretch of realization which all the past civilizations have pointed to. The city, which was the birthplace of civilization, such as we know it to be, will exist no more. . . . The peoples of the earth will no longer be shut off from one another within states but will flow freely over the surface of the earth and intermingle. The worship, investigation and subjugation of the machine will give way to the lure of all that is truly occult. This problem is bound up with the larger one of power—and possession. Man will be forced to realize that power must be kept open, fluid and free. His aim will be not to possess power but to radiate it.[25]

It is perhaps no accident that the diction of Miller's last sentence ("power must be kept open, fluid and free") echoes Whitman's "When Lilacs Last in the Dooryard Bloom'd," where the speaker apostrophizes the consoling song of the bird: "O liquid and free and tender! / O wild and loose to my soul . . ."). Brown's argu-

ment for the Dionysian ego, which had its real-world culmination
in 1969 in the Woodstock "event," anticipated Foucault's Dionysian
manifesto, *Histoire de la folie à l'age classique* (1961) by two years.
One reason, perhaps, for the belatedness of the French in discovering
Dionysianism is that the United States had an indigenous Dionysian
tradition going back to Emerson and Whitman, whereas the French
had to borrow their Dionysianism from Nietzsche. In discussing the
bizarre marriage of an Apollonian structuralism with a Dionysian irrationalism, J. G. Merquior notes that ". . . the best-known instance
of Foucault's Dionysian allegiance is his comment on Descartes's first
Philosophical Meditation in *Histoire de la Folie*. Foucault strives to
demonstrate that Descartes's famous 'evil genius' hypothesis actually
amounts to an arbitrary expulsion of madness from thinking. . . .
Foucault's discussion quickly became a locus classicus of the indict-
ment of rationalism as sheer epistemological 'arrogance.'"[26] Merquior then goes on to discuss Derrida's agreement/disagreement with
Foucault in *Writing and Difference*: "Reason, according to Derrida,
cannot be evaded; all we can do is deconstruct it, undermining its
pretence of clear, stable meanings . . ."[27]

But in a twentieth century context that includes the death camps
and Nazi genocide, both the "Apollonian" and the "Dionysian" present a troubled reality in the context of the Holocaust, for Nazism and
the Nazi genocide took place against a background that discredits
both the Dionysian and the Apollonian. Nazi Germany itself was a
culture gone mad, and we know that Hitler exploited Dionysian tendencies in the German *Volk*. At the same time, Reason was put to use
in organizing a brilliant bureaucratic structure designed to exterminate human beings. The death camp itself is the ultimate example of
Rationalism gone mad, and madness rationalized. Any talk of rationalism and madness that does not attempt to encompass the Nazi
years can only be idle chatter.

By 1968, Theodore Roszak was announcing *The Making of a
Counter Culture*, and in 1970, Charles A. Reich was anticipating *The
Greening of America*. In 1968, Hyatt Waggoner reinstated the centrality of Emerson and Whitman to the tradition of American poetry
and culture, especially their centrality as soul voyagers.

Focusing on Emerson [Waggoner wrote in 1968] seemed to me originally, and still seems, to throw more light on the question of what's American about American poetry than any other approach could have. . . . Our poetry has been, and continues to be, more concerned with nature than with society or culture, and more concerned with the eternal than with the temporal. . . . Deprived of the security offered by place, position, class, creed, and the illusion of a stable, an unchanging society, our poets, like our religious seekers, have had to discover meaning where none is given and test its validity personally. . . . The greatest of [American poets] have turned from society toward theology and metaphysics for their answers to the question [Edward] Taylor was the first to ask, "Lord, Who am I?"[28]

Waggoner went on to indicate how Whitman fulfilled the model of the poet called for by Emerson: "Whitman is our greatest exponent of the individual conceived as containing the possibility of self-transcendence, or growth beyond the determined and known. Like Emerson before him, he refuses to place a limit on the self's possibilities."[29] It is widely accepted that the flowering of the counterculture, with its mixture of religious and secular transcendences, experienced its zenith at Woodstock in 1969. Then history and human limitation started to reassert themselves.

I have presented a brief reminder of the dynamics of American literary and cultural criticism in the context of the fifties and sixties to give some sense of the magnitude of the "erasure" that has been enacted by recent "theorists" and historians of literary and post-structuralist theory. What is clear, I believe, is that American cultural criticism did not need Heidegger and the French antihumanist Heideggerians and Marxists to alert them to the evils and dangers of a postindustrial technological society and to the threat against democracy and the integrity of the individual constituted by a technocratic culture. In fact, the dominance of the cluster of ideas constituted by Marxism-Heideggerism-deconstruction imported from France constituted a serious step backward.

To make this point more strongly, I should like to consider some sentences written by Horace Kallen, an American of the Jewish faith, who came to this country from Germany.[30] Kallen was a progressive humanist whose life style was certainly very unlike that called for by the counterculturists. In 1969, at the age of eighty-seven, he published a tribute to Walt Whitman as the great poet of democracy. Kallen was one of the few, perhaps the only one at that time, who would dare connect Whitman's attitudes toward death to those of the twentieth-century existentialists. For Whitman, Kallen wrote, the years of "the modern" turned out to be the tragic years of the Civil War, but nonetheless, conscious of the fearful death toll taken by that war, "Whitman chanted . . . a paean and prophecy of human progress *en masse*, [of individuals] in equal liberty to form a free society of free men. . . ." Those who had lived through the twentieth century, however,

the talliers of these years of the modern, lived and suffered, still live and suffer . . . evil times. These years are years of the greatest, the bloodiest wars that mankind ever waged; years when cruelty and killing became articles of faith. . . .

Some who became existentialists bet their own lives on resisting this evil; the most celebrated is French Jean-Paul Sartre; others saw in the evil the purpose of an ultimate good; the most celebrated of these is German Martin Heidegger; others rejected it and fled it; the most celebrated of these is Karl Jaspers. All became aware that death was the ultimate issue of their lives.

Kallen then continued:

For Whitman, his role in the war was as momentous as Sartre's in the war against the form of ultimate evil we call Hitlerism. The commander-in-chief of freedom's army became for Whitman, beyond anything a flag could be, the precious symbol of the American Idea, ever thrusting forward to establish as living fact the equal freedom and fellowship of all mankind. "Here," Whitman had written long before, "here is not merely a nation but a teeming nation of nations." America is the race of races. Its poet must be the voice and oracle of their diversity: "The genius of the United States is not best or at most, save always in the common people—their deathless attachment to freedom—the air they have of persons who never knew how it felt to stand in the presence of superiors." Elsewhere our Good Gray Poet had written, "The noble soul rejects any liberty or privilege or wealth that is not open to every other man on the face of the earth." On the battlefields and in the hospitals of the Civil War, Whitman had come face to face with this nobility; he had suffered with its champions and victims the costs of it, and he had grown into a reverent love of Abraham Lincoln as their incarnation, their sacrificial avatar.[31]

It is unlikely that Kallen could have read Waggoner's book before he wrote his own tribute to Whitman. Yet Waggoner the antinomian Christian and Kallen the secular Jew were primarily children of the Enlightenment and humanists. Waggoner found in Whitman the poet of self-transcendence, the ultimate promulgator of the American ideology of what we may call "possibilism" (that is, of the ideology that each human being is a separate and integral individual protected by a Bill of Rights, and yet is, at the same time, a set of infinite and always unfulfilled possibilities). Kallen, ever mindful of the Holocaust and genocide (as a Jew, how could he not be?) focuses on Whitman's painful discovery of human limitation. After his traumatic encounter with death in his ministering to the Civil War wounded, and in the wake of his grief on hearing of the assassination of Lincoln, Whitman could no longer recapture the pure unrestrained joy in living of "Song of Myself." After citing the "Come lovely and soothing Death" passage of "When Lilacs Last in the Dooryard Bloom'd," Kallen comments that

Such now, was to Walt Whitman, the living inwardness of death. Whenever and however death happens, it is self-consummation, it is climax. It is life living itself out, using itself up, converting to joy of life all the fears, the dread and anxiety over loss, defeat, tragedy that so largely flow together in our awareness of death. . . . There is no cure for birth or death, George Santayana advises, save to enjoy the interval of existing. To enjoy it, Walt Whitman declares, is to die living and live dying, by loving.[32]

What Waggoner and Kallen each discovered in Whitman independently, almost at the same time, was not so different after all. The believing Christian and the secular Jew both found in Whitman a rare poet with the courage to face death and human mortality directly; both found consolation in the great bard of democracy, one in a message of love and transcendence, the other in a message of joy and love.[33] What bound them together as enlightened humanists (Christian or secular) surely was stronger than what separated them, and we can imagine them, now, as Melville once imagined himself and Hawthorne:

If ever, my dear Hawthorne, in the eternal times that are to come, you and I shall sit down in Paradise, in some little shady corner by ourselves; and if we shall by any means be able to smuggle a basket of champagne there (I won't believe in a Temperance Heaven), and if we shall then cross our celestial legs in the celestial grass that is forever tropical, and strike our glasses and our heads together, till both musically ring in concert,—then O my dear fellow-mortal, how shall we pleasantly discourse of all the things manifold which now so distress us,—when all the earth shall be but a reminiscence, yea, its final dissolution an antiquity.[34]

Whether from the viewpoint of the counterculture, of Christianity, or of progressive secular humanism, American thinkers of the fifties and sixties who read and loved American literature and American writers were reaffirming the integrity of the individual and were, at the same time, moving toward greater intellectual openness and toward an expansion of American democracy that would result in a greater tolerance for a greater diversity of persons.[35] By ignoring the writings of American humanists in the fifties and sixties, it was possible for Frank Lentricchia to present the influx of literary theory from France during the mid-sixties through the seventies as a great leap forward. To hear Lentricchia tell it, a new world came to term and was born in the period from 1966 to the early seventies:

When in late October of 1966 over one hundred humanists and social scientists from the United States and eight other countries gathered at the Johns Hopkins Humanities Center to participate in a symposium called "The Languages of Criticism and the Sciences of Man," the reigning avant-garde theoretical presences for literary critics in this country were Georges Poulet, . . . and, in the distant background, in uncertain relationship to the critics of consciousness, the forbidding philosophical analyses of Heidegger (*Being and Time*), Sartre (*Being and Nothingness*), and Merleau-Ponty (*The Phenomenology of Perception*).[36]

After explaining why structuralism did not establish itself in this country, Lentricchia then continued, "Sometime in the early 1970s we awoke from the dogmatic slumber of our phenomenological sleep to find that a new presence had taken absolute hold over our avant-garde critical imagination: Jacques Derrida. Somewhat startlingly, we learned that, despite a number of loose characterizations to the contrary, he brought not structuralism but something that would be called 'post-structuralism.' "[37]

This view of poststructuralism (and deconstruction) as a leap forward was to become, if it was not already, the orthodox position. But was the advent of poststructuralism really a move forward or was it a step backward? Thanks to books by J. G. Merquior, Luc Ferry, and Alain Renaut, we are now in a position to see the history of French theory of the sixties from a more authentic and less partisan perspective. Writing an inside narrative, Merquior contextualizes the structuralists and poststructuralists by following their tortuous, labyrinthine passage from structuralism to semiotics to hedonism to nihilism to poststructuralism. In Merquior's account, the tetrarchy (or pentarchy and friends) emerge looking much less weighty and profound than they appeared to American critics.[38]

Ferry and Renaut also contextualize the poststructuralists but they do so less in terms of pure structuralist theory and more in terms of the French student rebellions of 1968, and they focus more intensely on the antihumanist bias of the thinkers (principally Nietzsche, Marx, Freud, and Heidegger) who stand in one degree or another behind the quintet of Lacan-Althusser-Barthes-Derrida-Foucault and their entourage. It is not surprising, given their common ideational origins, that in spite of superficial differences and petty family quarrels, the members of the quintet cluster together to disseminate variations on a few sets of ideas. Among these are the notion of "the dissolution of the self"; the claim that the individual is a "fiction," or that the individual is the creation of bourgeois ideology, or that the "subject" must be deconstructed; the denial of transcendence (or of the transcendent subject); and the belief, derived from Nietzsche and filtered through Heidegger, that there are no facts, only interpretation.[39]

Maintaining the hegemony of post-structuralist-deconstructionist ideology has become more difficult for two reasons. First, the authority of at least three of the four main sources of poststructuralist-deconstructionist ideas—Marx, Freud, and Heidegger—has been seriously diminished in one way or another by scientific, economic, and political developments, and by personal and historical revelations about both Heidegger and Freud. That Marx, Freud, and Heidegger are all discredited is no longer in doubt. We see Marxism in total ruins as an economic system, repudiated everywhere except those places where it is sustained by brutal and murderous repression. Freud's claims for psychoanalysis as a science are now considered ludicrous, the accuracy of his data is seriously in question, and the ailments he diagnosed as "neurotic" (i.e., caused by infantile toilet training and sexual repression) are now considered physiological disorders, treatable with chemical intervention. In the case of Heidegger, his unshakable faith in Nazism, his shameful unwillingness to speak out against Nazism after the war, and his obtuse paralleling of mechanized agriculture with the death camps have made him a laughing stock to all but the most dedicated fanatics.

How seriously can one take a thinker whose thinking reveals to him no difference between mechanized agriculture and the extermination of women and children in order to achieve an ideal of racial and national purity (the second of which, at least, he certainly subscribed to)? In a speech delivered in Bremen in 1949 Heidegger said, "Agriculture is now a motorized food industry, in essence the same as the manufacturing of corpses in the gas chambers and extermination camps, the same as the blockade and starvation of the countryside, the same as the production of the hydrogen bombs."[40] This line of reasoning is enshrined in the thinking of the hermeneutist reader-reception schools and is exactly the line taken by revisionist historian Ernst Nolte. Nolte's basic premise is that history is hermeneutics, that is, all history is interpretation. By recontextualizing Auschwitz, that is by looking at it in a wider context (by decentering it, as the deconstructionists would say), it appears much smaller and more trivial, just another blip of cruelty in the vast history of man's cruelty to man.[41]

The hegemony of deconstruction is faltering as well, because it is becoming increasingly difficult for deconstructionists to continue to reconcile Heidegger's pagan spiritualism with Marxist dialectical materialism. What has emerged from this mixing of ideas is a plethora of contradictions: for example, there is no absolute truth, except the absolute truth that there is no absolute truth; consciousness (the subject) is historically determined, but, at the same time, there is no subject; the subject (read individual self) does not exist, but the deconstructionists must speak and act as if they were individual subjects; the post-structuralists-deconstructionists are opposed to all forms of authority (the authority of the text), except that they claim authority for their own writings (see Derrida's vicious denunciations of anyone who dares to disagree with him).[42] Language, they insist, speaks itself, but they sign their essays and books "Jacques Derrida," "Roland Barthes," etc., not "Monsieur Language." Are they plagiarists, then, or do they believe that language speaks itself, but speaks itself differently through different, and hence unique, individuals?

What is more difficult for even the most dedicated of deconstructionists to explain is why we should want to start rebuilding a postmodern world with two failed philosophies, one that led to the Soviet gulag, and the other that was powerless to reveal Auschwitz as an evil and in fact put itself at the service of an ideology that led to Auschwitz. It is only fair to say that Marx did not foresee, and certainly would not have approved, that his utopian ideas would lead to the Leninist-Stalinist gulag state. Similarly, Nietzsche might not have foreseen and would certainly not have approved of the use to which the Nazis put his ideas. But Heidegger, as we now know from Victor Farias's book, was part of the ideational context (call it a mass psychosis if you will) that led to Auschwitz, and he was encouraged to support Hitler's National Socialism (especially the populist version espoused by Ernst Roehm) by his philosophical beliefs in the spirit of the German *Volk* and in pan-Germanic and ultranationalistic ideas of blood and soil. As theologian Emil Fackenheim puts it, "What the Führer Adolf Hitler did in 1934 and 1935, respectively, to Germans and Jews, was no more than what the *Denker* Martin Heidegger had endorsed in advance when, on November 3, 1933, as rector of Freiburg University, he addressed his students as follows: 'The Führer himself and he alone is German reality and its law, today and henceforth.' . . . The indisputable and undisputed fact is, however, that when he endorsed in advance the Führer's actions as German 'reality' and 'law,' he did so not like countless others impelled by personal fear, opportunism, or the hysteria of the time, but rather deliberately and *with the weight of his philosophy behind it.*" [43] Hans Jonas stated the connection between Nazism and Heideggerian philosophy most succinctly: "But as to Heidegger's being, it is an occurrence of unveiling, a fate-laden happening upon thought: so was the Führer and the call of German destiny under him: an unveiling of something indeed, a call of being all right, fate-laden in every sense: neither then nor now did Heidegger's thought provide a norm by which to decide how to answer such calls—linguistically or otherwise. . . . Heidegger's own answer is, to the shame of philosophy, on record and, I hope, not forgotten." [44]

But the French intellectuals, who have chosen to demonstrate that they bear no grudge against the Nazis by letting themselves think in Heidegger's shadow, have endeavored to make us forget. Undoubtedly Heidegger's total obtuseness on the issue of Nazism as a culture of death, genocide, and enslavement, even after the war and when the obscenity of the death camps was well known, is most damaging to his reputation as a thinker. When Herbert Marcuse wrote to Heidegger on August 28, 1947, asking him to take an unequivocal "stand against . . . the identification of you and your work with Nazism. . . ," Heidegger answered, in part, that ". . . your letter just shows how difficult a dialogue is with people who have not been in Germany since 1933 and who evaluate the beginning of the National Socialist movement from the perspective of the end." To which Marcuse responded, "We knew, and I myself have seen, that the beginning already harbored the end; it was the end. Nothing has been added that was not already there in the beginning." [45] Is it possible that in 1948 Heidegger was still unaware that for some people, staying in Germany after 1933 meant a free ticket to Auschwitz, and is it to so forgetful a thinker that we wish to entrust our destiny?

I

Deconstruction in Its European Setting

CHAPTER ONE

Penelope's Web

In turning away from the urgent moral dilemmas posed by writers who bore witness to an ugly European past, and in subjugating themselves to the ideational structures that had helped to create that past, literary theorists inevitably committed themselves to trivializing not only literature, but life itself. We may permit Penelope's loom to stand as the paradigm metaphor for contemporary literary theorizing. What one critic (or "school" of critics) weaves by day, another unravels at night. Nor can we console ourselves with the notion that this weaving and unweaving constitute a dialectic, since no forward movement takes place. Nevertheless, the theory industry prospers, never completing the robe, never even progressing toward completion, just laboring assiduously till the eyes grow dim and the fingers falter.

The debate rages not on practical questions of method, but on questions of ontology, technology, and epistemology—philosophical issues that resolve into various sets of oppositions. When the poles of opposition are phenomenology and structuralism, the debate centers on the locus of "meaning," and by extension on the locus of reality and existence. In the realm of literary criticism, phenomenologists are split further between those who locate "reality" and "world" in the author's consciousness (intention) and those who locate these qualities in the mind of the perceiver/reader (reader-response). The phenomenological intentionalists argue for a "determinate meaning" intended by an author, while the phenomenological subjectivists argue for a "text" as a set of indeterminate meanings that come to life in the mind of reader/perceiver. The structuralist's alternative to author and reader is the language-system out of which texts emerge and in which they are cast. Both "phenomenologists" and "structuralists" are further agitated by the question of "referentiality." Extreme structuralists deny referentiality, as do extreme phenomenologists of both the authorial and responsivist persuasions. What we can "know" when we read, according to the two schools of phenomenological extremists, is either an authorial "intention" or our own consciousness: according to structuralist extremists, we know only something called "difference," distinctions between units of the total system.

That is to say, literary theorists are no longer concerned with such questions as "What does a poem mean?" or "What is a particular poet or novelist saying?" or "What makes a great work of art?" or "How are great works different from mediocre?"[1] Instead, theorists have turned their attention to such questions as "What is meaning?" and "What is language?" Is language (mind you, *language,* not merely poems) self-referential? Is "meaning" to be equated exclusively with "differences" (oppositions?) within language-systems (i.e., the signifier "table" is not designation for a physical entity: it is a sound designating a concept that achieves its value from the fact that it is unlike other sounds within the same system that designate other concepts). The questions are not new, nor is the radically skeptical mindset that generates them. What is new, I believe, is the insistence with which these questions have come to occupy the center of literary-theoretical concerns. More and more the theorists lean toward classically trained philosophical thinkers; they move further and further from poems, stories, novels, and any other work of literary and aesthetic merit.

This leaning toward philosophers, while it may result in the displacement of literary discourse by the discourse of professional philosophers, does not in itself result in more rigorously logical thinking or even in a significant change in critical method. What remains ever constant is that words beget words. And whatever "meaning" may be ontologically, or whatever may be its essence, in the practice of literary criticism "meaning" is always a set of words substituted for a set of words, whether those words (both sets) are an impression of the author's intention, the reader's comprehension, or qualities inherent in the language system itself.

The various strands of contemporary literary criticism and theory (reader responsism, or reception aesthetic; intentionalism; semiotics; deconstruction; indeterminacy; and poststructuralism) all have in common an implacable enmity toward "the New Criticism." Each movement makes a broad dual claim: on the one hand to be moving inexorably forward into new realms of knowing, and on the other to be effecting this movement forward by means of a frontal assault on some aspect of New Critical error. Intentionalists, for example, claim to be restoring to literature the author who was so unjustly whisked away by the doctrine of the "intentional fallacy." Reader responsists and reception aestheticists claim to be restoring the reader so precipitately removed by the doctrine of "the affective fallacy." All contingents claim to be doing heroic battle against the alleged New Critical dogma of "the autotelic text." And the most advanced school of critics, who seem to be developing a new doctrine of metadecadence that can be described as nothing less than "theory for theory's sake" or "theory in place of literature," have set themselves in opposition to all interpretation.

Before going into the particulars of the critical schools, I should like to make the point that the fortress New Criticism under attack is actually a convenient house of straw constructed by the new metatheorists themselves. The kind of criticism against which they launch their most furious attack was, by and large, not practiced by the major New Critics. Certainly such initiators of New Critical practice as T. S. Eliot, Cleanth Brooks, Robert Penn Warren, Allen Tate, and John Crowe Ransom were cognizant of author, reader, and historical background. But one of the oddities of the contemporary schools is that they continue to attack the straw-house fortress without ever citing a single New Critical essay, except for "The Intentional Fallacy" and "The Affective Fallacy."

If we look at actual essays written by New Critics, we find that they do not fit into the stereotyped views that have become hardened facts for the New Theoreticists. For example, consider the following questions, posited by Brooks and Warren in the revised version of *Understanding Poetry*, the bible of New Criticism: "What is the feeling which the poet is interested in giving the reader? What does he want the poem to mean to us?" Brooks and Warren here are explicating the anonymous ballad "The Three Ravens." They conceive the poem not as an authorless, readerless autotelic object, but as a meaningful utterance addressed by its anonymous author to a reader. They are clearly interested in presenting the poem as a statement made by a poet that is intended to elicit a response from the reader. Continuing their analysis of the poem, they point out that "the poet does not depend on the kind of general statement which we have given in our prose paraphrase. The material is arranged so that we feel the effect intended without the direct statement." Here we have an instance of the so-called heresy of paraphrase, but not propounded as dogma. Brooks and Warren want to caution the reader not to mistake the paraphrase for the poem. They conceive the prose paraphrase as a necessary crutch that must remain always subordinate to the poem itself. The reason for this is that the "message" communicated by the poet must be experienced by the reader in the temporal process of reading the poem. As Brooks and Warren put it in their concluding sentence: "The poem gives the theme its force."[2] I should add that this analysis of "The Three Ravens" is neither an exceptionally good nor exceptionally bad example of New Critical analysis.

Much as it may seem that I am defending the New Criticism, that is not my point. The new Criticism did have some unfortunate side effects: it may have become a vehicle for cultural and political ideologies we can no longer accept; it may have encouraged excessive intellectual narrowness; it may have privileged certain texts at the expense of others. For such sins the New Criticism is certainly entitled to take its lumps. What is distressing in the present situation, however, is that the contemporary theoreticists do not know what they are talking about and, ironically, instead of correcting the errors of the New Criticism, they are actually canonizing them in grotesquely exaggerated form: the ideologizing, the narrowness, the privileging of certain texts to the detriment of others are all present with a fury in the New Theoreticism. Moreover, the sins that the major New Critics did not commit but are accused of committing, such as concentrating on the autotelic text, are now being committed with a vengeance by the New Theoreticists.

Let us consider what happens when a critic at the subjectivist extreme of the spectrum undertakes an act of criticism. In a flagship essay that has now been printed in four different publications within a decade (first published in 1970), Stanley Fish sets out "to demonstrate the explanatory power of a method of analysis which takes the reader, as an actively mediating presence, fully into account, and which, therefore, has as its focus the 'psychological effects' of the utterance."[3] Fish's claim seems to be that he can explain (give the meaning of) a text (an utterance, a word, sentence, paragraph, poem, etc.) by examining ("focusing on") the "psychological effects" that the "utterance" produces on "the reader." To drop all coyness, I shall assume, in the absence of any assertion to the contrary, that "the reader" is Fish himself and that any given "psychological effect" is a nonrepeatable temporal event that takes place only at the moment of a given reading. Otherwise the power of Fish's method would be predictive rather than explanatory, since he would be making the claim that all readers in the foreseeable future exposed to the same text would have to experience the same specified psychological effect.

Let us see how Fish proceeds, how his "method" focuses on "psychological effect" and how it exercises its explanatory power. Fish chooses to implement his method on a sentence from a seventeenth-century meditation, Thomas Browne's *Religio Medici*. The sentence, which according to Fish "does not open itself up to the questions we usually ask," runs as follows:

> That Judas perished by hanging himself, there is no certainty in Scripture: though in one place it seems to affirm it, and by a doubtful word hath given occasion to translate it; yet in another place, in a more punctual description, it maketh it improbable, and seems to overthrow it. (p. 71)

Before examining Fish's analysis, I would like to point out that the diction with which Fish introduces the sentence ("A sentence that does not open itself up . . .") is characteristic of structuralism rather than reader-response criticism (that is, of objectivist rather than subjectivist critical approaches). The consequence of putting the sentence itself in the position of subject is to give the language system primacy over "the reader." That is, the "questions" seem to be inherent in the text rather than in the reader's response. Were it not for Fish's claim to logical rigor, his lapse would be of small consequence. Under the circumstances, however, his carelessness undermines his claim to logical and rhetorical precision.

Fish begins the analysis by asserting that

> Ordinarily, one would begin by asking "what does this sentence mean?" or "what is it about?" or "what is it saying?" all of which preserve the objectivity of the utterance. For my particular purposes, however, this particular sentence has the advantage of not saying anything. That is, you can't get a fact out of it which would serve as an answer to any one of these questions. (p. 71)

On several counts Fish's analysis is not only careless but unacceptable, even as reader-response criticism. He does not mention that Thomas Browne's sentence would strike an untrained twentieth-century reader as unusually long and as strange in diction and punctuation. Fish, who is an unyielding opponent of formalism and New Critical dogma, here commits one of the excesses often attributed to New Critical readings; he excludes historical context from his description of the reading act, assuming a static reader (the reader as a Platonic form) who is outside of history, and who is therefore always the same. But would a learned seventeenth-century reader, well versed in scripture, and accustomed to a rhetoric of balance and antithesis, experience the agonies of Fish's reader?

Since Fish started his career as a seventeenth-century specialist, his insensitivity to seventeenth-century style is surprising. He says, for example, that

> The strategy or action here is one of progressive decertainizing. Simply by taking in the first clause of the sentence, the reader commits himself to its assertion, "that Judas perished by hanging himself" (in constructions of this type "that" is understood to be shorthand for "the fact that"). This is not so much a conscious decision as it is an anticipatory adjustment to his projection of the sentence's future contours. (p. 71)

Fish's description of the reading process here is pure fantasy. There is no basis for his declaring peremptorily that "in constructions of this type 'that' is understood to be shorthand for 'the fact that.'" On the contrary, if we convert the full clause to normal twentieth-century syntax it would read, "There is no certainty in Scripture that Judas perished by hanging himself. . . ." In this sentence, "that" functions as a relative pronoun, and clearly Browne has inverted the syntax in order to catch the reader's attention and to give prominence to the mystery surrounding the death of Judas Iscariot, a mystery generated by two conflicting accounts, one in Matthew 27:5, and the other in Acts 1:18–19. These conflicting narratives in Scripture make it difficult to know whether Judas took his own life or whether he died a violent but not self-inflicted death. This striking inversion of the relative clause is what we may call Browne's "style."

Now we may ask what Fish is actually doing when he asserts that Browne's sentence "has the advantage of not saying anything." Is his claim that the sentence is "not saying anything" an assertion about the sentence, or is it an assertion about Fish's response to the sentence? If it were indeed the latter, then it would have been more accurate and candid of Fish to have said simply, "On the first reading I found myself unable to respond to Browne's sentence," or, "My initial response to Browne's sentence was perplexity, or blankness," or, "When I first read the sentence it was beyond my comprehension." That is, on the basis of his own theory, Fish can never be in a position to make the judgment that "the sentence is not saying anything." The most he can claim is that the sentence "is not saying anything *to him.* Clearly, the concatenation of words that Fish actually uses constitutes not a response to the sentence but an assertion about the sentence— and an erroneous assertion at that.

It is fairly clear that the sentence is saying something, and that it does supply an attentive reader who knows Scripture with the fact that since Scripture gives two contradictory accounts of the death of Judas, we cannot be certain, on the basis of the scriptural evidence alone, that Judas hanged himself; moreover, the difficulty of the scriptural evidence is compounded by lexical problems in the

Greek text. In trying, later in his analysis, to convince the reader that Browne's sentence is "not saying anything," Fish stoops to arguing by means of verbal pattern. "There are two vocabularies in the sentence; one holds out the promise of a clarification—'place,' 'affirm,' 'place,' 'punctual,' 'overthrow'—while the other continually defaults on the promise—'Though,' 'doubtful,' 'yet improbable,' 'seems'; and the reader is passed back and forth between them and between the alternatives—that Judas did or did not perish by hanging himself." While Fish claims to be analyzing reader response, he is actually analyzing the text, and he is treating the text in the way that he learned from the New Critics. To demonstrate that "the reader" is "passed back and forth," he attempts to convince us that there are two vocabularies in the sentence that work against each other. Of course we can test this claim in a way that we cannot test the claim about what happens to "the reader," and when tested the claim collapses. There is no substance to the assertion that "place," "affirm," "place," "punctual," "overthrow" constitute a vocabulary of "promise." Nor by the same token, do "though," "doubtful," "improbable," . . . "seems" constitute a vocabulary of "default." Rather, both so-called vocabularies work together to produce that rhetoric of checks and balances that has been described as the "Senecan amble."

In Fish's eagerness to persuade his reader that what he is doing is not interpreting Browne's sentence but describing the "event" that is his own dynamic "experience" of that sentence, Fish commits another rudimentary interpretive blunder. "The indeterminateness of this experience," he writes,

is compounded by a superfluity of pronouns. It becomes increasingly difficult to tell what "it" refers to, and if the reader takes the trouble to retrace his steps, he is simply led back to "that Judas perished by hanging himself"; in short, he exchanges an indefinite pronoun for an even less definite (that is, certain) assertion. (p. 72)

Of course, anyone who reads the sentence carefully will see that though Browne's use of the pronoun "it" is indeed confusing for a twentieth-century reader (perhaps for a seventeenth-century reader as well), the reason for the confusion is precisely that while the "it" sometimes refers to the initial clause, at other times the "it" refers to Scripture ("it seems to affirm—i.e., "Scripture seems to affirm; "it maketh it improbable"—i.e., Scripture maketh . . .), and in at least one instance the referent is not clear ("hath given occasion to translate it"). But if we sort out the pronouns, then the meaning of the sentence is clearly as I have given it above.

A little later in his essay, Fish analyzes his response to the Miltonic line, "Nor did they not perceive the evil plight." I shall not go into Fish's gyrations about double negatives and whether "they" did or did not "perceive." I would, however, like to call attention to his conclusion: "The reader's inability to tell whether or not "they" do perceive and his involuntary question (or its psychological equivalent) are events in his encounter with the line, and as events they are part of the line's *meaning*, even though they take place in the mind, not on the page." (p. 73) If Fish had not told us he was a reader-response critic, we might have thought we were reading the New Criticism of Brooks and Warren. In fact, if we remove the assertion that the events take place only in the mind of the reader, Fish's conclusion sounds suspiciously like the "heresy of paraphrase" of the New Critics. This heresy, as Cleanth Brooks explains it in *The Well-Wrought Urn*, is precisely to substitute a prose statement of the "theme" of the poem for the experience of the poem itself. According to Brooks, it is only the total experience of the paradoxes, ambiguities, imagery, and totality of the poem itself that is its meaning. As Brooks puts it, the "beauty" of the poem is "the effect of a total pattern . . ." (p. 194) "Paraphrases," Brooks writes, "are useful as pointers and short-hand references," but should not be mistaken for the poem itself. (p. 196) That is why he finds, "form and content, or content and medium, are inseparable" (p. 199).[4] As we can see, Fish is a New Critic in reader-response clothing.

Fish maintains that

there is no direct relationship between the meaning of a sentence (paragraph, novel, poem) and what its words mean. Or, to put the matter less provocatively, the information an utterance gives, its message, is a constituent of, but certainly not to be identified with, its meaning. It is the experience of an utterance—*all* of it and not anything that could be said about it, including anything I could say—that *is* its meaning. (p. 72)

This seems to suggest that there can only be experience, that all experience is self-enclosed, and that meaning is never communicated, and, to close the circle, that we can never know whether there is any correlation between "what the words [of a sentence] mean and what the reader "experiences." If nothing Fish can ever say about "it" (the experience or the meaning?) is the "meaning" of a sentence, then we are left in an infinite regression of experiences. Fish "experiences" Sir Thomas Browne's sentence and then makes an utterance about his experience, which is neither his experience nor the meaning of Browne's sentence. Another reader then experiences Fish's sentence, and makes an utterance about it, but nothing that reader says is that reader's experience or the meaning of the sentence either, and so on. Moreover, if it is only the "experience of an utterance" that is its meaning, then suppose that in reading Browne's sentence, a reader "experiences" a headache. Would that reader, then, be obliged to say that the sentence, "That Judas perished by hanging himself . . . etc.," means "I have a headache?"

Apparently fearful that equating "meaning-of-a-text" with "process-of-reading-a-text" might not have been a sufficiently extreme position, Fish has taken to denying (1976) that texts exist at all; "The answer to the question 'why do different texts give rise to different sequences of interpretive acts?' is that they *don't have to,* an answer which implies strongly that 'they' don't exist." Again: "The other challenging question—'why will different readers execute the same interpretive strategy when faced with the "same" text?'—can be handled in the same way. The answer is again that *they don't have to,* and my evidence is the entire history of literary criticism."[5] And if one asks why readers should accept Fish's description of "meaning" and "the reading process," that too can be handled in the same way—*they don't have to.* Fish's position is not as radical as he would make it seem. He argues for what French critics have been calling the "writerly" text. That is, if any given text is susceptible of an infinite number of interpretations, then no text exists as "itself" but only as

a text created by any given reader (which is to say, by any given interpretation). And since any given interpretation becomes in its turn
a text subject to other readings (interpretations), the concept of "a
text" gives way to a concept of process. Ironically, the "postmodern" onslaught on New Criticism brings us back to one of the New
Criticism's favorite philosophies—Heraclitian flux.

Another theorist who has attempted to restore the lost reader who
was, in fact, not lost, is Wolfgang Iser. In an essay entitled, "The
Reading Process: A Phenomenological Approach" (1972), Iser deployed two pieces of heavy philosophical artillery: Edmund Husserl,
the father of phenomenology, and Roman Ingarden, who spent the
years in wartime Poland, where a genocide was being conducted in
the name of German ideology, writing a treatise on "The Controversy over the Existence of the World". Firing these heavy guns, Iser
comes up with two contradictory models of what he calls "the literary
work." According to one model, the literary work is a totality made
up of the "text created by the author" and "the realization accomplished by the reader." But in his very next sentence Iser outlines a
second model in which "the literary work cannot be completely identical with the text, or with the realization of the text, but in fact must
lie halfway between the two." [6] Here, the "literary work" is no longer
the totality made up of created text and accomplished reading but a
mysterious entity "lying" in some undesignated and indeterminable
space midway between text and reading.

Rather than pursue this quixotic attempt to pinpoint the locus of
the existence of the "literary work" (i.e., does the "literary work"
exist in the intention of the author, in the physical text, in the mind
of the reader, or in some Platonic "space" where all three, or some
combination of the three, converge?), let us examine the method that
Iser claims his models of "the reading process" generate: "As a starting point for a phenomenological analysis," he writes, "we might
examine the way in which sequent sentences act upon one another.
This is of special importance in literary texts in view of the fact that
they do not correspond to any objective reality outside themselves." [7]
Iser's authority for this astonishing assertion of the "autotelic text" is

not a New Critic, but the philosopher Roman Ingarden (whose own sentences, of 1939 to 1945 at least, certainly could not be accused of corresponding to the objective reality around him). The problems inherent in Iser's gropings never disappear from reader-response criticism, and indeed, as this form of criticism "develops," new problems emerge.

Jonathan Culler attempts to effect a fusion between a systematic, scientific "semiotics" on the one hand and a theory of subjective reader-response criticism on the other. He brings about this fusion, not without some slight of hand, by asserting that the "semiotics" he is calling for "would be a theory of reading, and its object would not be literary works themselves but their intelligibility."[8] But such a theory would violate both of Iser's models. How can a "theory of reading" that disregards "literary works" tell us anything about the "intelligibility" of the works? Such a theory would have as "its object" readers, not "intelligibility." In fact Culler's call for a "theory of reading" whose object would be "the intelligibility of the text" is little more than self-delusion. Though he argues against the alleged New Critical autotelic text, he nevertheless embraces it in its most concentrated form in the person of Michel Riffaterre. In *The Semiotics of Poetry* Riffaterre develops, with consummate brilliance and finesse, the position that all poetry is "intertextual," a network of poems that refer always and only to one another, and never to a "physical" world; in other words, an autonomous poetry and autonomous language in place of autonomous poems. Therefore poetry, like language itself as conceived by Saussure, is an autotelic system—i.e., units in the system can be related only to other units in the same system, never to anything outside the system. It does not bother Culler that Riffaterre interprets poems, because he also describes "the processes by which readers interpret poems." Furthermore, Riffaterre not only analyzes poetic figures but indicates that "an important meaning of figures is what they tell us about figurative language." Finally Culler approves Riffaterre's "interpretations" because they "are so engaging that one cannot wish them eliminated."[9]

Culler does not ask whether it would have been possible for Riffaterre to describe the process by which readers interpret poems without "interpreting" poems, or to discover what it is that "figures . . . tell us about figurative language" without first "interpreting" a particular poem to determine what particular "figures" mean in that poem. Culler seems to think that he is paying Riffaterre a compliment; he does not realize how damaging it is to Riffaterre's entire enterprise for his interpretations of individual poems to be treated as if they were fluffy little French bonbons, twinges of Gallic charm, rather than models of poetic reading. Culler seems unable to decide between reading as a hedonistic psychologism (the pleasure to be derived from Riffaterre's "engaging" interpretations) or as a grimly puritanical theoreticism. Beneath Culler's call for an end to interpretation, while at the same time advocating "reader-response," lies another seeming contradiction. Reception-aesthetic (reader-response) theorists of the Constance school, such as Iser and Hans Robert Jauss, acknowledge a debt to the hermeneutic theories of Hans Georg Gadamer, for whom there is only interpretation.

This indecisiveness may be as much a reflection of the two antithetical "philosophies" that have been used to prop up reader responsism as it is of Culler's personal confusion. Iser seeks backing for his responsism in what he claims is Husserlian phenomenology but what is actually a reductive psychologism that would have been repugnant to Husserl. Stanley Fish, on the other hand, whose reader responsism Culler favors, claims to derive his support from the behavioristic language philosophy of John Austin through John Searle. Fish turns Austinian behaviorism into its opposite, psychologism, by maintaining that not only do people "do things with language" (such as marry, christen, promise) but language does things to people. In short, as a consequence Fish concludes that literary criticism should be the study of what literature does to readers. This is apparently what Culler has in mind when he declares that "the task of literary theory . . . is . . . to offer a comprehensive theory of the ways in which we go about making sense of various kinds of texts." [10] But how could such a theory be arrived at, and to what end, without interpretations? How could anyone offer a theory of "the ways in which we go about making sense of texts" if there were no one "making sense of texts"?

In a recent adaptation of the Fish-Culler approach to American literature, Steven Mailloux prefaces a reading of Hawthorne's "Rappaccini's Daughter" with the claim that all previous interpretations of the story are "inadequate" because "only a temporal analysis of the reader's response can fully explain how each part of an author's text relates to those parts before and after it."[11] Aside from the fact that this claim is demonstrably false and illogical, it is also impossible to implement. For one thing, a blow-by-blow analysis of the reader's response would perhaps explain the reader's response, but it would not necessarily explain how the parts of a text are related to one another. Obviously a reader could respond to a text without being cognizant of the relationships between its parts. Second, every description of reader response is subject to an insurmountable time lag—what may be called the Tristram Shandy dilemma. The reader-response critic is inevitably writing after the fact. No matter how fast he writes, and even if he records his response as he is reading, there must always be a lag between the actual response and the recording of the response. Hence we never get the reader's actual response but only a recollection of the response; therefore, even with the best of intentions, a reader can only tell us what he *thinks* his response was, or what he remembers it to have been.

In addition to the question of reliability raised by this time lag, there is also a question of credibility. What reason do I have to trust Iser, Fish, or their followers, whose personal responses, by their very nature, cannot be tested or verified? Let me cite an example of credibility lag from Mailloux's reading of "Rappaccini's Daughter." He opens his "temporal analysis" of the reader's response by asserting that "the reader encounters the first enigma of Hawthorne's text in its title: 'Who (and soon what) is Rappaccini's Daughter?' "[18] In saying this, however, Mailloux does not actually render a reader's response: he merely makes an assertion about what he apparently believes the reader does or should "encounter." Mailloux does not indicate whether he himself encountered this "dilemma" on first reading the story, or whether he believes "the reader" should or must become cognizant of this "dilemma" on reading the title for the first time. In fact, that a first-time reader would respond to the title by perceiving a dilemma seems highly unlikely. Or, if a dilemma is perceived, why not the dilemma "Who is Rappaccini?" As a consequence, I must doubt that Mailloux himself experienced such a response. On the other hand, it is certainly possible, and even likely, that Mailloux did recognize this dilemma after reading the critical analyses of the story, for these do indeed focus on the questions of "Who and what is Rappaccini's daughter?" As one "humanist critic" put it way back in 1955, "Not Rappaccini but Rappaccini's *daughter* is (Hawthorne's) subject." [13]

As Mailloux's "temporal analysis" of his alleged response continues, another problem comes to the surface. What happens in case a declared response does not accord with the text? For example, Mailloux writes that he responds to the text as follows: "The landlady tells Giovanni that the mysterious garden belongs to Rappaccini." [14] According to Iser this would be the "accomplished reading." But in this instance there seems to be a disjunction between the text created by Hawthorne and the reading accomplished by Mailloux. The former reads: " 'Does this Garden belong to the house?' asked Giovanni. 'Heaven forbid signor, unless it were fruitful of better pot herbs than any that grow there now,' answered old Lisabetta. 'No; that garden is cultivated by the own hands of Signor Giacomo Rappaccini, the famous doctor.' " [15] The landlady, then, does not tell Giovanni that the garden *belongs* to Rappaccini, but merely that the garden does not belong to her house, and that Rappaccini cultivates it with his own hands. A quibble, perhaps, except that, given Hawthorne's penchant for ambiguity and what Matthiessen called "multiple choice," this detail has implications for the "symbolic" interpretations of the tale. If this parodic Eden "belongs" to Rappaccini, then we would be inclined to see him as a divine creator in the symbolic structure. But if he merely "cultivates" the garden, that would suggest that he is more in the position of Adam in the Garden of Eden.

The ultimate weakness of reader responsism, however, is that it does not really make a difference in the way we read or interpret particular works. Mailloux concludes about "Rappaccini's Daughter" that "the end of the discourse, then, serves as the final test of the reader's discernment, a test the reader passes if he rejects Baglioni's narrow attribution of guilt to Rappaccini alone and replaces it with a judgment that all three male characters are morally responsible for the death of an innocent." [16] The notion, to begin with, that Hawthorne could have conceived himself as writing "Rappaccini's Daughter" as an exam to test the discernment of the reader contradicts everything we know of Hawthorne as a writer and a person. Moreover the relative degree of guilt and innocence of all four principals is exactly what is at issue in the story, and the assertion that a reader passes the discernment test by finding the "three males morally responsible" for Beatrice's death is an unfortunate and limiting reduction of the story. Such a reading is less a matter of the technique of "reader-response" interpretation than it is a matter of a new sensitivity to female perspectives generated by the feminist movement, and of appropriating new possibilities of interpretation created by feminist criticism.

In his reading of "Rappaccini's Daughter," Mailloux commits several sins generally attributed to the New Critics. He reads the story in a historical and intellectual vacuum, disregarding Hawthorne's customary fictional techniques and his cultural milieu; he ignores the reader of Hawthorne's time; he dwells, as any New Critic might, on Hawthorne's ambiguity, although he does not call it that; he uses the phrase "the reader," but this reader remains an abstraction devoid of feelings or of any specific identity; finally, this reader who is taking a "discernment exam" is not credited with having any taste or any sense of literary values.

Edward S. Casey is a phenomenologist who approaches literature not so much from the perspective of a hypothetical reader but from the perspective of one who engages in the act of "imagining." [17] Following phenomenological procedures, Casey plucks "imagining" out from among other "mental acts" and then examines all its facets, as one might examine a three-dimensional object in space. To conduct this examination, Casey must first observe his own mind in the act of imagining, describe what he has observed, and then project his observations of a single mind examining itself in the process of imagining as if those observations were empirically valid truths.

Casey's first step is to represent, and subsequently comment on, three "direct descriptions of several imaginative experiences—descriptions which were written down immediately after the experiences took place." These "imaginative experiences" are then narrated "in the present tense in order to convey as fully as possible the vividness of the original experiences." [18] The descriptions of the three imaginative experiences involve "white dolphins" in the first instance, "the cry of a flamingo" in the second, and a forthcoming "seminar on Rawls's Theory of Justice" in the third. Casey's description of the first episode specifies not only what he "imagined" but the physical context in which the act of imagining takes place: "I am seated at a long library table. I close my eyes. Immediately a school of white— very white—dolphins appears. There are perhaps between five and ten of them though they cannot be enumerated with precision." [19]

Casey's representation of himself in the act of imagining raises a number of questions. For example, how do we know Casey is being completely candid and honest; that is, how do we know he actually did imagine, or, more precisely, as he seems to be telling us, actually did "visualize" the "images" bodied forth in his descriptive utterance, since we have absolutely no way to test the veracity of his utterance? And what connection, if any, is the reader to infer between Casey's descriptive language and a "visible world out there?" Is Casey's utterance a "representation" of an "actual scene," presumably "derived from," or "in imitation of," or "reflecting" a "physical world," or does he conceive himself merely as having "imagined" a "scene" that may not be related to a "physical world" at all? Would it not be possible for an inventive writer to string these very words together without having imagined anything but the words themselves? It is exactly such a possibility that James Joyce seems to intimate at one point in his *Portrait of the Artist as a Young Man.* In one scene Stephen is waiting for his father, and having grown impatient, he starts wandering through the streets of Dublin. He sees a squad of "christian brothers," and the sight of them precipitates a long meditation, in the course of which,

He drew forth a phrase from his treasure and spoke it softly to himself:
—A day of dappled seaborne clouds.
The phrase and the day and the scene harmonised in a chord of words. Was it their colours? He allowed them to glow and fade, hue after hue: sunrise gold, the russet and green of apple orchards, azure of waves, the greyfringed

fleece of clouds. No, it was not their colours: it was the poise and balance of the period itself. Did he then love the rhythmic rise and fall of words better than their associations of legend and colour? Or was it that being as weak of sight as he was shy of mind, he drew less pleasure from the reflections of the glowing sensible world through the prism of a language manycoloured and richly storied than from the contemplation of an inner world of individual emotions mirrored perfectly in a lucid supple periodic prose.[20]

Joyce portrays the relationship between the literary artist and words as parallel to the relationships between a painter and paints, between a composer and sounds. The medium gives pleasure for its own sake: in a painting, the beauty of color, in music, the beauty of harmonious sound. At first glance, Joyce seems to be intimating that it is language that generates the world. But, finally, he does not deny the existence of a physical world, or of a connection between that world and language. Rather, he intimates that language is the middle ground between mind and world, partaking of both, a mirror of world as well as a mirror of the inner self. If there is any doubt that the elements of this trinity (mind, language, world) are functionally and inextricably intertwined with each other, Joyce brings Stephen's meditation to a close by reversing the process initiated at its beginning:

Disheartened, he raised his eyes towards the slowdrifting clouds, dappled and seaborne. They were voyaging across the deserts of the sky, a host of nomads on the march, voyaging high over Ireland, westward bound.

Now Joyce boldly rearranges the very words that he has just told us were drawn from "his treasure," and uses them to convey a "transparent" description of scene ("dappled seaborne clouds," to "clouds, dappled and seaborne"). Joyce the artist is fully aware of the complexity of the interrelationships between the inner self and the outer world, between perception and the physical world, between language and imagination, imagination and world, world and language.

But what is it that Casey, the philosopher, thinks he is doing when he sets his imaginings into language? Does he believe he is presenting a "transparent" description of visual images (pictures) that have crept into his consciousness without having been willed to appear (drawn from his treasure, so to speak), or does he believe, rather, that he is writing a poetic description that will evoke certain reader responses? Why do white dolphins "appear" when Casey closes his eyes? Why this image of purity and freshness and beauty—dolphins that are not only white but "very white," that is to say, not only pure but very pure? Why white dolphins and not green chickens? Where did these dolphins come from, and where is it that they "appear?" How are they related to the long white table? Is numerical vagueness a necessary adjunct to acts of imagining? Why did Casey have to close his eyes? Is the closing of the eyes part of the mental activity called "imagining"? Does the "autonomous imagination" function only when the eyes are closed? If so, then the imagination would seem to be not independent and free, but subject to the tyranny of the visual organs. Why does Casey think we need to know that he is seated at a long library table at the moment his imaginings take place? Is being seated at a long table a necessary prerequisite for the initiation of the act of imagining? Could it be said that if Casey had never actually seen white dolphins before he would be imagining, but if he had seen them he would be remembering?

What does Casey mean when he says that a school of dolphins "appears"? I have the feeling, in reading Casey's description of his imaginative experience, that he equates imagining exclusively with visualizing. He does not raise the question of whether converting images (thoughts, visions, etc.) into linguistic utterances may itself be part of the imagining process. Suppose one speaker says, "I close my eyes. I see the sunrise. The sky is pink, streaked with orange." While another says, "I close my eyes. But look, the morn in russet mantle clad / Walks o'er the dew of yon high eastward hill." Would we say that both of these speakers have performed an act of imagining, or only the second? When there is a conflict between philosophical ways of thinking and the mental act that he calls "imagining," Casey, as a philosopher, always gives precedence to the philosophical ways of thinking.

Robert Magliola presents a closely argued account of the strengths and weaknesses of the phenomenological approach to literature. His chapters on such individual critics as Martin Heidegger, Roman Ingarden, and Mikel Dufrenne are informative; most useful, perhaps, is a chapter in which Magliola vigorously contests E. D. Hirsch's extreme intentionalist position that even the most complex literary text is susceptible of only one valid interpretation.[21] I shall return to this extreme form of intentionalism, but first I would like to give some indication of what strikes me as one more major deficiency in the phenomenological method.

Although reader-centered phenomenological critics attempt, in theory, to discover the text-reality that can be perceived by a reader, what they often do in practice is to deflect attention away from the meaning of the text in order to focus exclusively on the techniques of reading. Whereas the formalists and the New Critics concentrated on the technique of writing, the reader-centered phenomenologists concentrate on the technique of reading. As a result literary criticism shifts from the genuine crisis of the creating of the text to the illusory crisis of the understanding of the text. The agony of the writer is displaced by the angst of the reader. In his discussion of Roman Ingarden, Magliola provides an example of this "crisis orientation." He points out that "Ingarden proceeds to raise thorny hermeneutical problems: '. . . there arises the difficulty of how one can convince oneself, on the basis of the text alone, that the text and, in particular, the nominal word meanings entering into it contain an implicitly potential stock. In short, how can one know whether one (or more) meanings which belong to a word's potential stock are actually operative in the text?' Ingarden suggests what he considers a useful procedure. First, of course, one should consult (independently from the text) the whole scale of meanings a given word has in a given *langue*.'[22]

An examination of both Ingarden's assertion and Magliola's commentary is revealing. Why should there "arise the difficulty" that Ingarden describes? Ingarden creates a crisis and a problem, both of which are falsifications of the normal act of reading. We do not ordinarily have to convince ourselves that words are meaningful, even in a difficult text. Perhaps certain problematic texts short-circuit a competent reading, but even in moderately difficult texts, competent readers are usually capable of coping with a certain level of ambiguity and even of syntactic dislocation.

To complete Ingarden's handling of this "problem," Magliola summarizes or paraphrases Ingarden's solution ("First, one should consult . . ."). He interprets Ingarden's utterance and then represents it in abbreviated form, ostensibly in language that he believes is more lucid than Ingarden's. Presumably Magliola does not experience a crisis in understanding Ingarden's text. If he did, he would not be able to paraphrase and interpret Ingarden so confidently.

Moreover Ingarden's solution of the crisis, as represented by Magliola, is itself startlingly simple. Confronted with a problematic text, the reader tries to find all previously established meanings of problematic words, and then feeds those meanings back into the context, trying to determine which, if any, of them work. The reader scans the lexicon and selects the appropriate meanings. What Ingarden and Magliola have done, then, is to describe a process that competent readers have engaged in from time immemorial. It is as if the phenomenologist, instead of telling us *what* a text means and *how* texts mean, provides us instead with a minute mechanics of the reading process. But just as human beings are able to chew their food without knowing the complete physiology of mastication, so they can read without knowing the complete mechanics of reading.

At the theoretical antipode from reader-response criticism is intentionalism.[23] Whereas Fish adopts the extreme reader-response position that there is no "text," only reader responses (or as many meanings-of-a-text as there are acts-of-reading), so the most uncompromising intentionalists hold that all texts, regardless of who is reading them, have "only one correct interpretation" and a single determinate meaning which is the author's intention. According to P. D. Juhl, "a literary work has one and only one correct interpretation," and "an interpretation cannot account for the features of a text unless it is a statement about the author's intention."[24]

Although Fish and Juhl take diametrically opposed views, it is one of the oddities of their opposition that both of them call on the speech-act philosophy of John Searle to support their positions. What they agree on is that literature is a form of speech act. What they cannot agree on is the very core of the philosophy itself—what constitutes a speech act. While Fish uses speech-act philosophy to support the claim that a literary work *does* something to the reader, and therefore is susceptible of a range of interpretations (which is to say, meanings), Juhl asserts that "If a literary work is a speech act, it cannot have logically incompatible meanings." [25] What is ironic in all this is that speech-act philosophy itself has shown but meager capacity to deal with problems of semantics.

Despite their divergences in the application of speech-act philosophy to literature, the reader-responsist and the intentionalist are united by method. To demonstrate that the meaning of a text is the series of acts that constitute reading that text, Fish "analyzed" a sentence by Thomas Browne; that is, he substituted another set of sentences for Browne's sentence. To demonstrate his theory of interpretation, Juhl also "analyzes" a text. Specifically, he substitutes a set of sentences for the Wordsworthian line, "Rolled round in earth's diurnal course." Discussing the line, Juhl takes up a problem that had already been identified and debated: Is there a contradiction between the phrases "rolled round," which may suggest either violent motion or gentle motion, and "diurnal course," which suggests a "slow orderly motion"? [26]

If we look closely at Juhl's procedure we see that the concept of intention is thornier than he recognizes, and that he too fails to break away from "formalist" methodology. He tries to wriggle out of difficulty by saying, "I shall not argue for or against this claim . . . ," that is, the claim that the line is "more coherent" if "rolled round" is taken to connote "slow and gentle motion" than if it is taken to mean that "the woman is 'being whirled about.' " [27] Having picked up the controversy and the contradictory connotations from previous criticism, Juhl absolves himself of the need to make a choice. By contending that he will "not argue for or against this claim," he eliminates the need to justify the connotations one way or another on the basis of context, usage, syntax, or the lexicon, thereby liberating himself to concentrate on "intention," and to pretend that the question of the text itself is irrelevant. We can detect a similar self-deception in Juhl's description of the way he uses the word *intention:* "I am using the term in this sense of an author's intention in writing a certain sequence of words—in the sense, that is, of what he meant by the words he used." [28] But how are we to decide "*what he meant by the* words he used" except by determining what the "words he used" mean? And how do we determine this except by considering context, syntax, and lexicon?

In fact, his denial notwithstanding, Juhl does argue for one of these interpretations. Juhl prefers "slow and gentle motion" as the meaning of "rolled round" because he believes that such an interpretation brings the phrases "rolled round" and "earth's diurnal course" into harmony, thus making the line "more coherent." Now, in order to justify the notion of "coherence" as dependent on the notion of "intention," Juhl launches a most bizarre argument. If, Juhl asserts, the poem "is not by Wordsworth but has been accidentally typed out by a monkey randomly depressing keys on a typewriter," then we would not have been able to choose one interpretation over another, because we could not assume that the line is purposeful. "All we can now say," Juhl asserts, "is: The words 'in earth's diurnal course,' rather than some other words, qualify 'rolled round' because the moneky just happened to hit those keys there." [29] This argument is not very convincing and is in some ways irrelevant. If we can suppose a monkey typing this line by "randomly depressing keys on a typewriter," then we can also suppose that a reader not aware of this phenomenon might well decide to interpret the poem as if it were purposeful. If we are going to get into the business of drawing significant conclusions on the basis of absurd suppositions, let us suppose we discovered that the opus we call the Shakespeare plays had been dictated to an amanuensis by a parrot. Would we then destroy all those plays as nonsense because they were not the result of an authorial intention? Moreover, with regard to the Wordsworth poem, how can Juhl be sure that Wordsworth "intended" the line to be "harmonious"? The biographical evidence would suggest that during the period of his life when Wordsworth probably wrote the Lucy poems (assuming that this is a Lucy poem) he was in a state of flux and uncertainty, and it may well be that his "intentions" when he wrote the poem were ambivalent.

What I want to stress is not only that Juhl's argument is neither logical nor compelling, but that he, like Fish, while striving to free himself from the New Criticism, is still struggling in the New Critic's net, as is apparent by the very nature of the questions he continues to ask. Is there anything to be gained by running over the old ground again of whether this presumed Lucy poem is an affirmation of pantheistic order in the universe or a lament over human mortality? If we are to break away from purely formalist questions, then we should ask whether and why it is important to know what Wordsworth (the poem?) means. For example, would it make a *difference* to Juhl whether the poem affirms pantheism or deplores mortality? Would Juhl alter his own religious or philosophical beliefs on the basis of this poem? Is Wordsworth's "intention" sufficiently important to Juhl that he would change his way of living to bring his life into accord with that "intention"?

What must be underscored here, a question that Juhl avoids, is that "intention" is an important concept *only* if readers believe that poets are authoritative, and that what they say is more significant and will have greater impact on our lives than the sayings of philosophers, bankers, lawyers, politicians, scientists, etc.

One reason for the long-term dominance of the New Criticism was the ability of the major critics (not the second-liners who were later used as straw men) to convince their public that for them there was no human activity or form of discourse that took precedence over poetry. It is difficult to feel such confidence about theorists like Fish, Iser, Culler, Mailloux, and Juhl, who are more interested in establishing rhetorical strategies than in knowing what a given poem (or poet) is saying. It is really a matter of little import whether a critic's rhetorical strategy is to say "The meaning of *The Waste Land* is that life is a completely joyous experience," or, "In *The Waste Land* Eliot intended the meaning that life is a completely joyous experience," or "The reader responds to *The Waste Land* by feeling the sense of life as a completely joyous experience."

Thus, despite the magnitude of the theoretical gap separating the reader-responsists and the intentionalists, they have several things in common. Though both start in a genuine effort to justify the importance of literature, at some point the "justification" starts to become an end in itself, with the consequence that "philosophy" of a sort pushes out literature. Fish would restore a human dimension to literature by attacking the positivistic strain in American formalism (especially Wimsatt and Beardsley's highly influential essay, "The Affective Fallacy") in such a way as to reinstate the reader in the reading process. Juhl would restore the human dimension by attacking the other flank of formalism (Wimsatt and Beardsley's more powerful and even more influential "The Intentional Fallacy") so as to reinstate the author. But ironically, both of them fall prey to the most sterile and positivist eddy of Wittgensteinian ordinary-language analysis: speech-act philosophy. Wandering in this valley of dry bones, Fish and Juhl lose sight of their original purpose. "Philosophy," or at least one narrow school of philosophy, begins to displace poetry; and instead of justifying literature, they trivialize it. Finally, having set out to free literary criticism from formalist method, as well as dogma, both Fish and Juhl turn out to be formalists in disguise.

Perusing the performances of Anglo-American critics, we see that there is a minimal transference from theory to practice, and that the theories have little power to generate new understanding of particular works. What we wind up with, in most instances, are New Critical readings in Continental dress. For example, Mailloux's reader-response approach to "Rappaccini's Daughter" recounts much that had already been said about the story, except that in Mailloux's account the phrase "the reader" becomes the subject of utterances about the story. Instead of saying "The first enigma in the story is . . . ," Mailloux chooses to say "The reader encounters the first enigma." This strategy enables Mailloux to re-present standard interpretations of the story, but to give them a different "look" by changing the rhetorical emphasis. In other words, having said that a literary work is an encounter between text and reader, or that it is an act of communication, the critic is still left with the task of telling us what "the reader" thinks or feels the author is saying. Culler is shrewd in this regard: recognizing his limitations as a reader, he makes a virtue of them, avoiding the problem of theory and practice by shunning all interpretation.

The continuing problem for contemporary theory, then, has been the inability of theorists to bridge the gap between literary theories and the practice of literary criticism and literary history. Introducing a collection of essays by Hans Robert Jauss published in 1982, Paul de Man pointed to a "lack of compatibility between literary theory and practice that plagues the study of literature everywhere."[30] This persistent alienation of contemporary literary theory not only from critical practice but from literature is reflected in Frank Lentricchia's postmortem on the New Criticism, which appeared in 1980.[31] Lentricchia provides what is in many ways an excellent description of the rapid changes in critical movements, from the New Criticism to poststructuralism, that took place during the postwar period. But while he takes great care in articulating the philosophical intricacies of the postwar theoretical movements, Lentricchia caricatures the American New Criticism, pitting the stereotype of the New Critics' autotelic poem against what he sees as a more complex European deep-thinking philosophical historicism.[32] Lentricchia gives especial prominence to the thinking of the authoritarian Martin Heidegger and to the historiography of the antiauthoritarian Michel Foucault.

Lentricchia looks to Foucault's historicism for a methodology that will overcome "the traces of the New Criticism" still to be "found . . . in the repeated and often extremely subtle denial of history by a variety of contemporary theorists,"[33] and he concludes his chapter on "Structuralism" by invoking the problem of the postmodern shift from Heideggerian hermeneuticism to Foucauldian historicism: "The long temporal unity of historical consciousness," he writes, "the very basis of shared tradition and the bond of a community of meaning: are these determinations of established power and the effects of a massive repression? These are questions that cannot fairly be posed to [Hans Georg] Gadamer; these are questions for Michel Foucault."[34] But Lentricchia believes, with Foucault, that these are rhetorical questions to which the answer is an unequivocal "yes." For Lentricchia it is a truism that "The long temporal unity of historical consciousness, the very basis of shared tradition and the bond of a community of meaning . . . *are* . . . determinations of established power and the effects of a massive repression."

Foucault provides a "historicist mode of writing which stresses 'phenomena of rupture . . . [and] discontinuity,' " rather than a historical method which would "celebrate the idea of 'tradition' itself . . ."[35] As an example of how this Foucauldian historicism might work, Lentricchia draws a parallel between the delay in accepting Gregor Mendel's theories of genetics and the long wait Robert Frost had to endure before his poetry received any sort of public recognition.

The implication is that if one would not speak truth "in a void," as Mendel did . . . or if one would not write poetry in a void as did Robert Frost . . . then one had better assent to the rules of discursive policy by placing oneself within the confines of those systems that determine biological or poetic truth for one's time. To refuse to conform is to accept a place . . . alongside society's more dramatically visible outcasts: the criminals, the insane, racial minorities, and the indigent, who are brutally and unhesitatingly subjected to the power that divides and silences.[36]

In this example of discontinuity, at least, Foucaldian methodology does not seem to contribute something new to literary history. On the one hand, the Foucauldian observation is an assertion of the obvious phenomenon that the known and the conventional are more acceptable than the unknown and the unconventional. On the other hand, we may ask whether there is a legitimate parallel between the belated reception of Mendel's theory and the deferred public acceptance of Frost's poetry, and whether the instance of either Mendel or Frost represents evidence of the sinister workings of domination and power. The geneticist Gunther S. Stent has argued that a scientific discovery like Mendel's may not be recognized as such in its day because it is "premature," which means that other scientists do "not seem to be able to do much with it or build on it."[37] In other words, the neglect of original work in science is often arbitrary, not necessarily conspiratorial. To conclude that Mendel and Frost became indistinguishable from "criminals, the insane, racial minorities, and the indigent" is the result of accepting Foucault's paranoid vision as a basis for the writing of literary history.

Lentricchia attributes the acceptance of Frost's poetry in his lifetime to "a modernist revolution [that] . . . had stripped power from the honorific norms that had denied 'poetry' to Robinson and Frost. . . . The dramatic rise of both Robinson and Frost after 1913," he continues, "was not the result of a collective coming to good sense on the part of magazine editors, critics, contemporary poets, and other instruments of a repressive poetic discipline that had confined Robinson and Frost to speaking in a void."[38] But this is more paranoia. It is not clear that modernism was triumphant by 1913. As late as 1917, Ezra Pound had to browbeat Harriet Monroe into publishing "The Love Song of J. Alfred Prufrock" in *Poetry*. And except for a few discerning readers like Edmund Wilson, *The Waste Land* was greeted with jeers and incomprehension in 1922.

The tendency to distort literary history in this way is a consequence of falling into the deconstructionist habit of putting abstract ideas in the syntactic position of grammatical subjects. But it was not the "modernist revolution" that changed the norms of poetry and made Frost's work acceptable. That revolution was carried out by human beings, some of whom were "magazine editors, critics, and contemporary poets." And it was those editors, critics, and poets, not a disembodied revolution, that changed the norms; they found value in Frost's "unconventional" poems and managed to convince other critics, editors, and readers that the poems were worthy of attention. And also there may be something in Frost's poetry itself that explains its eventual acceptance. Once published, Frost's poetry gave pleasure to a substantial number of readers.

The new literary history, we are told, will emerge as "genealogy . . . a subtler . . . historicist strategy, an impure determinism which can account, at once, for the repressive force of the historical conditions of discourse . . . and for a (continuous) emergence from those conditions of a newer . . . formation of power." The Foucauldian literary historicist, then, will be a "genealogist," and for this "genealogist . . . the first order of business . . . is the 'dissociation of the self, its recognition and displacement as an empty synthesis, in liberating a profusion of lost events.' "[39] But this determinist literary history not governed by cultural constructions of the self raises some puzzling questions, not least of which is: Who, or what, selected Frost as an example of a poet before his time? Was this, after all, a deliberate choice that the genealogist made acting as a discrete and empowered individual, or does Lentricchia really think of himself as "an empty synthesis [lacking an] ontological foundation" for whom the choice of Frost was made by "genealogy" itself? If "genealogy" made the decision, why did it choose Frost rather than Whitman? Surely, in its time, Whitman's poetry was more revolutionary and more un- and even anticonventional than Frost's.

The irony has been widely observed that though Whitman aspired to become the voice of the common people, his poetry was repugnant to a vast majority of midnineteenth-century American readers. And Whitman was indeed identified with "criminals, outcasts, and the insane," partly because he himself seemed to be making this identification in the poetry. What is perhaps more interesting about Whitman as an example of a poet before his time is that his long experience as a printer and newspaperman empowered him to become publisher, publicist, disseminator, typesetter, distributor, and even reviewer of his own poem.[40] Yet for some reason, Foucauldian literary "genealogy" did not discover the obvious example of Whitman, perhaps because this particular literary historian really is an individual self with his own "ontological foundation" who happens to have written a book on Frost and not on Whitman.

Based on assumptions of rupture and discontinuity, Foucauldian historicism would discourage historians of American literature from tracing "influence" or writing books about an Emersonian or Adamic tradition "running through Whitman, Stevens, Roethke, and Ginsburg." Historians of American literature would avoid "a repetitious continuity which celebrates the individual authorial will . . . and which dissolves, in the process, the myriad changing forces, poetic and otherwise, that shaped the identities of figures as culturally separated as Emerson and Roethke."[41] But must we agree with the Foucauldian genealogist that celebrating the individual authorial will would inevitably dissolve "the myriad changing forces . . . that shaped the identities" of different poets? Just the opposite seems to be the case. That is, can we recognize changing aesthetic and cultural forces without also recognizing "individual authorial will" as both a symptom and cause of those changing forces? Should we not say, actually, that American literary histories in search of a unifying tradition are themselves generated by cultural forces, and are, in their own way, declarations of independence? Since the nineteenth century, American writers and critics have felt a need to discover in American writing something that would distinguish it from the British tradition, with which it shares a vocabulary and a grammar but no longer a common history, peoplehood, social structure, geography, experience, and aspirations. And do we not find those differences embodied in the "individual authorial will?"

Would it not be ironic if American literary historians, having liberated themselves from a British tradition, were now to enslave themselves to a methodology rooted in French political and cultural traditions? What is liberating for Foucault, writing in the tradition of a basically stable and racially, religiously, and ethnically homogeneous culture with a long established language and an ancient tradition of class hierarchy and repression, may turn out to be stifling and unproductive for American literary historians, who write out of a dynamic, continually evolving culture that is racially, ethnically, and religiously heterogeneous and that has long been liberated from a rigid class structure. Need we remind ourselves that American fiction writers claimed that they had to write romances because they could not find in their culture the class structure and the class conflicts that were the necessary stuff of the novel?

From within Foucault's traditionalist and highly stratified culture it is a bold and innovative gesture to assert decenteredness, but from within an antitraditionalist American pluralistic culture there may be a greater need to seek out continuities than differences. Adopting Foucault's historiography would make it impossible to find those continuities that help us to understand the still evolving American character. Foucault, as an exquisitely sensitive student of French history, cannot help being influenced by two uniquely traumatic events in that history: the first of these events is, of course, the French Revolution, in which a cruel and oppressive monarchy was succeeded by an even more cruel reign of terror; the second is what is sometimes referred to as the humiliation of 1940 to 1944, in which it became clear that there were at least as many collaborators as there were active resisters in occupied France, and that an admiration for authoritarianism and repression was still as strong a force in French character as the love of democracy.[42] For example, when Foucault writes that "Humanity does not gradually progress from combat to combat until it arrives at a universal reciprocity, where the rule of law finally replaces warfare; humanity installs each of its violences in a system of rules and thus proceeds from domination to domination,"[43] are these not the words one would expect from someone whose identity has been shaped in the shadow of the eighteenth-century Reign of Terror and the Nazi occupation of 1940 to 1944?

A genealogical American literary historicism would be anomalous, because Foucauldian genealogy is more than a mere methodology. All methodologies carry their own ideological baggage, and the baggage of genealogical historicism is an implacable hatred for liberal democracy in general, and for American culture in particular, as both the paradigm and disseminator of liberal democracy. In his essay, "Nietzsche, Genealogy, History," Foucault announces that "genealogical analysis shows that the concept of liberty is an 'invention of the ruling classes' and not fundamental to man's nature or at the root of his attachment to being and truth."[44] Enlarging Louis Althusser's concept of an "ideological state apparatus" that imposes its restraints covertly by training individuals to police themselves, Foucault develops an elaborate scenario of a condition in which those who enjoy illusory freedom in the liberal democracies are actually more constrained than those who live in police states (Tell that to the East Europeans!).

The hated target of "genealogy," both as an ideology and a method, is the middle class. This should come as no surprise, since the middle class has long been an object of derision to French intellectuals of both the right and left. Genealogy has always a single goal: to expose the ways in which the so-called ruling class in liberal democracies dominates and oppresses. But while the oppressors are clearly defined by Foucauldian genealogy, it is somewhat more difficult to identify the oppressed. It can't be the individual who is oppressed, because in Foucauldian genealogy "the individual" as a living entity does not exist; the term being nothing more than an expedient construct of the oppressors. Nor can it be a specific class that is oppressed, since in being inscribed by the ideological state apparatus, the dominating class is as oppressed as those it dominates. "The body," as Foucault sees it, "is the inscribed surface of events . . . the locus of a dissociated self . . . and a volume in perpetual disintegration."[45] When Foucault talks about the body and history he often sounds like an embittered Norman O. Brown. But where Brown, writing in the tradition of Whitman, celebrated the unrestrained joys of the Dionysian ego, Foucault, writing in the tradition of de Sade, broods over the cruel pleasures of the Apollonian ego. He declares that genealogy must be "an analysis of descent," whose ". . . task is to expose a body totally imprinted by history and the process of history's destruction of the body," and "to reestablish the various systems of subjection . . . the hazardous play of dominations."[46]

Foucault has only disdain for the interwoven ideals of the "free individual," liberal democracy, and the rule of law. In the Introduction to *Discipline and Punish* he writes, "This book is intended as a correlative history of the modern soul and of a new power to judge; a genealogy of the present scientifico-legal complex from which the power to punish derives its bases, justifications, and rules. . . ."[47] This is the essence of genealogical historicism; for whatever reason, wherever the genealogist looks he sees only the punished and those who punish them. The legal system itself, in the genealogist's view, exists only to punish. At some point in the eighteenth century, according to the genealogist, a transition took place from coercion by means of the state apparatus, such as police and military, to coercion by means of "discipline." "Discipline," for the genealogist, is the internalization of the repressive state apparatus, which is now built into a newly created entity called "the individual." In the genealogist's view, the microcosm of the liberal democratic state is the prison: "How could the prison not be immediately accepted when, by locking up, retraining, and rendering docile, it merely reproduces, with a little more emphasis, all the mechanisms that are to be found in the social body? The prison is like a rather disciplined barracks, a strict school, a dark workshop, but not qualitatively different."[48]

It may be that this picture Foucault has presented is an accurate portrait of French society. But in absolute terms, his words sound like the musings of a depressed soul, reminiscent of that most depressed of princes, Hamlet. It will be recalled that in his first encounter with

Rosencrantz and Guildenstern, Hamlet inquires, "What have you, my good friends, deserved at the hands of Fortune that she sends you to prison hither?" The dialogue continues, we all know, with Hamlet declaring, first that "Denmark's a prison," and then that the whole world is "a goodly one in which there are many confines, wards, and dungeons, Denmark being one o' the worst." When Rosencrantz disagrees, Hamlet makes his famous answer, "Why, then 'tis none to you; for there is nothing either good or bad but thinking makes it so. To me it is a prison." Whereupon, Rosencrantz responds, "Why, then your ambition makes it one. " 'Tis too narrow for your mind." [49] May we not say the same for the genealogist that, seeing the world through the restrictive paradigm of discipline, he can perceive it only as a prison? And should we not ask what kind of literary historicism is likely to emerge from such tunnel vision?

What William James would have called a more healthy-minded view of the human condition [50] is presented by a biblical commentator who has suggested that the two creation stories in Genesis represent two aspects of the human form. In the first, a human creature is created "in the image of God" and is told to "subdue" the earth and to "have dominion" over all other living things (Gen. 1:28). This creature represents the human's existence as a majestic, dignified being. In the second creation story, the human creature is "formed . . . out of the dust of the ground, and [God] breathed into his nostrils the breath of life; and man became a living soul" (Gen. 2:7). This second human, who is placed in a garden and told to "cultivate it and keep it" (Gen. 2:15), represents a passional being in search of redemption. This dual human has been described as follows:

Cathartic redemptiveness, in contrast with dignity, cannot be attained through man's acquisition of control of his environment but through man's exercise of control over himself. A redeemed life is by its nature a disciplined life. While a dignified existence is attained by majestic man who courageously surges forward and confronts mute nature in a mood of defiance, redemption is achieved when humble man makes a movement of recoil, and lets himself be confronted and defeated by a Higher and Truer Being. [51]

In American mythology, the majestic human is represented in the Declaration of Independence and the Bill of Rights, while the human seeking redemption is to be found in the Puritan doctrine of sin and salvation. If we set aside, for a moment, the notion of a "Higher and Truer Being" wholly unacceptable to the genealogical historicist, then the dual human resolves into the inner conflict of a creature who takes pride in his ability to gain mastery over the universe, and yet recognizes himself, at the same time, as "this quintessence of dust."

The classic American writers have focused on this inner conflict as the price that must be paid for becoming a free individual. For the genealogical historicist, "discipline" is the ultimate instrument of subjugation, but for an American writer like Thoreau, discipline is the means of coming to terms with the physical world and it is also a prerequisite for the liberation of the self. Is not the whole of *Walden* a lesson in acquiring the discipline that will make one free? And what, specifically, is the story of the Kouroo artist, if not a parable of the liberation and expansion of the individual through self-discipline? [52] For the genealogist, "The general juridical form that guaranteed a system of rights that were egalitarian in principle was supported by all those systems of micropower that are essentially nonegalitarian and assymetrical which we call the disciplines"; but Thoreau writes that, "As we grow old, we live more coarsely, we relax a little in our disciplines, and . . . [thus] cease to obey our finest instincts. But we should be fastidious to the extreme of sanity, disregarding the gibes of those who are more unfortunate than ourselves." [53]

Melville, as usual, summarized the conflict in the dual human succinctly: "If we obey God," says Father Mapple, "we must disobey ourselves; and it is in this disobeying ourselves, wherein the hardness of obeying God consists." [54]

Since the injunction to rewrite American literary history from the viewpoint of a "genealogical historicism" calls for us to cleanse ourselves of the ideology of liberal humanism, one would expect that before doing so we would want to measure this ideology more fastidiously against the ideology clamoring to replace it. But Lentricchia, who is not fastidious in this respect, seeks salvation in Foucault's Americaphobic ideology:

Literary discourse in the wake of Foucault no longer needs to be forced into contact with political and social discourses, as if these were realms outside of literature which writers must be dragged into by well-meaning critics. For as an act of power marked and engaged by other discursive acts of power, the intertextuality of literary discourse is a sign not only of the necessary historicity of literature but, more importantly, of its fundamental entanglement with all discourse. In its refusal to center power either in a dominant discourse or in a subversive discourse that belongs only to poets and madmen, Foucault's latest work gives us a picture of power-in-discourse that may move critical theory beyond its currently paralyzed debates.[55]

Since the "literary discourse" of any given period does, after all, overlap with the "literary discourse" of other periods, as well as with "political discourse" and "social discourse" of its own period and other periods, poetry enters into the world of history in spite of itself. The practice of literary criticism and of literature itself can now break out of a narcissistic self-referentiality and return to a consciousness of history. Yet Lentricchia's own account of the philosophical forces that have brought us to the brink of this new "historicism" reflects a characteristic blindness to recent history, thus creating a historical void in which Martin Heidegger, a crucial player in the development of contemporary theory, is severed from an unfortunate but crucial historical context. It is generally agreed that the conflux of postwar French theories that is now labeled postmodernism has been fueled by the philosophizing of Martin Heidegger. In the case of Derrida, the debt is openly acknowledged. In the case of Foucault, the Heideggerian influence is more elusive. Nevertheless, we can see it quite clearly in the following characterization by Lentricchia:

What Foucault calls "effective history," then, is not a new historicism, but the old one disturbed, questioned, its duplicities and its techniques illuminated. Our contemporary historicity may perhaps be no more, or less, than the deconstructive project in its strangely divided identity: decadent and phlegmatic, and yet bravely energetic and full of hope; paralytic and corrosively self-ironic, and yet awesomely productive and full of assurance.[56]

If Lentricchia is correct about Foucault, then there can be no doubt that this "old [historicism,] disturbed, questioned, its duplicities and its techniques illuminated," is a Heideggerian historicism. And if there were any doubt of the Heideggerian roots here, they are removed by the peroration, which identifies itself not only in the notion of "the deconstructive project," but which reeks, in its diction, of the Heidegger *Rektoratsrede* of 1933, when Heidegger called on German university students to follow their Führer bravely and energetically, and filled with self-assurance. In short, Lentricchia, through Foucault, presents Heidegger and his philosophy-aesthetics in a "privileged" manner that sets Heidegger himself above criticism and outside of history.[57]

Martin Buber, Heidegger's compatriot and fellow philosopher, was not deceived by Heidegger, and recognized that he was not beyond history. In 1938 Buber expressed a searing insight into Heidegger's *Being and Time* that may now be perceived as prophetic. Buber was close enough to Heidegger not to be overawed by him, and wise enough to perceive the dehumanizing strain in his philosophy. In *Between Man and Man*, Buber pointed out that: "The man of 'real' existence in Heidegger's sense, the man of 'self-being,' who in Heidegger's view is the goal of life, is not the man who really lives with man, but the man who can no longer really live with man, the man who now knows a real life only in communication with himself."[58]

For Lentricchia, Heidegger's infatuation with National Socialism may as well be nonexistent. Heidegger's postwar silence on Nazism (when he might have spoken openly without fear of retribution) is also of no import to Lentricchia. Discussing Heidegger as a *historicist*, Lentricchia's reveals a lack of historical perspective that is characteristic of postmodernist literary theorizing:

The bridge between early and late Heidegger is "The Origin of the Work of Art" . . . and the bibliographical history of this piece is a clue to the value he placed upon it. Given initially as a single lecture at Freiburg in the fall of 1935 (Just a few months earlier he had given the lectures that would constitute *An Introduction to Metaphysics*) and repeated at Zurich in January of 1936, "The Origin of the Work of Art" was expanded into three lectures which were delivered in Frankfurt late in 1936.[59]

Though an advocate of historicism, Lentricchia does not find it worth mentioning that while Heidegger the historicist was busy getting his essay on the origin of art exactly right, barbarism was overtaking what had been the world's most advanced culture.[60] At the very moment that the culture he was living in and supported was making everything the artwork had stood for in European civilization obsolete (in 1935 the infamous Nuremburg laws were being passed), Heidegger was busy looking for the artwork's origin. In Heidegger's highly touted essay, "The Origin of the Work of Art," appears a most enlightening paragraph:

> Thus we are compelled to follow the circle. This is neither a makeshift nor a defect. To enter upon this path is the strength of thought, to continue on it is the feast of thought, assuming that thinking is a craft. Not only is the main step from work to art a circle like the step from art to work, but every separate step that we attempt circles in this circle.[61]

It is apparently not within the scope of Lentricchia's "historicism" for him to point out that while Heidegger was preparing to gorge himself methodically on a "feast of thought" that would enclose him (as Buber foresaw) in narrowing circles of the mind, his countrymen were methodically enclosing their fellow citizens in narrowing circles of barbed wire. I do not want to be misread here; I am not accusing Heidegger of actually participating in the Nazi program of genocide, though he apparently was never bothered very much by it, either. I am trying instead to point out that a genuine complex "historicism" would undertake to explain why the soul of German (and to some extent European) culture, philosophy, and literature was powerless to prevent (and may even have contributed to) Germany's—and Europe's—descent into a most brutal barbarism. Not one of the theorists or philosophers named by Lentricchia, and certainly not Lentricchia himself, makes even the slightest attempt to explain the importance of high culture's impotence in meeting the challenge of barbarism from within. Lentricchia's failure to deal with or even recognize the existence of this question makes a mockery of his historicism. That so-called historicism is as self-enclosed as Heidegger's "feast of thought"; what Lentricchia is calling for, and what is being practiced by the poststructuralists he seems to admire, is not genuine historicism but a mystique of historicism, not history but a dream of history, not a recognition of past horrors that must be reckoned with, but a circular world of thought to feast on.

Another telltale indication of the gap between literary theory and critical practice may be found in the organization of *After the New*

Criticism. While the first part, "A Critical Thematics, 1957–77," is devoted to pure theory (or pseudo-philosophy), the second part, called "The American Scene: Four Exemplary Careers," contains four major chapters, each discussing the work of an "American" literary critic whose theorizing has made an impact on literary criticism and theory. The organization, the heading, and the choice of those careers that are considered exemplary are all instructive. According to Lentricchia, the four critics who have achieved "exemplary" careers on "the American scene" are: Murray Krieger, E. D. Hirsch, Paul de Man, and Harold Bloom. No doubt the terms Lentricchia used to head the second half of his book were chosen deliberately. While the designation *exemplary* would suggest that these critics are to be emulated, the noun *careers* suggests, rather, that what brings these names together is not the originality or the importance of their theories, but rather their ability to achieve success in an American academic setting. With the exception of de Man, none of the critics named can be said to have had a significant and lasting impact on the study of literary theory.

Hirsch's *Validity in Interpretation*, attempting to demonstrate that a work can have only one correct interpretation, has added many a day to the longevity of Penelope's tapestry, but in the long run, the theory is too extreme to be tenable. Bloom's reputation as a commentator on Romantic poets and Romanticism will live on. Using New Critical methods of close reading, Bloom reversed the New Critic's alleged low valuation of the poems of the British Romantics. (I say "alleged low valuation," because there is much evidence to indicate that the New Critics did not devalue Romantic poems; such evidence would include Cleanth Brooks's essays on Wordsworth's "Intimations Ode" and Keats's "Ode on a Grecian Urn" in *The Well Wrought Urn*, and Robert Penn Warren's enabling essay on *The Ancient Mariner*.) Let us grant, however, that in rebelling against "the New Critical Father," Bloom added much to our understanding of Romantic poetry. In turning his own rebellion against "the Father" into a "theory" that purports to be the key to understanding all literature, however, Bloom took an eccentric and counterproductive turn. *The Anxiety of Influence* attempted to reverse the hitherto conventional understanding of "influence." Whereas influence studies once had the purpose of showing how a "major" writer borrowed material that had been lying inert from a "minor" writer (or sometimes even from another "major" writer) and then brought it to life, Bloom reversed this convention, so that the critic would now have to study "later" writers as always the lesser progeny of giants; the later writers' lifelong task in writing was destined to be a labor of freeing themselves from the dominance of their "precursors." As to the work of Murray Krieger, no one, I believe, would argue that it has exerted a major influence on literary theory. Of the four who have, in Lentricchia's view, made "exemplary careers," only de Man, as the promulgator of deconstruction, the dominant "literary theory" of the eighties, still seems to be an important theorist.

Lentricchia himself, when he talks about specific works as opposed to careers, identifies with admirable conciseness the weaknesses of these critics. About Krieger he advises: "The surface solution of 'thematics' is only asserted, not argued." On E. D. Hirsch as a student of German philosophy he has this to say: "Hirsch appears to me to have misunderstood Heidegger and Gadamer about as badly as it is possible to misunderstand them." (Lentricchia's own understanding of them, as we have seen, is less than perfect.) Of Bloom Lentricchia writes: "In the end Bloom's critique of Derrida becomes anxiety-ridden rhetoric, not argument; assertion, not analysis." In his chapter evaluating the work of de Man, Lentricchia is brilliant. While he failed to spot the Nazism in Heidegger, he deserves credit for having been the first, so far as I know, to point out both the contradictions and the authoritarianism in de Man's criticism. "What we witness" in de Man's critical discourse, writes Lentricchia, "is a strange discrepancy between a frightfully sobering theory of literary discourse and the actual practice of a critic whose judgments, authoritative in tone and style, betray the theory." He also points out that de Man "does not argue in any formal sense of the logic and truth of his position. One has the impression of a critic who . . . intends to put across his interpretation mainly by crafty rhetorical maneuvers." What the four exemplary American careers seem to have in common, then, is that they are all based on either misunderstanding of the philosophers they work with, or by the absence of logical argument.[62]

More important, except for the career of de Man, these "careers" were not really built on the discovery or creation of new theoretical directions. In fact, one might almost say that one of those careers was blighted by the encounter with de Man and almost overwhelmed by "theory." Lentricchia refers to de Man as the "resident Godfather, the *capo di tutti capi*" of the "Yale Mafia" and asserts that "Bloom's latest thesis about literary history . . . was announced by de Man three years before the appearance of *The Anxiety of Influence*." [63] But de Man's most damaging effect on his colleagues at Yale was not, I believe, his "thesis about literary history," but his having convinced them that no distinction should be made between poetry and criticism, that both are equally creative activities. This sad deception has almost been the undoing of both Bloom and Geoffrey Hartman, another Yale "mafioso," both of whom came to see themselves as the equal of poets. Hartman had publicly abetted Bloom in this cruel self-deception in a review of *The Anxiety of Influence*. "Six essays," he wrote, "emerge from this dense, eloquent and experiential brooding, flanked by two prose poems and accompanied by a synoptic intro-duction and an interchapter on 'Antithetical Criticism.'" [64] It is, no doubt, this kind of ridiculous mutual puffery that first led William Pritchard to refer to certain members of the Yale English department as a "hermeneutical mafia." [65]

One cannot help wincing at the excess and insensitivity of Hart-man's language. Surely he must realize that he has deified Bloom, representing him as nothing less than the *elohim* of Genesis 1:2, Childe Harold as God "brooding" on the face of the waters. And as God's brooding brought a universe out of the waste and void, so the great Harold has also "created" a world, having brought six essays, two prose poems, a synoptic introduction, and an interchapter out of his eloquent brooding. The literary critic now challenges not only the primacy of the poet, but the preeminence of the great God Absolute himself.

What is the logic of the claim that there is no qualitative difference between the critic and the poet? The claim is based on two Bloomian syllogisms. The first goes as follows:

> All poetry consists of responses to other poems.
> All literary criticism is a response to poems.
> Therefore, all criticism is poetry.

It follows from this, as well, that all who write criticism are poets. By syllogism, then, Bloom is a poet. The second syllogism that motivates Bloom's late criticism runs:

> All mortals have oedipus complexes.
> All poets are mortals.
> All poets have oedipus complexes.[66]

But unlike other mortals, poets are concerned not so much with their flesh-and-blood fathers as with their poetic progenitors; hence they spend all their creative energies trying to get out from under *the* "precursor," who for the English poets is Milton. While it is true that the British Romantic poets were almost obsessed by the thought of Milton and by their desire to write an epic poem, it is also true that the most pervasive influence on English (and American) poets for the last three hundred years has been exercised not by Milton but by Shakespeare and the Bible (of course, one reason for the power of Milton's own influence was undoubtedly his choice of Scripture as the primary source of his own great epic poem). On Shakespeare as precursor Bloom has surprisingly little to say,[67] and on the Bible nothing, even though *Paradise Lost* obviously could not have been written had not scripture preceded it.

Let us, however, grant that Bloom wants to synthesize rhetorical, religio-mystical, aesthetic, and Freudian terminology by making each translatable into the other, so that kabbalistic "breaking-of-the-vessels" is equivalent to the principle of "rhetorical substitution"— and "in psychic terms is the metamorphic element in all defenses, their tendency to turn into one another, even as tropes tend to mix into one another." But instead of synthesis Bloom comes up with New England chowder. All the "writers" that Bloom reads with approval become poets because he approves them. Hence "Freud, in the context of poetic interpretation, is only another strong poet, though the strongest of modern poets, stronger even than Schopenhauer,

Emerson, Nietzsche, Marx, and Browning."[68] What gets lost in all this is the concept of poetry as a distinct entity—and the sense that poetry was once related to the beautiful. Bloom, like Hartman, strives mightily to establish literary criticism as a form of "primary" writing.

The argument for criticism as a primary activity is doomed to fail, however, because it is repugnant to common sense. The critic must start by recognizing that whereas the great poet (novelist, playwright, etc.) converts energy into matter by translating undifferentiated experience into language, the critic starts with that which has already been shaped by the time the critic arrives on the scene; the critic's task is to test the validity, beauty, accuracy, power, human value, etc., of these shapings. In the course of analyzing, assimilating, and evaluating the shapes, he may have recourse to self-analysis. That is, the verbal constructs the critic is dealing with may rouse new feelings about the "inchoate out-there," upon which the critic now has to impose another "shaping" corresponding to the "poetic shaping" that evoked the "new" response. But always the critic has the poet's primary verbalization to lean on. To the extent that a poem is shaped out of, or is wholly dependent on, other poems, it may be described as "entropic." That is, to the extent that "verbal arrangements" represent only other verbal arrangements, they begin to reflect a decline in creative energy.

Bloom's theory of "anxiety," of course, has the element of entropy built into it. If all literature is exclusively—and indeed can only be—a response (positive or negative) to previous literature, then there is bound to be a "loss" of energy in making the transfer from the early work to the later. If Blake's verbalizing of reality is totally dependent on Milton's prior verbalizing of reality, then Blake can never be better than a less energized (which is to say, a second-rate) Milton. The flaw in the theory is that it does not allow for a new influx of energy. Such influxes may come in various ways. For example, a writer may combine several sources (as Bloom himself tries to do) in such a way as to arrive at a higher level of linguistic energy than any of the single sources. Or a writer may bypass a predecessor to go directly to a higher source of energy. A later writer may take his inspiration from the Bible itself and not bother with Milton. Or he may tap new sources of energy that were unavailable to either the Biblical writers or Milton. Nor can we discount the possibility of an influx of energy from "Nature" itself (which is what Emerson hoped for). Otherwise, how would one explain the fact that *King Lear* transcends all its known sources, or the fact that *Moby-Dick* is a greater and more original epic than *Paradise Lost*?

Although Bloom denies that his criticism "has something in common with anything now miscalled 'Freudian literary criticism,' " it is nevertheless a hidebound psychological criticism, which is to say it diverts interest away from literature and the text by focusing on the presumed psychological determinants that brought forth the poem. Unfortunately, despite its obvious weaknesses, Bloom seems to be overcommitted to, even Ahabically obsessed by, his theory, which he has taken to repeating. In a book dealing with the mystical Jewish doctrine of the Kabbalah, Bloom writes, "If Kabbalah can be interpreted, as I think it can, as a theory of influence, then *keter* is the paradoxical idea of influence itself."[69] That he should attempt to impose his theory on a body of mystical literature that he has never, by his own admission, studied, and that he knows only at third hand, is a measure of Bloom's total turn away from poetry as a thought bodied forth in language. Whatever poetic qualities the Kabbalah literature may possess, Bloom shows no interest in such qualities. With staggering single-mindedness, he limits himself to the Kabbalah literature only as it reflects a "swerve" away from, or a repudiation, as he sees it, of encroaching scripture.

Although Bloom is not, properly speaking, a mystic, he has, nevertheless, come to believe in a mystique of influence. The center of a poem for Bloom no longer resides in its language but in a "vision" or attitude that seems to be independent of the language of the poem. Like Emerson, he believes in a "metre-making argument" that makes an actual poem irrelevant. Hence the following theory of the way in which poems are related to each other:

Only weak poems, or the weaker elements in strong poems, immediately echo precursor poems, or directly allude to them. The fundamental phenomena of poetic influence have little to do with the borrowings of images or ideas, with sound patterns, *or with other verbal reminders of one poem by another* [italics mine]. A poem is a deep misprision of a previous poem when we recognize the later poem as being absent rather than present on the surface of the earlier poem, and yet still being in the earlier poem, implicit or hidden in it, not yet manifest, and yet there.[70]

The "belated" poem displays the influence of the precursor poem by being wholly unidentifiable with it as far as actual language is concerned. For example, if the language of the precursor poem is PL1, then the language of the belated poem may be anything that is not PL1. But in terms of vision, if the vision of the precursor poem is PV1, then the vision of the belated poem may be PV1, PV1a, PV1b, ad infinitum, in which 1, 1a, 1b, etc. may stand for repetition of 1, "continuation" of 1, completion of 1, repudiation of 1, etc.

While his career does not qualify as exemplary for Lentricchia, Geoffrey Hartman, too, shows the ill effects of the de Man-Derrida influence. Take, for example, Hartman's ominously titled collection of antistructuralist essays, *The Fate of Reading*. A very heavy title. And weightiness it is that characterizes this book: elephantine puns and jokes, pontifical pronouncements, and specious pseudo-soul-searching. The opening sentence of the leading essay, "The Interpreter: A Self-Analysis," runs: "*Confession.* I have a superiority complex vis-á-vis other critics, and an inferiority complex vis-á-vis art." But feelings of inferiority are very little in evidence in the book. With poststructuralist trendiness, Hartman pretends to analyze himself in the act of analyzing the work of art, but with minimal results. His self-analyses are invariably banal. For example, does the reader really care to know that when Hartman "was young (real young) what came in through the senses was so profuse and arbitrary I had no need of heaven and hell"?[71] Is this really Hartman analyzing himself in the act of analyzing, or is it, rather, a middle-aged Hartman imagining the young Hartman as an ersatz young Wordsworth? Hartman seems to think he can outdo Wordsworth, consummate genius of the "Egotistical Sublime," at this game. But his attempts to establish the illusion that he is a poet in his own right, or at least possessor of a poetic sensibility, usually fail. The essays as a group remind one of the clown who runs around the stage threatening people with a gun. When he finally squeezes the trigger, out comes a flag with the word

BANG written on it. Hartman keeps threatening to fire his gun, that is, tell us something new about literature, but all that ever happens is that the innocuous flag pops out. The main thrust of the essays is Hartman's attempt to clear a space for himself—and for the interpreter in general—as poet. One hopes, however, that Hartman is not serious, because while he can make some legitimate claim as an interpreter of poems, he is clearly no poet.

With rare exceptions, literary critics are not poets, and they are not usually very good philosophers, either. By the same token, philosophers are not necessarily good literary critics. Lentricchia describes the situation accurately in pointing out that Krieger, Hirsch, de Man, and Bloom misinterpret the philosophers they discuss and do not frame very strong logical arguments to support their theories. The same can be said of Iser, Fish, and Juhl—and about Lentricchia himself. His sentimental call to the reader to rally round the flag of Foucauldian "historicism" is hardly an example of incisive logic. Moreover, Lentricchia's "historicism" itself, derived from theories of intertextuality, is merely one more "fiction of desire," as much cut off from mimesis and reality as any other "mythic structure" or "structure of consciousness."

Literary theorists play philosophers' games with minimal skills, and they dabble in philosophical discourses they do not necessarily control. All too often, the discourses of twentieth-century philosophy, especially as those discourses have developed in postwar France and Germany, are self-deceiving and antihuman. They have been forged in the shadow of a guilt that will not go away, and that has not yet been faced. In seeking to turn away from the truth of a painful past they resolutely mock the idea of truth itself. Of all European thinkers, Heidegger, the source of "deconstruction," must surely be the least authentic. Quite aside from what he did or did not do during the war, his behavior after the war sets him among those who must surely be the least admirable specimens of thinking beings, those Germans who could never bring themselves to acknowledge that a crime against humanity had been committed. That so many thinkers could have remained detached from reality while their countrymen were turning Europe into a continent of death camps, that "philosophers" could sit in the eye of the whirlwind, thinking sublime thoughts, oblivious to the disintegration of human values occurring before their eyes— these realities are the scandal of twentieth-century European philosophy. Nazism, the existence of the death factories, and systematic genocide—all were powerless to deter European philosophers from continuing to try to erect sublime philosophical systems. But an even worse scandal is the fact that instead of trying to make sense of this madness after the war, European philosophers, and none more than Heidegger, pretended that nothing had happened. Maybe such immunity from mundane daily events is to be expected of philosophers. They claim, after all, a special license to dwell in ideal worlds.

Literature, unlike philosophy, claims no such license, and literature, as a rule, has been more forthright in at least making some attempts to record the guilty European past. But this literature, usually relegated to a largely ignored pigeonhole designated "Holocaust Literature," still remains largely excluded from "the canon," especially by those who spend all their energies trying to get a handle on Heideggerian "Being." In an essay entitled "Ruins and Poetry," Czeslaw Milosz describes Polish poetry of the years between 1939 and 1945 as a record of the disintegration of the culture. The Polish poets, he observes, "perceived Europe sinking in consecutive stages into inhumanity," and they also perceived this sinking "as the end of European culture, and its disgrace."[72] To this inhumanity and disgrace recorded by the poets the philosophers were blind, and they have labored strenuously to remain blind. Equally blind are the literary theorists who pursue these philosophies.[73] In their zeal to extirpate the alleged blemishes in the New Criticism, and in their dabbling in philosophy in hope of finding weapons with which to smite the dreaded father, the New Theoreticists have assumed the blindness of the European philosophers. Turning their backs on the poets, proclaiming themselves philosopher-poets, the theoreticists wander in their own elysian fields, hopelessly alienated from art, from truth, and from humanity.

CHAPTER TWO

Paul de Man and the
Politics of Deconstruction

During the fall and winter of 1987–1988, three seemingly dispa-
rate events occurred that made it increasingly difficult to ignore
the link between deconstruction and Germany's National Socialist
past. The events were the continuing investigation of the wartime
activities of former Secretary General of the United Nations, Kurt
Waldheim, who had concealed the extent of his knowledge of, and
possible participation in, Nazi atrocities carried out in the Balkans;
the accidental discovery of Paul de Man's collaborationist writings;
and the heated debate generated among French intellectuals by the
appearance of Victor Farias's *Heidegger et le Nazisme*. So as not to be
misunderstood, I should say that what I take the three events to have
in common is the concealment of a shameful European past that must
be uncovered, always in the face of intense and hostile opposition.

In reporting the discovery of Paul de Man's anti-Semitic writings
for pro-Nazi newspapers, a *New York Times* story from Dec. 2, 1987,
stated that "The findings about a man respected at Yale and elsewhere have shocked scholars." The surprising news that he wrote for
Nazi journals may serve to remind us not only of de Man's buried
personal past but of a European past that has been buried just as effectively. One suspects that those same scholars who were shocked to
learn about de Man's past would be equally surprised to learn about
the existence of German death camps. Certainly, one would be hard

pressed to acquire such knowledge by reading *PMLA* or the proliferating number of literary journals devoted exclusively to deconstruction, postmodernism, metafiction, and literary theory. Anyone who derived his or her knowledge of literature and the world only from the journals de Man and his followers would be likely to publish in and read would most likely dwell in blissful ignorance of the recent European past and would never in the least suspect that the various literary and critical "postmodernisms" may be related to the historical events of the thirties and forties.

For years I had been puzzled by this strange phenomenon, but thought it a mere coincidence, or perhaps a reflection of the "unworldliness" of literary critics who preferred fictional to real worlds. In the light of the Waldheim affair and the indifference toward their past shown by the Austrian people in electing a former Nazi to high office; in the light of the insensitivity of the Pope in conferring "respectability" on this same former Nazi; in the light of Claude Lanzmann's revealing documentary film, *Shoah*, and the ensuing denials and debate surrounding the film; in the light of the trauma and echoes of French collaboration surrounding the trial of Klaus Barbie; in the light of the Roques affair, in which a doctoral dissertation questioning the existence of Nazi death camps was accepted at a French university; in the light of German revisionist historians who complain of "a past that will not pass," and who in place of denying Nazi atrocities outright seek to mask the guilt of "civilized," systematic, and planned state-of-the-art genocide by submerging it beneath the current of general human cruelty and the mainstream violence of human history; in the light of all these developments, one can no longer consider the promotion of deconstructionist literary criticism, with its concomitant relegation of Holocaust literature to the margins of literary history, to coincidence or daydreaming.

Once one ponders the audacity of the omission, and the immensity of the abyss this omission opens in Western "literary history" as now conceived and written, then the connection between de Man's deconstruction criticism and his past, far from being shocking, starts to make a great deal of sense. Despite the deconstructionist critics' insistent claims that they not only deconstruct texts but also probe into the deepest corners of their own consciousnesses, the deconstructionist de Man was apparently guarding a secret from himself as well as from his naive American graduate students and, as it turns out, equally naive academic peers, a secret that had to be kept by European intellectuals, the dark secret that European high culture in its most advanced phase not only was powerless to prevent the construction and implementation of the death camps, but actually provided the ideological base on which the death camps were built.

Moreover, the European intellectuals, the supreme products of this high culture, must hide from the rest of the world and from their own consciences the fact that they not only did nothing to shield the victims from slaughter but were willing and eager contributors to the Nazi project of annihilation (*Vernichtung*) and accomplices to Hitler's proposed enslavement of the rest of the world. As Leszek Kolakowski, among others, has pointed out, the Nazis did not keep their ideology or their evil intentions a secret. What lurks behind de Man's urbane, sophisticated, and obscurantist philosophical criticism, then, is the shame of the European intellectuals who participated in and profited from genocide, whether out of greed, or opportunism, total commitment to Nazi racist ideology, or even out of sheer hate. Nor is de Man the first European intellectual to hide behind self-deceiving distortions and obscurantism. Even Hannah Arendt sought to protect German culture by ascribing guilt to the victims instead of the criminals. The sad fact European thinkers are still loathe to face is that neither European humanism, nor philosophy, nor religion, nor learning, nor music, nor art helped to prevent the degradation that European culture wrought upon itself.

The convenient myth is that Nazism was a movement restricted to the uneducated masses, and that the killers were ignorant brutes recruited from the lumpenproletariat and the petit bourgeoisie. Only inconvenient facts interfere with this comforting myth. We need but consider the career of none other than the Angel of Death of Auschwitz himself, Doctor Jozef Mengele. Dr. Mengele was the proud product of a European education. He considered himself a scientist and a man of culture. Victims testify that he was fond of quoting the poetry of Hölderlin. Of course, Mengele was only one of many; more cruel, perhaps, and certainly with a greater flair for the dramatic, than some of his peers. Robert Jay Lifton asserts, in *The Nazi Doctors*, that ". . . When we turn to the Nazi doctor's role in Auschwitz, it was not the experiments that were most significant. Rather it was his participation in the killing process—indeed his supervision of Auschwitz mass murder from beginning to end."[1] There is also the story, retold by Elie Wiesel, of how the Jewish historian Shimon Dubnow was murdered by an SS officer who had been a pupil of Dubnow's in Heidelberg. Wiesel goes on to say that in doing research on this incident he and the students in his seminar ". . . discovered that most of the killers of the four *Einsatzkommando* (killing squads) had college degrees. They had Ph.D. degrees in philosophy and literature, in the sciences. They were doctors. There were two opera singers, and one of them, may God save us all, had a . . . Ph.D. in Divinity."[2] In *Hitler's Professors* (1946), Max Weinriech demonstrates, with a massive show of evidence, that "German scholarship provided the ideas and techniques which led to and justified this unparalleled slaughter."[3] In the 1982 *Sewanee Review*, I questioned the worship lavished on sometime Nazi Martin Heidegger by de Man and his followers, by pointing out that ". . . while Heidegger . . . was busy getting his essay on the origin of art exactly right, barbarism was overtaking what had been the world's most advanced culture."[4]

We still know little about de Man's activities once he stopped worrying in print about how the Jews were polluting European literature. The *New York Times* story tells us: "The young de Man quit the newspaper in 1942, entering publishing until he left for the United States in 1947 . . ." We do not know why de Man left his native land, but it is common knowledge that many known Nazi sympathizers left the place of their birth when the situation there started to become unpleasant. Perhaps de Man was simply ashamed of his past and wanted to eradicate it by starting life anew in a new country.

At any rate, shifting attention away from the representational writings of poets, essayists, and fiction writers, and focusing, instead, on the question of *how critics read* would give de Man the opportunity to conceal his past, even from himself. In the foreword to *Blindness and Insight* (1971), the book that vaulted him into academic prominence, de Man announces his intention to deal with criticism rather than primary creative works: "Because critics deal more or less openly with the problem of reading, it is a little easier to read a critical text as *text*—i.e., with an awareness of the reading process involved—than to read other literary works in this manner." Is de Man's purpose here, as elsewhere in his writings, to sow confusion?

In addition to deflecting literary criticism away from literature and its humanistic moral implications, de Man launches an attack on the concept of "the past." Like so many deconstructionists, de Man has founded his poetics on a version of Saussurean linguistics. There is no need to repeat Saussure's definition of the sign. It is enough to point out here that what might make Saussure's linguistics so alluring to a critic trying to blot out the past is its synchronic tendencies.

This will to obliterate the past is evident in de Man's essay, "Literary History and Literary Modernity." [5] Most of the essay recapitulates Nietzsche's essay, "Of the Use and Misuse of History for Life," [6] in such a way as to demonstrate Nietzsche's rejection of "history." In a typical turn, however, de Man finds that the seeming rejection of the past is actually, at a deeper level, a discovery of the impossibility of forgetting the past. In Nietzsche's ". . . description of life . . ." de Man writes, "it [i.e., life] is a temporal experience of human mutability, historical in the deepest sense of the term in that it implies the necessary experience of any present as a *passing* experience that makes the past irrevocable and unforgettable, because it is inseparable from any present or future." [7] For an instant, it seems as if de Man is saying that deeper than the urge to forget is the need to remember. But it is soon clear that "the past" that must be remembered has melted into an eternal present (". . . the past . . . is inseparable from any present or future.") I have not space here to enter into all the evasions and involutions of this labyrinthine exercise in obfuscation, but should like merely to cite the closing sentences as evidence that de Man's purpose in writing an essay on literary history is to destroy not only literary history but history itself:

To become good literary historians, we must remember that what we usually call literary history has little or nothing to do with literature and that what we call literary interpretation—provided only it is good interpretation—is in fact literary history. If we extend this notion beyond literature, it merely confirms that the bases for historical knowledge are not empirical facts but written texts, even if these texts masquerade in the guise of wars or revolutions.[8]

The bad faith in this passage is so clear and the indeterminate qualifiers and half-truths so obvious ("*good* literary historians," "*what we usually call* literary history," "provided only it is *good interpretation*," etc.) that I shall content myself with pointing out that the claims de Man makes in this passage rest on neither logic nor empirical evidence. To say that "what we call . . . good literary interpretation" is "[*what we call?*] literary history" is merely to raise a series of questions, such as, What is literary interpretation? What is good, as distinguished (presumably) from bad, literary interpretation, and who is to decide what is good or bad? Who is the "we" that "call" . . . ? In what sense can a synchronic entity (interpretation) be equated to a diachronic entity (history)? But de Man proclaims this highly questionable and actually nonsensical utterance as if it were a universally accepted absolute truth. It is also apparent that he slides from positing "literary history" as an indeterminate and possibly indeterminable entity, to positing it as a clearly definable entity that can be pinned down (i.e., in the first instance, he talks about "what we usually call literary history" and in the next about something that "is in fact literary history." Finally, de Man's disingenuous claim that he has somehow confirmed "that the bases for historical knowledge are not empirical facts but written texts," is a half-truth at best. To a large extent "written texts" themselves become the "empirical facts," and a good historian tries to establish their accuracy. But written texts are not always the historian's only evidence. The assumption underlying this assertion, which de Man has stated explicitly in another essay, is that all written texts are merely components of a sign-system in which "the actual expression" never "coincides with what it signifies." If one accepts this assumption, then history itself, and with it de Man's own past, has been obliterated.

What is surprising is the eagerness with which de Manian deceptions have been taken up by younger American literary critics, and even by de Man's colleague, Geoffrey H. Hartman, who, himself having escaped the Nazis, should have known better. In an essay entitled "History Writing as Answerable Style," Hartman asks, with sublime naivete, "Can history-writing, or interpretation in touch with it, become a new medium—a supreme fiction which does not reduce being to meaning but defines a thing sharply in 'the difficulty of what it is to be'?" Elsewhere in the same essay, Hartman apes de Man with what is a most determinate proclamation coming from an advocate of semantic "indeterminacy": "History-writing, therefore, while inherently 'critical' is not inherently 'judgmental': it is judgmental only by the claim that human beings could act without blindness, without that which makes them finite enough to act. But this claim is not made when history is told by historians, by critics rather than gods."[10]

Hartman seems to be saying that since historians, like the actors in history, are "fallen" beings (i.e., capable of acting only out of that "blindness" that defines their "finiteness"), history should always be "a supreme fiction" that does not "reduce . . . to meaning." How would such a historiography deal with the memory of the Nazi death camps and the Nazi past? No revisionist could ask for a more comforting paradigm for the writing and understanding of history.

It is not surprising, perhaps, that we should be able to hear echoes of deconstructionist "historiography" in the German revisionist historian Ernst Nolte's infamous article, "The Past That Will Not Pass Away," which appeared in the *Frankfurter Allgemeine Zeitung,* June 6, 1986. " 'The past that will not pass,' " he writes, "can only mean the Nazi past of the Germans. The issue implies the thesis that every past passes away, and that this not-passing-away involves something very exceptional. On the other hand, the normal passing away of the past cannot be seen as a disappearance." In a penetrating commentary on the revisionists that appeared in the June 1987 issue of *Encounter,* Josef Jaffe pointed out that "If the past could not be laid to rest, it had to be reconstructed. If images of cattle-cars and crematoria refused to subside, then the films must be taken in hand by the professionals for reediting and retouching. If the ancestral stain could not be scrubbed off, perhaps the crimes could be made to pale in the blinding light cast on those of others."[11] Two observations may be in order. One is that instead of the historian's "ancestral stain," de Man, we may infer, had a personal stain to scrub off. Secondly, while the historian must "reconstruct" the past to wash off the stain, the man of letters must "deconstruct" it, so that the past may be said never to have existed, or to exist only as a "supreme fiction" or a "rhetorical strategy," which would then mean, of course, that the past could be "reconstructed" or "rerhetorized," as a film may be re-edited and retouched, to eliminate the "images of cattle cars and crematoria."

It is not without some sense of irony and dismay that one perceives de Man's friends and colleagues beginning the process of reconstructing *him*. As the *Times* story puts it, "Some scholars said they detect anti-Nazi nuances in Professor de Man's favorable reviews of Jewish authors such as Kafka or the French historian Daniel Halevy." It would certainly constitute a self-imposed blindness and would actually be unfair to de Man to let ourselves be taken in by such feeble rationalization; for as soon as we recognize de Man's suspect past, his work starts to take on new meaning, and we can perceive a coherence and cogency that were not there before. To see this coherence we need only re-examine the essay "Criticism and Crisis" (1967), which contains in somewhat more than a nutshell the *donnée* of his entire *oeuvre*.

De Man opens the essay by announcing that "Well established rules and conventions that governed the discipline of criticism and made it a cornerstone of the intellectual establishment have been so badly tampered with that the entire edifice threatens to collapse. One is tempted to speak of recent developments in continental criticism in terms of *crisis*." I shall not concern myself with the accuracy of these assertions, which, despite the imperiousness with which they are stated, seem to me highly questionable (e.g., Were there ever "well established rules and conventions that governed the discipline of criticism," and if there were, had they not been "badly tampered with" well before the 1960s, in fact, at least as early as the eighteenth century?). Rather, I would like to call attention to de Man's strategy of deflection. A sheltered American critic, I believe, might be forgiven for being innocent enough to perceive a "crisis" in literary criticism as an apocalyptic event. But is it possible that de Man could have been as naive as a sheltered American? Since he wrote for a pro-Nazi newspaper for more than a year, we must assume that he read Nazi ideology and propaganda. The *Times* story cites Raoul Hilberg, the Holocaust historian, as saying that "almost all educated Belgians knew by 1941 or at the latest, 1942, that Jews were being sent eastward to be exterminated." Is it possible, then, that as late as the mid-sixties de Man should not have understood that the crisis in Western culture was (and is) not a crisis of literary criticism, but of the ease with which Europe was Nazified, and that it was not the rules of criticism that had been tampered with but the rules of civilized human behavior? That is, "the edifice" of European culture "threatens to collapse" not because the rules of literary criticism have changed but because of Auschwitz.

What we now know of de Man's past may help in answering one of the enigmas of the essay: Why did de Man choose Husserl (a Jew) as his example of a philosopher whose "privileging" of "post-Hellenic European consciousness" blinded him to his own Eurocentrism and prevented him from doing justice to non-European cultures? After all, was Husserl the only Eurocentric philosopher? Oddly, de Man finds no Eurocentrism or blindness in Heidegger's exegesis of Hölderlin, and takes for granted the validity of Heidegger's ". . . intention to collect and found Being by means of language," [12] even though Heidegger never questioned his own belief that he could discover Being using only one European language. Knowing that de Man was concealing a suspect past, perhaps even from himself, we must be struck by both the pathos and the irony of de Man's contention that it was Husserl who failed to live by one of the cornerstones of his own thinking: "Husserl conceived of philosophy primarily as a self-interpretation by means of which we eliminate what he calls *Selbstverhülltheit*, the tendency of the self to hide from the light it can cast on itself." [13]

It may have been de Man himself, after all, who had most to fear from "the light . . . the self . . . can cast on itself." And perhaps that is why he had to conclude his essay on "Criticism and Crisis" in a spurious nihilism:

The 'virtual focus' [that is, Levi-Strauss's substitute for the subject] is, strictly speaking, a nothing, but its nothingness concerns us very little, since a mere act of reason suffices to give it a mode of being that leaves the rational order unchallenged. The same is true of the imaginary source of fiction. Here the human self has experienced the void within itself and the invented fiction, far from filling the void, asserts itself as pure nothingness, our nothingness stated and restated by a subject that is the agent of its own instability." [14]

What is at issue is not nihilism itself, but the insincerity of the nihilism expressed here, which is that of a clever child who has learned to play with words. This is not the kind of felt nihilism that a writer like Melville expresses with fear and trembling in the chapter in *Moby-Dick* on "The Whiteness of the Whale." It is, once again, a nihilism in bad faith.

Among the unidentified scholars cited in the *Times* story were some who ". . . defended [de Man] as having been a young man, influenced perhaps by an uncle, Henri de Man, who was a minister in the collaborationist Belgian government . . ." These defenders were apparently innocent of the knowledge that men much younger than de Man, and in many instances not as well educated, were able to tell right from wrong, and were willing to risk their lives fighting in the Resistance. There is one writer a little older than de Man, Jean Amery, who "presents" himself "in a double capacity, as a Jew and as a member of the Belgian resistance movement," who published an essay entitled "At the Mind's Limits" [15] at about the same time de Man must have been writing his essay on "Crisis and Criticism." Although academe has not chosen to pay attention to Amery's essay in the way that it has chosen to honor the works of de Man, Amery is a more forthright and honest writer. His learning seems to have been no less formidable than de Man's, but his experience was in a sense both poorer and richer. He was captured by the Gestapo, tortured, and shuttled through the death-camp system, including Buchenwald, Bergen-Belsen, and Auschwitz.

Instead of playing with verbal variations on nothingness and instead of contemplating Being, Amery was forced by the culture that had once nurtured him to learn a new skill: survival. In this paragraph from "At the Mind's Limits," Amery describes graphically a new reality, created by German culture, that renders the chatter of Heidegger and de Man irrelevant. In contrast with de Man's circuitous and self-deceiving language, the unrelenting truth of Amery's strong and authentic words may wake literary critics and historians from the deep sleep into which they have been lulled by de Man and his self-blinding followers:

All those problems that one designates according to a linguistic convention as "metaphysical" became meaningless. But it was not apathy that made contemplating them impossible; on the contrary, it was the cruel sharpness of an intellect honed and hardened by camp reality. In addition, the emotional powers were lacking with which, if need be, one could have invested vague philosophic concepts and thereby made them subjectively and psychologically meaningful. Occasionally, perhaps that disquieting magus from Alemannic regions [Heidegger] came to mind who said that beings appear to us only in the light of Being, but that man forgot Being by fixing on beings. Well now, Being. But in the camp it was more convincingly apparent than on the outside that beings and the light of Being get you nowhere. You could *be* hungry, *be* tired, *be* sick. To say that one purely and simply *is*, made no sense. And existence *as such,* to top it off, became definitively a totally abstract and thus empty concept. To reach out beyond concrete reality with words became before our very eyes a game that was not only worthless and an impermissible luxury but also mocking and evil. Hourly, the physical world delivered proof that its insufferableness could be coped with only through means inherent in that world. In other words: nowhere else in the world did reality have as much effective power as in the camp, nowhere else was reality so real. In no other place did the attempt to transcend it prove so hopeless and so shoddy. Like the lyric stanza about the silently standing walls and the flags clanking in the wind, the philosophic declarations also lost their transcendency and then and there became in part objective observations, in part dull chatter. Where they still meant something they appeared trivial, and where they were not trivial they no longer meant anything. We didn't require any semantic analysis or logical syntax to recognize this. A glance at the watchtowers, a sniff of burnt fat from the crematories sufficed.[16]

CHAPTER THREE

Martin Heidegger
and Pagan Gods

Postmodernism, postmodernist literary criticism and philosophy, and deconstruction are slowly dying from the revelations emerging about their founders. The antics of apologists for de Man's collaboration with the Nazis and Heidegger's commitment to the National Socialist movement only bury the apologists and deconstruction itself deeper in the morass of their own and the movement's moral obtuseness. The revelations themselves are now old hat—Ortwin de Graef's discovery of de Man's anti-Semitic comments in the Belgian newspapers *Le Soir* and *Het Vlaamsche Land,* and Victor Farias's presentation of the ugly facts in the case of Mr. Heidegger. It is the later apologetics by loyalists like Geoffrey Hartman, Christopher Norris, and Richard Rorty, and, as expected, Jacques Derrida, among others, that have taken a bizarre turn, but a most useful one, nevertheless, for the sake of truth. For these bizarre defenses indicate how fully "deconstructionists" are committed to doublespeak and to strategies that advance their own narrow agendas, without regard to fairness or justice.

Consider, for example, the extraordinary defense of de Man mounted by Jacques Derrida in *Critical Inquiry*. His essay is an exercise in unadulterated narcissism, dripping with self-pity. An estimated thirty million civilian victims and the destruction of an entire culture are as nothing compared to the pain Derrida himself experienced on first learning of de Man's anti-Semitism. Time and again, the reader is asked to try to understand Derrida's pain.

Now, we know that Derrida is the most subtle of the scholars in the field, a master of reversive readings that he calls deconstructions. Therefore, it comes as no surprise to see him demonstrate that silence is not really silence but a scream of anguish; that concealment is actually confession; that lying is a higher form of truth-telling; that anti-Semitic statements turn out under close scrutiny to be philo-Semitic utterances in disguise; that being a collaborator with the Nazis is not very much different from being a resistance fighter against the Nazis; that those who are repelled by de Man's collaboration with the Nazis are actually Nazis themselves; and that any one who does not accept these Derridean subtleties is a simpleton.[1] Only the most subtle of reasoners could weave so intricate a net. But this is not all. Condemning the biographical fallacy that would extend the early de Man's possible blemish into the later de Man's work, Derrida nevertheless presents his own subtle biographical argument (at the same time subtly denying that he is doing so), assigning a saintly essence to de Man's personal identity that would make any hint of anti-Semitism or even collaborationism an impossibility.

No. It is even more than that. Mr. Derrida is not the most subtle of reasoners for nothing. He converts a colloquium at the University of Alabama into a Last Supper, and de Man into a man of sorrows, acquainted with grief and despised of men. In what can only be called a gesture of obscenity, the collaborator is turned into one of the victims, a crucified savior. "Is it not de Man," Derrida asks, "who speaks to us 'beyond the grave' and from the flames of cremation?" Derrida must be answered here with a resounding NO! De Man does not speak from "the flames of cremation" any more than the Waffen SS buried in Bitburg. To utter so obscene a lie is to repeat the behavior that led to the crematories to begin with, and is a callous desecration of the memory of the victims. Whatever virtues we may attribute to de Man—intelligence, practicality, a strong self-preservation instinct, analytic prowess—we dare not credit him with martyrdom. De Man decidedly does not speak from the "flames of cremation." On the contrary, we now know that when de Man had to choose between the cremators and those to be gassed and cremated he chose to align himself with the cremators. De Man, in fact, would drown the voices of those who speak from "the flames of cremation" in a sea of evasions and deflections from truth, as would Derrida himself.

Interestingly, the unrelenting foe of the Logos and of the logocentric tradition in Western thought now appropriates nothing less than the Logos to himself. As the colloquium is the Last Supper, so the participants in the colloquium become the disseminating disciples to de Man's Christ and Derrida's Jacques the Baptist. Deconstruction itself now becomes the Logos, the word of God, the Holy Spirit incarnate in the body of de Man: "Even those who would like to reject or burn de Man's work know very well and will have to resign themselves to the fact, that from now on it is inscribed, at work, and radiating in the body of the corpus of our tradition." "Our tradition," no less, says the man who has proclaimed "the end of metaphysics!" Is it not clear that we are in the presence, here, of a pseudoreligion that demands, like all religions, total faith and submission? One wonders about the participants at the colloquium, who have been reduced to a faceless, nameless mass in the shadow of Derrida's ego. How do they take this attempt to send them forth as evangelists of a new Faith? Do they take the assignment of this mission as a compliment to their trustworthiness or as an insult to their intelligence? Do they fail to recognize the cheap rhetorical tricks that are being foisted on them? Do they accept in silence Derrida's attempt to make them accessories to his project of victimizing the victims one more time?

Derrida and the other defenders of de Man want to keep playing the game of pretending that moral issues are, after all, only a matter of rhetoric; they try to clothe moral shabbiness in dazzling eloquence and elaborate rationalization. Yet how weak the case for de Man appears when we see the depths to which his defenders must stoop to defend him. In his essay, Derrida creates an elaborate historical context in which de Man is essentially a quasidivine person who did no more nor less than what he was forced to do by circumstances of the times. But in his brilliant summation of the evidence against Kurt Waldheim, presented in a made-for-television trial, prosecutor Allan A. Ryan sets quite another, and more accurate, historical context, which provides a powerful antidote to the moral obfuscations of the academic narcissists. He cautions the five justices who make up the commission not to

be lured into a search for *the* one officer responsible for each of these crimes. [The commission] will not find him, for that officer does not exist. And if it goes off on such a futile search, this commission will fall precisely into the trap set by the array of unrepentant witnesses who came before this commission. To a man they said, "It was not my job, I knew nothing." "I was in intelligence, but this had nothing to do with intelligence." "I was in operations but this had nothing to do with operations." "I was on the general staff. What did I know?"

You see what they are doing. They are inviting you to search for the tiny black pinhead of malignancy that is responsible for all the cancer. Do not be misled. History and the evidence show us, Nazi crimes poisoned the entire system. Germany could not have done it without its collaborators. The SS could not have done it without the military. The commanding general could not have done it without his staff and his troops. The 1A could not have done it without the 1B and the 1C. The colonels could not have done it without the lieutenants, or the lieutenants without those who wielded the weapons.

For two years Kurt Waldheim has been urging the world to do what Nazis have done since 1945, to slice the responsibility into such tiny pieces that no one can be held responsible. If we believe that, what do we believe next? That these millions of dead were victims of a natural disaster? [2]

In the real world that Ryan lives and functions in, moral issues are important. In this world, Paul de Man, like Waldheim (although in a lesser capacity), permitted himself to become an accessory to the Nazi crimes, not by "transmitting orders," but by helping to circulate the poison that infected the entire society. He was part of that chain of complicity that Ryan articulates so eloquently, one of those collaborators who made it possible for Germany to keep the death-camp furnaces running on human fuel. He was not, is not, a crucified Savior who took upon himself the suffering of mankind.

As is the case in the defenses of de Man, the display of ingenuity required to reconstruct Heidegger may turn out to be as interesting, and incriminating to both Heidegger and his defenders, as the recent revelations about his Nazi sympathies. If de Man may be said to have been one of those who circulated the poison, Heidegger, we may now see, was one who helped to concoct it; worse, while concocting it he made it taste like nectar. Reviewing Victor Farias's book, *Heidegger et Nazisme*, in *The New Republic*, Richard Rorty presents a spirited but ultimately shocking defense of Heidegger's Nazism. Granting what cannot be denied in the light of the Farias book, that ". . . as a human being, Heidegger was a rather nasty piece of work— a coward and a liar, pretty much from first to last," Rorty cautions that "there is no way to correlate moral virtue with philosophical importance . . . ." since "being an original philosopher . . . is the result of some neural kink that occurs independently of other kinks. The only reason we think that good moral character is more important for professors of philosophy than for professors of other subjects," Rorty continues, "is that we often use 'philosopher' as the name of an ideal human being: one who prefectly unites wisdom and kindness, insight and decency. . . . But 'philosopher' is not the right name for this ideal." Amazingly, Rorty seems willing to trash philosophy in order to save Heidegger. Yet having diminished philosophy to a matter of trivial game-playing and neural kinkiness, Rorty nevertheless goes on to argue that we must continue to study Heidegger because, just as "we have gotten a lot out of the Gospels, . . . I suspect that philosophers for centuries to come will be getting a lot out of Heidegger's original and powerful narrative of the movement of Western thought from Plato to Nietzsche."[3]

Rorty's own argument is a striking example of the contaminating effect that Heidegger seems to have on other thinkers. Normally a lucid and rational thinker, Rorty falls into a series of hopeless contradictions in his defense of Heidegger, and even loses judgment sufficiently to compare the thinking of this xenophobe, who we now know was so deeply involved in the ideology of hate, to the Gospels which convey the message of love and universal brotherhood. Rorty adds that if we read Heidegger in a way that Heidegger would not have wanted to be read (that is, if we read him coolly, denying him our total commitment and acceptance), then we may "pull out, from the tangle we find on the pages, some lines of thought that might turn out to be useful for our own purposes," and we will "think of Heidegger . . . as one more source for a description of *our* experience . . ." [my emphasis]. Since Rorty's review appeared in *The New Republic*,

I assume he is writing for American readers. But in what sense can open-minded, pluralistically oriented, universally tolerant American readers take the writings of this ultra-nationalist German "as one more source for a description of *our* experience . . ."? Or what "useful purposes" may be served by the philosophizing of a thinker who is a "coward and a liar, pretty much from first to last?"

What, we may ask, does it tell us when those who would defend de Man and Heidegger in public have to become even grosser obfuscators and self-deceivers than de Man and Heidegger themselves were in order to defend them?

It must be understood, as those who think and write from within the cozy confines of Heideggerian-de Manian-Derridean hermeneutics seem unable to understand, that Auschwitz was not only *anus mundi*, as it was called by victims and tormenters alike; it is the symbol of the total collapse of a high culture that included, and fattened on, the philosophizing of Heidegger, as well as the collaboration of the de Mans. The question thus becomes not one of whether or not Heidegger and de Man were nice persons (the terms into which Rorty and Derrida translate the question). Nor is the question, as Thomas Sheehan puts it in the *New York Review of Books*: "If the man himself was—to put it minimally—a Nazi sympathizer, is his philosophy also in some way fascistic? Does his thought, in whole or part, lend itself to political reaction or at least a nondemocratic view of the world?" "Nondemocratic view of the world" indeed! Rather, the question is one of the extent to which Heidegger's powerful thinking may be an ineradicable part of that fatal stain in German culture that led not simply to a "nondemocratic view of the world" but to Auschwitz, which is to say to a criminal state, to the unrelenting and systematic deployment of modern technology and age-old bureaucracy for the purposes of dehumanizing both murderers and victims, with the ultimate intention of carrying out total genocide on certain "races" (namely, Jews and gypsies), and of brutally enslaving Slavs and other "inferior" peoples.

It is not just a matter of Heidegger's personal quirks or even of his character. It is a matter of what Heidegger believed, and the further question is whether it is advisable or possible to separate what a philosopher thinks from what he believes. Once we start to consider Heidegger's thinking in terms of his beliefs we cannot fail to be struck by the close parallel between those beliefs and the Nazi program of aggression, genocide, and enslavement (not merely "nondemocracy"). It is clear, for example, that though Hitler hated Jews and would have been prepared to exterminate them on the basis of his hatred alone, he also hated them as the originators of Christianity, which he, like Nietzsche, found to be a decadent religion. Can we overlook the fact that Heidegger's undermining of metaphysics and his desire to burrow his way back to a pre-Socratic revelation of Being by means of the German language is a philosophical parallel to Hitler's political agenda of returning to a pre-biblical, pre-Christian past as represented by Arminius the Cheruscan? And do we not find this philosophical and political agenda paralleled in music, in Wagner's *Ring Cycle*?

We must remember, as so many have been working so hard to make us forget, that Nazism was not the momentary aberration of a single madman, but was a mass movement by virtue of which, as both Hitler and Heidegger believed, the German *Volk*, "rooted in soil and blood," was fated to impose its will on Europe and the rest of the world to save humankind from sinking further into what they saw as the "evils" of liberty, equality, fraternity, and human rights. Summarizing his response to a letter from a German correspondent who wrote that the Germans had been intoxicated by Hitler's "beautiful words," only to find, later, that "we were riding a criminal and a traitor," Primo Levi wrote to the German: "that above all, on my shelf next to Dante and Boccaccio I kept my *Mein Kampf*, 'My Struggle,' written by Adolf Hitler many years before coming to power. That dread man was not a traitor, he was a coherent fanatic whose ideas were extremely clear: he never changed them and never concealed them. Those who voted for him certainly voted for his ideas. Nothing is lacking in that book: the blood and land, the living space, the Jew as the eternal enemy, the Germans who embody 'the highest form of humanity on earth. . . .'"[4]

Is it possible that a man of Heidegger's intelligence would have joined the Nazi party without having read *Mein Kampf*? And is it conceivable that so powerful a thinker could have read *Mein Kampf* without recognizing Hitler's racist mentality and his unconcealed racist policies? And could so deep a thinker have taken on the rectorship of a great university without realizing that in doing so he was not only approving, but becoming an accomplice to, the implementation of the murderous racist policies that Hitler had enunciated in *Mein Kampf*? Is it possible, further, that there should be no connection between the Nazi effort to murder God in Auschwitz and Heidegger's attempt to deconstruct the metaphysical tradition in Western philosophy, which is to say his attempt to destroy that fusion of Hellenism and Hebraism which is Christianity? In fact, are we not bound in all honesty to say that the real-world endpoint of Heideggerian (and now Derridean and de Manian) deconstruction of the logocentric tradition is precisely Auschwitz?

What has not yet been acknowledged is that we must understand Auschwitz to understand Heidegger, not the other way round. But we cannot understand Auschwitz as long as our philosophers, men of letters, and literary critics ignore the writings of the victims and think and write only from the perspective of middle-class leisure and "high" culture represented by Heidegger. It is, as survivors tell us, impossible to know Auschwitz without having been there; nevertheless, an understanding of the "postmodern" era cannot begin without the acknowledgment of Auschwitz. An understanding of contemporary developments in literature and philosophy will be possible only when we scuttle the vague and misleading category, "postmodern," for the historically rooted term, "post-Auschwitz." For though we cannot say what is meant by postmodern, except that it is somehow antithetically related to modernism, I believe we can identify what is intended by the term post-Auschwitz. In brief, the post-Auschwitz age is one in which the nineteenth-century prophecies of Marx and Nietzsche have been realized in the Soviet gulag, on the one hand, and in the Nazi death camps on the other.

But postmodernist and deconstructionist literary theory, which take an avowedly Heideggerian stance, cannot deal with this recent past, nor can postmodernist theorists acknowledge that postmodernism is the direct historical legacy of Europe's Holocaust past.[5]

Hence we should not be surprised to find that Stephen W. Melville's deconstructionist-motivated *Philosophy Beside Itself: On Deconstruction and Modernism*, as the achronological subtitle suggests, is conceived antihistorically and in defiance of cause-and-effect. Without regard to the rupture constituted by the years 1939 to 1945, the two literary movements are considered in terms of one another. The title, however, is misleading. At least it was to me. There is more chronological organization and discussion of influence (though it is not called that) than one is led to expect. And there is certainly less of modernism, at least of literary modernism. Modernism, here, is represented by Hegel, Wittgenstein, and Heidegger (the last named can actually go either way); deconstruction by the usual suspects: Derrida and de Man, and a less usual one, Stanley Cavell. The book is, in fact, saturated with Derrida, and written in the shadow of de Man. How saturated with Derrida? The index is headed by a "profound" Derridean riddle (the first time I have ever seen an epigraph appended to an index): "*Differance* is neither a *word* nor a *concept*." How deep in de Man's shadow? The author's preface ends on a note of servile gratitude: "There is a last debt, undischargable. It is of course to the late Paul de Man." [6] Why "of course"? Has undischargable indebtedness to de Man become a predestined condition for all humankind?

As a consequence of his immersion in Derrida and de Man, Stephen Melville is not at all concerned with the fact that modernism was a historically rooted cultural phenomenon enveloping a murderous but not quite barbarous war, and preceding the fully barbarous war that put an end to whatever illusions about Western culture may have been left after World War I. He also glosses over the fact that modernism was a highly fertile literary movement. Although there is an endnote indicating that the author "earned his Ph.D. in Comparative Studies in Literature," nothing seems further from his mind than literature. While almost two whole pages of the bibliography are taken up by Derrida and de Man, there is, in a book purporting to deal with modernist literature, nary a mention of any of the following: T. S. Eliot, Ezra Pound, E. E. Cummings, Wallace Stevens, HD, Anais Nin, Ernest Hemingway, William Faulkner, Robert Frost, James Joyce, Virginia Wolfe, John Dos Passos, F. Scott Fitzgerald, Sherwood Anderson, or

Gertrude Stein. Needless to say, Melville takes no note of Heidegger's Nazism, nor of the possible connections between his acceptance of Nazi ideology and his project of deconstruction.

Whatever else Stephen Melville may have learned from Heidegger, Derrida, and de Man, he was without doubt an apt student of the pretentious declaration. The examples that follow hardly require comment: "I am myself very much a product of Derridean subversions—neither fully critic nor fully philosopher, at once uneasily and joyously adrift between departments and disciplines. . . ." Or, again, "By presenting Derrida in such a thoroughly Hegelian context, I have been led into a systematic neglect or disparagement of Kant that is based upon what is, finally, neither a particularly deep nor a particularly generous reading of him."[7] But this pretentiousness is not as harmless as it may seem, for it leads inevitably to a dangerous inauthenticity, and to an eclipse of moral consciouness. It is not amusing to read that

It may be that we can now feel the grammatical sense behind what might be called the "modernist imperative"—the way in which the modernist must say "must" without being able to know whether or how he or she really means it. . . . It is more nearly the case that with this "must" I commit myself to philosophy, its history and its discipline, in the only way that I can, which is: at risk and with no authority beyond that commitment and the conviction it may compel. . . . The force of such a "must" does not lie in me, but elsewhere. . . .

I am then at risk here. I am in the position of arguing for the Emperor's clothes."[8]

Here we cannot be so indulgent of what first appears mere academic pomposity. In what sense is Stephen Melville "at risk"? What does "risk" mean to him? What does it mean to the philosophers he so admires? In normal speech, to be "at risk" means to be in danger of some harm or injury. Yet we know that when Heidegger had to choose between safety and risk he chose safety. Apologists for Heidegger have offered as a defense for his not having opposed the Nazis that it would not have been the safe thing to do (we now know, of course, that he did not oppose the Nazis because he supported their project). At any rate, it is the case that if Heidegger did recognize

Nazism as an evil, he chose not to risk opposing it. We can say no less of de Man. And no doubt we may assume that Stephen Melville, too, would not resist evil (even though he counts himself "a product of Derridean subversions"), for even if he were capable of recognizing a monstrous evil, he would inevitably conclude that the "must" that might induce him to resist that evil did "not lie in me, but elsewhere," as did those who gave tacit approval to genocide by not opposing it. What better statement can we find of this moral blindness than Stephen Melville's own admission: "Among the things we do not, in the end, know is what nakedness—or clothing—is." [9] But let us hope that Melville speaks only for himself and other deconstructionists, and not for the whole of humankind. Surely there are some people who can still tell the difference between a person who is clothed and one who is naked.

It is, as Herman Melville's Ishmael points out, "a thing most sorrowful . . . to expose the fall of valor in the soul." Hence, one can take little pleasure in the spectacle of Stephen Melville's deludedness. This ultimate tunnel vision of pursuing "intellectual liberation" through a narrow tube of Heidegger seen through Derrida seen through de Man is reminiscent of a Yiddish proverb: "The worm that has burrowed into the horseradish thinks there is nothing better." All too many deconstructionists dwell, without knowing it, in an enclosed Heideggerian room that Martin Buber has described as ". . . a strange room of the spirit [in which] we feel as if the ground we tread is the board on which a game is being played whose rules we learn as we advance . . . and which persist only through a decision having once been reached to play this intellectual game." [10]

Buber, who understood Heidegger and Heidegger's culture intimately, who, as a German Jew, as a philosopher and theologian, had the advantage, so to speak, of being both inside German culture, and at the same time outside it, was able to swallow Heidegger and eliminate him in timely fashion. But for American comparatists and philosophers, Heidegger becomes a source of incurable cerebral constipation.

Though the Heideggerian deconstructionist terminology suggests "largeness," a movement outward into all-encompassing ideas, the methodology of the deconstructionists strikes one as being a burrowing downward and inward into a vortex of the self, a narrowing rather than a widening of human experience and consciousness. On the book jacket of *Heidegger: Thought and Historicity*, Christopher Fynsk is identified as a comparatist, but he is a comparatist, like Stephen Melville, whose interest in literature seems minimal. True, the book contains a long chapter on Hölderlin, but Hölderlin is there only because Heidegger decided that Hölderlin spoke Being (in complementarity to Heidegger himself, who *thought* Being). "My own approach to Heidegger's interpretations of Hölderlin," Fynsk writes, "is shaped primarily by the guiding concern of this volume: the question of finitude as it presents itself in relation to the self-definition (or self-affirmation) of the human Dasein in a project of Being." [11]

Although Fynsk is a shade more attuned to Heidegger's political sins than Melville, he nevertheless interprets Heidegger's ambiguous, gnomic adumbrations of his political beliefs as expressions of Heidegger's opposition to National Socialism. But what does Heidegger have in mind when he writes that

The struggle for planetary sovereignty and the unfolding of the metaphysics that sustains it bring to fulfillment an age of the earth and of historical humanity; for here there are realized the most extreme possibilities of world domination and of the effort undertaken by man, to decide upon his essence purely out of himself.[12]

Fynsk interprets this passage in apocalyptic terms: "The danger that lies in the foundations of the modern world must emerge fully—the eclipse of Being must be complete—before the glimmer of another understanding of Being can emerge." But what is this other "understanding of Being," and whose apocalypise is this "struggle for planetary sovereignty" if not Hitler's?

Later in the book, Fynsk cites Heidegger's assertion that

It is enough if we gather from the reference that the variously named conflict of the Dionysian and Apollonian, of holy passion and sober representation, is a hidden stylistic law of the historical determination of the German people and that one day we must find ourselves ready and able to give it shape. . . . By recognizing this antagonism, Hölderlin and Nietzsche early on placed a question mark after the task of the German people to find their essence historically. Will we understand this cipher? One thing is certain: history will wreak vengeance on us if we do not.[13]

Fynsk concludes that "These words of 1936 underscore powerfully the fact that Heidegger's turn to the problem of art and Dichtung is part of his confrontation (however indirect) with the fact of National Socialism." But do not Heidegger's words lead us to the quite opposite conclusion that he was not "confronting" National Socialism but abetting it?

From the standpoint of literary criticism (as opposed to philosophy or pure aesthetics) Fynsk's book has its culmination in the final chapter, "Hölderlin's Testimony: An Eye Too Many Perhaps." Here we should expect the great revelation. The reader hopes to discover something new. Here we expect to have demonstrated for us the way in which poetry can still transcend the diminished world in which twentieth-century humans dwell. We expect Fynsk to show us the way in which Hölderlin (through Heidegger) spoke Being, to discover how his poetry can be put to the constructive task of replacing the dead God. Such expectations remain frustrated. Except for the reader who already is disposed to make a leap of faith, Fynsk's interpretations of Heidegger's readings of Hölderlin's poems do not discover Being or God. But then the reader who is already disposed to make the leap of faith does not need Heidegger, Hölderlin, or Fynsk. A reading of Hölderlin's poem, "In Lovely Blueness," truly a poem of great purity and loveliness, is a case in point. Fynsk comments that in Hölderlin's poem, "Man's purity, which is the basis of his resemblance to divinity, exceeds any natural appearance of purity. . . . Natural beauty brings forth man's figurality (his purity), but his purity exceeds the natural image." [14] Is there anything in this conceptualization of man's place in the universe that we cannot find anticipated in scripture? Man is created in God's image as a spiritual being, and to that extent he has the potential to be pure, and to rule over the rest of Creation ("his purity exceeds the natural image"). Hölderlin's expression, *"als der Mensch, der heisset ein Bild der Gottheit,"* echoes the biblical *"Und Gott schuf den Menschen Ihm zum Bilde, zum Bilde Gott schuf er ihn."*

Fynsk continues: "Heidegger reads the lines 'Is God unknown? Is He manifest as the sky? This rather I believe' as implying that the appearance of God in the manifestness of the sky is an appearance of God as unknown. The measure provided by the godhead, he concludes, consists in precisely this appearance of a concealment." [15] But is this not the common biblical motif of the hidden God found in the oft-repeated biblical formula, "Hide not Thy face from me . . . ?" Fynsk's (and Heidegger's) refusal to acknowledge the biblical echoes in Hölderlin, with his consequent inability to understand that Hölderlin derives his consciousness of "the Holy" from the Judeo-Christian tradition, calls attention to a major flaw in Heideggerian studies: an unwillingness to acknowledge the vital role that Hebraism has played in Western notions of "the holy" and of transcendence.

We must be impressed by the hubris of this obsessive burrowing into an ever-narrowing dead-end vortex, especially since the burrowers intimate, at the same time, that the dead end opens into the possibility of a new transcendence unrelated to the Judeo-Christian tradition. Consider Fynsk's annunciation, "My own approach to Heidegger's interpretations of Hölderlin is shaped primarily by the guiding concern of this volume: the question of finitude as it presents itself in relation to the self-definition (or self-affirmation) of the human Dasein in a project of Being." [16] Age-old problems of the mysteries of language, poetry, revelation, the finite and the infinite, flesh and spirit, human limitation and divine transcendence, the profane and the sacred, are funneled down to an interpretation of the lucubrations of two white German males, one a poet, one a philosopher and a Nazi, writing in a single European language, as though those two alone held the key to all mysteries.

Fynsk concludes that "Hölderlin reveals exactly what Heidegger himself announced in his earlier work when he said that our deepest and most authentic finitude refuses itself to the measure of our freedom." It never occurs to Fynsk that this scenario may be just a little too neat. May we not infer from it that Heidegger forces Hölderlin's text to say what he wants it to say, disregarding the biblical origins of

Holiness in Hölderlin, so as to be able to claim confirmation for his own "project of Being?" [17]

If there is light at the end of this tunnel, it may be provided by Stanley Corngold. In *The Fate of the Self: German Writers and French Theory*, Corngold undertakes the task of undeconstructing the deconstructionist fiction of the nonexistence of the self. "I conclude," he writes, "that the main tendency of the new French criticism is an attack on the self as it has been understood since German idealism as the agent of its own development." [18] Corngold uses the techniques of deconstruction to establish the point that each of seven German writers who is taken by Derridean and de Manian deconstructionism to be an example of the dismantling of the self, "has given an account of the self. . . . Each author elaborates a conception of the self whose conatus is to communicate itself and to come to light within its work." The argument for each of the seven authors is too elaborate and detailed to go into here. Nor is it necessary to do so, for the existence of the self can no more be proven than the nonexistence of the self. One can only marvel at the fact that it should be necessary to expend so much human energy to prove what is apparent to any sane, living human being.

What is important about Corngold's book, then, is not so much that he convinces us that the "self" exists (which, so long as we are sane, we know intuitively), but that he has managed to preserve his own human integrity and sanity in the belly of the beast. Two acknowledgments, one in the acknowledgments section and one in the introduction of *The Fate of the Self*, tell the story. In the acknowledgments Corngold announces, "My greatest debt, both personally and for the light he brought to these authors, is to the late Paul de Man. His seminars on Rousseau and Hölderlin and Heidegger . . . were full of a bliss of intelligent reading." [19] But a little later, in the introduction, Corngold adds that "The story in this book . . . is told with the collaboration of many other authors—of Lionel Trilling, for one, whose *Opposing Self* I read thirty years ago while a student at Columbia College. Rereading it now I am astonished at what I find. [Trilling's] essays all, in one way or another, take account of the idea that preoccupies this literature and is central to it . . . —the idea of the self." [20]

Corngold's real purpose is not simply to assert the existence of the self, but to demonstrate that a humanist self and humanist values can be salvaged from the devastation wrought by deconstruction.

Corngold's effort to counteract the deconstructionist assault on the self is noble, but unfortunately too restricted, that is, too concentrated on a narrow canon of writers to the detriment of history. But his effort can help us to clarify the issues. The deconstructionists claim, and let us grant that they believe it, that the assault on the self, or on what they call the totalizing subject, is an attack on all forms of totalizing, including the totalitarian state. But the evidence of recent history must give us pause. As Erich Kahler has shown in *The Tower and the Abyss*, which, though written in the fifties, remains the most brilliant, the most comprehensive, and the most accurate description of the Holocaust in all its dimensions, the quintessence of Nazism was precisely an assault on the concept of the existence of the self carried to its logical extreme.[21]

In Corngold's attempt to reassert the existence of the self by using the methods of reading designed precisely to destroy that existence, and in his wistful invocation of Trilling, he helps bring into focus what is at stake in the current debates on method and over politically motivated revisions of the canon. His recollection of Trilling reminds us of the price we have paid in accepting the ascendency and hegemony of comparatism in the guise of Franco-Prussian criticism and theorizing. And the moment we start to remember, the significance of the loss becomes frightening.

What has been effectively eclipsed by the Franco-Prussian hegemony is the gentle, constructive humanism of Matthew Arnold that once informed the study of literature.[22] There were vulnerabilities, to be sure, in Arnold's humanism, the most obvious of which may have been its incapacity to envisage or comprehend the blackness of darkness that was to erupt in central Europe and envelop the globe. Yet for all its shallowness and for all the contempt in which it is held by arrogant young critics, Arnoldian humanism did not lead, as did profound Heideggerian brooding, to the death camps. Arnold understood (as Heidegger, de Man, and Derrida clearly did or do not) the need for the Western mind to maintain a proper balance between the Hellenic and the Hebraic. It is inconceivable that Arnold would have accepted genocide with the same indifference as Heidegger and de Man, nor that he would have devoted his time and energy to pondering the origins of the work of art in a state that was committing genocide. To give credit where it is due, the British, whose intellectual and ruling class had been schooled in Arnoldian humanism, were the only Europeans to resist Nazism effectively and voluntarily, and at great cost to themselves. To the glory of the British, they did not make a deal with Hitler, even though they could have. And is it not to the shame of current Anglo-American criticism and philosophy to be goosestepping to the Franco-Prussian drum, diminishing what was noble while glorifying and elevating to dogma the ignoble, the cowardly, and the deceitful?

CHAPTER FOUR

Paul de Man and the
Poetics of Prevarication

A man's power to connect his thought with its proper symbol, and so utter it, depends on
the simplicity of his character, that is, upon his love of truth and his desire to communicate it
without loss. The corruption of man is followed by the corruption of language.
—Ralph Waldo Emerson, *Nature*

We have been silent witnesses of evil deeds . . . we have learnt the arts of equivocation and pretence; experience has made us suspicious of others and kept us from being truthful and open;
intolerable conflicts have worn us down and made us cynical. Are we still of any use? What we
shall need is not geniuses, or cynics, or misanthropes, or clever tacticians, but plain, honest,
straightforward men. Will our inward power of resistance be strong enough, and our honesty
with ourselves remorseless enough, for us to find our way back to simplicity and straight-
forwardness?"
—Dietrich Bonhoeffer, "After Ten Years. A Reckoning Made at New Year, 1943"

I wrote "Paul de Man and the Politics of Deconstruction" in December 1987 at the invitation of George Core, editor of the *Sewanee
Review*.[1] The state of the de Man affair is still unresolved, and the
swelling tide of essays and books still pouring forth on both sides of
the issue is an indication that literary critics and theorists believe there
is much at stake. For me at least, the discovery of de Man's youthful collaboration with the Nazis (coming almost simultaneously with
even more damaging revelations about Martin Heidegger) was the
smoking gun. For more than a decade I had been pointing out that one
could detect certain affinities to totalitarian ways of thinking in what
later came to be called postmodern theory and literary criticism. I had

also raised the question of why contemporary criticism and theory was so monumentally silent about the recent past. The discovery of de Man's collaborationist past, along with the equally intriguing discovery of Heidegger's steadfast commitment to Nazism, provided me with the answers I had been looking for.

Now de Man's work and his life have become a focal point for the struggle between those who wish to preserve the humanist tradition of literature as a body of works that reflects the highest aspirations and values of Western culture, and those who announce that they wish to bring about what they refer to as the end of metaphysics and the destruction of Western values (as though those values had not already been destroyed by history and Auschwitz). The task of bringing the de Man affair up to date would be formidable were it not for the fortunate fact that recent defenses of de Man break little new ground, continuing, for the most part, along the lines laid down by Jacques Derrida in his long essay in *Critical Inquiry*.[2]

The main lines of defense, which remain unchanged, were neatly summarized by Roger Kimball as follows:

(1) Yes, it's regrettable that Paul de Man wrote those articles, but after all, he was very young at the time. . . . (2) It's unfortunate that the prominent newspaper *Le Soir*, where the majority of his early journalistic efforts appeared, should have been openly collaborating with the Nazis—still, de Man was ambitious and naturally seized the opportunity to write for the prestigious paper; besides, only a few of his articles were explicitly anti-Semitic. . . . (3) It's true that he wondered in an article that appeared in March, 1941 . . . whether Jews "polluted" modern literature, and that he envisioned the establishment of a Jewish colony "isolated from Europe"; we must remember, however, that this was not as vicious as much anti-Semitic writing for *Le Soir* at the end of 1942, before people knew about the Nazi death camps. (4) While it's lamentable that he never acknowledged his deeds—that he went so far as to claim on at least one occasion that he had been part of the "Belgian resistance" to the Nazis during the War—perhaps his difficulty in coming to terms with his own past helps to explain his tough-minded resistance to the bewitchments of language later in life.[3]

Though the main lines of defense have remained constant, nevertheless several new items should be mentioned, two of which are worthy of extensive comment.

The University of Nebraska has issued two bulky volumes, one of which reprints de Man's wartime writings, and the other which includes fifty essays for and against de Man, with some new documentation, including a self-exonerating letter that de Man wrote to the Harvard Society of Fellows when they got wind of his wartime activities.[4] James Atlas retells the de Man affair for the general public in the *New York Times Magazine*, Sunday, August 28, 1988. The summer 1989 issue of *Critical Inquiry*, which has served as one of the major organs in this country for the dissemination of de Man's subversions of liberal humanism, contained six replies to Derrida's original apologetic, an outraged response by Derrida, and another defense of de Man by Shoshana Felman. And the summer 1989 issue of *World Literature Today* published a review-essay by Leon S. Roudiez on the two University of Nebraska volumes. The Nebraska volumes, plus de Man's writings, were also reviewed by Denis Donoghue, in the *New York Review of Books*, June 29, 1989.[5]

This listing is far from exhaustive, and even so, it is hardly possible to comment in detail on all the items just mentioned. The Atlas *New York Times Magazine* piece, and the Roudiez and Donoghue reviews, however, raise some issues worth looking into. In the initial phases of the de Man affair, his defenders condescendingly labeled their adversaries journalists, as if it were only lowly journalistic types, incapable of understanding de Man's profundities, who were calling attention to the scandal of his collaborationist past. It was also suggested that these journalistic attacks were part of an orchestrated conspiracy by the Establishment press to discredit de Man and undermine deconstruction itself.

Anyone who had accepted the press conspiracy hypothesis would have been greatly surprised by James Atlas's journalistic version of the story, which he entitled, "The Case of Paul de Man." If anything, Atlas proved that academics do not have a monopoly on moral obtuseness. His apologetic is the more shameful for having been presented as an "objective" examination of the "facts" in the "case." Raising the question in a sub-headline of whether, "in his youth, the eminent critic was a pro-Nazi journalist or an immature opportunist," Atlas eventually concludes not only that de Man was nothing worse than an "immature opportunist," but that being an opportunist under the Nazi occupation was not reprehensible.

There is no point going over old ground, but it should be said that while de Man certainly was an opportunist, the term "immature," which Atlas appears to take as an exonerating adjective, hardly seems to apply to de Man in 1941. Men much younger than he and not as well educated were mature enough to tell right from wrong. Many of them fought in the Resistance, and many paid with their lives for their belief in human decency and for their efforts to preserve some shred of it in wartime Europe. Jean Amery, a Jew and a member of the Belgian resistance movement, who was captured by the Gestapo, tortured, and shuttled through the death-camp system, wrote a series of profound meditations about his experiences, trying to understand the culture of death that the Nazis had created. The honesty and truthfulness of his writing stands in stark contrast to the obfuscations of his contemporary and fellow Belgian, de Man. Another sparkling demonstration that it was possible to make moral choices and that one did not have to be a collaborator is Jan Karski. His book, *Story of a Secret State*, is an understated account not only of his own heroism but of the heroism and self-sacrifice of those Poles who were not opportunists, who suffered torture and risked their lives rather than advance their own careers in exchange for collaborating with a genocidal regime.[6]

Atlas dismisses any significant connection between de Man's youthful anti-Semitic writings and deconstructionist theory on the basis that de Man was not "the inventor" of deconstruction. While it is probably true that de Man did not invent deconstruction, nevertheless, he found in the techniques of deconstruction a useful device for creating an intricate and elaborate set of evasions that would help him to nullify his own guilt-ridden past. It is no coincidence that there are such close resemblances between de Man's "historiography" and the revisionist historian Ernst Nolte's infamous article in the *Frankfurter Allgemeine Zeitung*, "The Past That Will Not Pass Away" (6 June 1986). And it is no wonder that de Man's obfuscations should have had a tremendous appeal to European intellectuals, many of whom did no more nor less than de Man himself. In fact, this is perhaps exactly the point that one must make about de Man: he is not unique.

Post-war Europe was awash with de Mans, a continent of displaced victimizers as well as displaced victims, from former death-camp officials to petty collaborators, all rubbing shoulders with each other in the ruins of war, all trying to melt into the general chaos and return to business as usual, as though nothing had happened.

Atlas ends his essay on what is apparently intended to be an idyllic note that strongly intimates the Nazi past should be declared over and done with. He is riding a bus to Antwerp, and as he ruminates on what he has found out about de Man he decides, with a comfortable sense of philosophical detachment, that

Others joined the Resistance, or kept out of things. De Man worked for a Nazi newspaper and implied that Jews were dispensable at a time when his employers were preparing the "final solution." He was innocent of history, and his innocence assured his complicity.

But these were episodes in a life, however nefarious, I reflected as I rode the bus into Antwerp when the conference was over. They were human failings, venial sins.[7]

It is not clear how Atlas arrives at the conclusion that de Man was "innocent of history," whatever that means. Perhaps he is suggesting that de Man was not fully aware of what he was doing. But such inattentiveness or unawareness does not seem to be consistent with de Man's character. He may not have known the full consequences of what he was doing, but he certainly knew that what he was doing would advance his ambitions; writing for pro-Nazi periodicals, he must have known what Nazism stood for, and in this sense he was probably not "innocent of history." It is also true that de Man's "venial sins," as Atlas calls them, were only episodes in a life. But that is true of all human acts: each one is nothing more than an episode in a life. Yet in de Man's case the episodes start to add up to a life of deception. De Man's "failings," Atlas finds, were "human," the implication being that collaborators were "only human" in advancing their careers at someone else's expense. In reducing de Man's "immature opportunism" to a mere human failing, Atlas adopts one of the tenets of deconstructionist ideology: human activities have no inherent "value"; value itself is merely another human fiction to be deconstructed. By the same token resistance fighters were also "only human" in their courage and heroism, and therefore there really is not much difference between collaborators and resistance fighters, both simply having acted out their particular "humanness" rather than having made moral choices.

"As for what he did," Atlas asks, "how can any of us know what we would have done under those same circumstances?" But what does Atlas imagine de Man's circumstances might have been? This attempt at exoneration on the basis of extenuating circumstances reflects an unfortunate inability to grasp just what the Holocaust of 1939 to 1945 was all about. The "circumstances" would exonerate de Man if he had had to face the kind of impossible choices that were confronting Europe's Jews at this time. Were the "circumstances" that if de Man did not write for *Le Soir* he or members of his immediate family would be tortured or killed? Atlas seems to assume that de Man was in the same position as someone like the physician Janusz Korczak, who deliberately chose to accompany the orphans in his charge to the gas chamber so they would be comforted. But de Man, as far as we know, did not have to make a choice of this kind. He did not have to write for *Le Soir* to save his own life or the lives of members of his family; it was, rather, only a matter of advancing his career. We know that while many chose to follow the path of opportunism, a noble few chose to resist the ideology of hate and racism. The reason that we should not casually rationalize away the behavior of the collaborators as normal human frailty is that in doing so we also diminish the heroism of the resisters. The question raised by the de Man revelations is not whether de Man was simply a fallible human being like the rest of us, but whether we should "privilege" the ideas and thinking of someone who not only disseminated racist policies for opportunistic reasons but who never gave any sign of regretting having done so.

If academics do not have a monopoly on moral obtuseness, however, they are certainly without competition in their capacity for self-deception. Professor Emeritus Leon Roudiez, whose review of *Wartime Journalism, 1939–1943*, and *Responses: On Paul de Man's Wartime Journalism*, is valuable as an informed and relatively un-biased evaluation of the mass of both new and old data on de Man, nevertheless suffers from the academic's blindness of insight. So skillful has de Man been in interweaving truth, half-truth, evasion, half-lie, and lie, that even astute experienced readers are taken in by his deceptions. In fact, paradoxically, the more sophisticated the reader, the more likely he is to be taken in by de Man's subterfuges. A case in point is a deception de Man employs in a 1955 letter to the Harvard Society of Fellows, written in answer to charges brought against him anonymously. In the letter de Man referred to his uncle, Hendrik de Man, as "my father." The passage is a clever enough piece of skulduggery to be worth quoting at length:

My father, Hendrik de Man, former Belgian Minister and Chairman of the social-democrat party, is a highly controversial political figure. Because of his attitude under the German occupation, he was sentenced in absentia after the war and died in exile in Switzerland last year. He remains an extremely debatable case and, for reasons that go to the roots of internal Belgian political problems, his name arouses extremely strong feelings at least in some Belgians, apparently still today.

I certainly am in no position to pass judgment on him, but I know that his mistakes were made out of a lack of machiavellism and not out of lack of devotion to his ideals. He did what he thought best for his country and his beliefs, and the final evaluation of his acts is a matter of history. One can find his own justification stated in the last two chapters of his autobiography, published last year in Germany under the title *Gegen den Strom.*

I hear now that I myself am being accused of collaboration. In 1940 and 1941 I wrote some literary articles in the newspaper "le Soir" and, like most of the other contributors, I stopped doing so when Nazi thought control did no longer allow freedom of statement. During the rest of the occupation, I did what was the duty of any decent person. After the war, everyone was subjected to a very severe examination of his political behavior, and my name was not a favorable recommendation. In order to obtain a passport, one had not merely to produce a certificate of good conduct, but also a so-called "certificate de civisme," which stated that one was cleared of any collaboration. I could not possibly have come to this country two times, with proper passport and visa, if there had been the slightest reproach against me. To accuse me now, behind my back, of collaboration, and this to persons of a different nation who can not possibly verify and appreciate the facts, is a slanderous attack which leaves me helpless.[8]

Atlas comments on the matter of de Man's having represented his uncle as his father that it is only the discovery of Paul de Man's birth certificate that "clears up one mystery in a life where even the matter of paternity has been in doubt." Needless to say, "the matter of paternity has been [a] mystery" only because de Man, for whatever reason, chose to make it one. Atlas goes on to speculate about the reason for de Man's peculiar misremembrance: "What could have motivated de Man to claim that his uncle was his father? Was it to deflect blame from himself? To enhance his ancestry?" Actually, either one of these would do, but the point is that in a letter presenting itself as a document intended to "clarify and explain my situation," de Man not only mystifies his situation still further, but tells what any reasonable person in possession of the facts would perceive as a deliberate perversion of truth. When the information in de Man's letter to the society is filtered through the deconstructionist-tinted reading glasses of Roudiez, however, prevarication is transformed into its very opposite; Roudiez perceives not a calculated lie, but an inadvertent confession by de Man of his sentimental attachment to his uncle. He begins his review with the following "facts":

Paul de Man, who died in New Haven in December 1983, was born in Antwerp in December 1919; his uncle Henri de Man became a well-known politician and socialist theorist, and, especially after Paul's brother was killed in an accident in 1936 and his mother committed suicide exactly one year later, the two were quite close—so much so that in 1955 in a letter to the Society of Fellows at Harvard, in which he responded to charges of wartime collaboration (which he denied), he wrote, "My father, Hendrik [Henri] de Man . . ."[9]

Atlas speculates that de Man may have been trying to deflect blame from himself or to appeal to the society's elitism. It seems very clear that he is doing both, skillfully playing on the sensibilities of the Fellows. With the benefit of hindsight, de Man's rhetorical strategies become transparent. He expresses his shock at the thought that anyone might bring allegations against him, then immediately shifts the focus of blame to his uncle. The allegations could not have been related to anything Paul de Man did, they must be aimed at him as some sort of vendetta against his father/uncle. Here, too, de Man is less than candid. He does not specify what his "father's" difficulties were. As de Man surely knows, "controversial" is an honorific term for American academics, and it was especially so in the fifties. Weren't all those victims of Joe McCarthy's red-baiting considered "controversial" too, and weren't many of them innocent academics who were being tarred by the brush of guilt by association? And now, as de Man represents it, someone is trying to do to de Man what McCarthy has been doing to American academics.

The words Nazi and collaborator are never used, and the "innocent" de Man registers amazement on discovering that his father's name can still "arouse extremely strong feelings at least in some Belgians, apparently still today [less than ten years after the cessation of the slaughter]." His "father's" problem, according to de Man, was not a matter of being a collaborator, but merely a matter of "attitude." De Man is gambling on the shelteredness of American professors, a high-odds roll of the dice that the members of the society will not have a sense for the intense anger and even vindictiveness certain Europeans still harbor toward Nazis and collaborators (though one would certainly have expected greater sophistication from Poggioli). Having for the most part lived sheltered lives in American groves of academe, would the members of the society suspect that people are now living in Europe who themselves might have been tortured and maimed by Nazis and collaborators, and whose relatives might have been carted off in cattle cars for gassing and cremation, and that these people would still harbor strong feelings about someone suspected of collaborating with the Nazis?

De Man continues his diversionary tactics in the next paragraph. Now there can be no doubt that his father is the target, and someone must be trying to get at the "controversial" father through the "innocent" son. It is the father, Hendrik, who must be judged, not Paul de Man. But who can judge him? Certainly not his own son. One thing for sure, though, the father was not Machiavellian—that is, he was no opportunist. He was an idealist. Ironically, that was probably true. Hendrik de Man probably was an idealist. Of course, so was Hitler. And now Paul is about to become the victimized son of a victimized idealist father. But Paul knows what it means to be an idealist in the twentieth century, even if the innocent Fellows of the society do not. What did the father do, after all? Only "what he thought best for his country and his beliefs," even if, in the Europe of 1941 to 1944, that sometimes meant sending women and children to be gassed. His idealism is even on record (as is Hitler's for anyone who wants to read *Mein Kampf*). Clever Paul. Did he think the Harvard fellows would rush out to read his father/uncle's book? Did they?

So the son declares the uncle/father, who is not even being accused of anything, innocent of opportunism. And now how about the son? "I hear now that I myself am being accused of collaboration. In 1940 and 1941 I wrote some literary articles in the newspaper 'le Soir' and, like most of the other contributors, I stopped doing so when Nazi thought control did no longer allow freedom of statement." More memory lapses at best, or perhaps misrepresentations, or maybe more lies. That is the problem. How does one describe language deployed in this way? "I stopped [writing for *Le Soir*] when Nazi thought control did no longer allow freedom of statement." That may be an accurate statement, but the question of "Nazi thought control" is not the issue here, since, as Paul neglects to mention, *Le Soir* was a pro-Nazi publication to begin with. De Man says he wrote "some literary articles" in 1940 and 1941, but he actually continued to write for *Le Soir* well into 1942, and he also overlooks his contributions to the pro-Nazi *Het Vlaamsche Land*, which are less likely to be discovered if anyone were going to bother checking his story. Nor does he mention that his "literary articles" included at least one that was virulently anti-Semitic. He also implies that his reason for discontinuing his contributions was related to "Nazi thought control," which may not be a misrepresentation, but which suggests that he was writing articles that might have been offensive to the Nazis. "During the rest of the occupation," de Man continues, "I did what was the duty of any decent person." And what was that? There are some people who might interpret doing "the duty of any decent person" under Nazi occupation to mean joining the resistance. Maybe he did do the decent thing, but the available evidence suggests otherwise.

Then follows what amounts to at least a half-lie. It is simply not true that "After the war, everyone was subjected to a very severe examination of his political behavior." We now know—and de Man, who was there, surely knew—that the examination procedures were extremely haphazard and erratic. Europe was in chaos. Anarchy prevailed. Records had been lost, misplaced, burned, bombed, destroyed, stolen. Displaced persons in every condition of being (that is, everyone from those who were well-fed and clothed to those who were naked and dying of starvation), speaking a babel of languages, were roving aimlessly across the Continent. Nazis rubbed shoulders with survivors of death camps. It was simply not possible, even if the will had been there, to subject "everyone to a very severe examination of his political behavior." And then again, a de Manian obfuscation: "My name was not a favorable recommendation," as though it were only his uncle/father's name and not his own activities that were in question.

De Man's next misrepresentation, the assertion that he would not have been able to enter the country had there been the least suspicion that he might have been a Nazi or a collaborator, is one that he likes so well he repeats it for good measure. Earlier, in "clarifying" the conditions under which he entered this country and his present status with the Department of Immigration, de Man had written:

On September 28th 1954, I was informed by the Department of Immigration that, in order to obtain a permanent status, I would have to exit from the U.S. and re-enter under the sponsorship of my wife. . . . I wish to point out that, in order to obtain this permission which is considered a privilege, one has to establish good moral character. This means that my entire history, here and abroad, was investigated by the Immigration Service and found to be satisfactory. I foresee no difficulties in accomplishing the formalities leading to my reentry and subsequent naturalization.[10]

Once again, de Man is betting on the innocence and inertia of the Fellows. He knew, but the Fellows probably did not, that the clean bill of moral health he attributes to himself and the rigorous examination of character he depicts here and in the paragraph denying the accusations against him were pure fictions (in fact, so far was de Man from having a "good moral character" at this point that he might have been committing bigamy at the very time the immigration procedures were being conducted). A more authoritative and accurate picture of American immigration policies after the war is rendered by Allan A. Ryan, Jr., who was the director of the Office of Special Investigations from 1979 to 1983:

The overwhelming majority of Nazi criminals came through the front door, with all their papers in order. They came here not by conniving with lawless government officials but by the infinitely easier method of simply deceiving the honest ones. They were the beneficiaries of a law that virtually excluded Jews while welcoming their oppressors [the Displaced Persons Act of 1948, under which de Man may have entered this country]. And these immigrants were not merely "ex-Nazis," or Nazi sympathizers, or Nazi collaborators. They were the war criminals, the handmaidens of Nazism who had personally, and quite willingly, taken part in the persecution of millions of innocent men, women and children. They had no assistance from anyone in particular; they did not need it. All they needed was the ability that any twelve-year-old might possess to tell a lie; we did the rest. And we did it with all democratic processes intact and functioning.[11]

De Man knew that his record was only as clean as the evidence he gave to the immigration authorities. As he probably lied and evaded to them, so he was also now lying to the Fellows, but with the, for him, delicious added twist that now his earlier perjuries were being presented as evidence of his current purity. For anyone who takes the trouble to read this letter in its entirety and in the light of the information now available to us it is an astonishing document. It provides us with a deeper insight into what made de Man tick than all his critical and theoretical essays put together.

Nevertheless, with all the evidence now available, and after examining the evidence in the two Nebraska volumes, including de Man's letter to the Harvard Fellows, Leon Roudiez can still conclude that "we are not now, and, in all likelihood, shall never be . . . in the position of being able to pass judgment on Paul de Man." That is because, according to Roudiez, though we have many facts, "facts are usually meaningless in themselves and need to be interpreted." Moreover, Roudiez continues, facts must not only be interpreted, but to be interpreted, they must have a context. And what shall be the context for de Manian facts? Should we include his mother's suicide, and what the suicide meant to de Man's mother? "Or", he goes on,

what was the meaning, for Paul de Man, and what is the meaning for the rest of us, of the five-hundred-word article "Les Juifs dans la littérature actuelle"? S. Heidi Krueger writes, "If we read it in isolation, it is almost impossible to tell where it stands with regard to the situation of the Jews" (*R*, 305). It requires interpretation, and interpretation requires a context—the three other articles on the same page, the entire contents of *Le Soir*, the events in Brussels, in Belgium, and in Europe that occurred at the same time, and also the context of the present-day reader. Does a Jewish reader interpret it the same way as a non-Jewish reader? Does a person whose relatives or friends were sent to Auschwitz interpret it the same way as a younger person for whom Auschwitz, Dachau, and Treblinka are just words on the page of a history book? How important are those five hundred words when set against the whole of what Paul de Man has written? It is all a matter of interpretation, and each interpretation will probably reveal more about the interpreter than about de Man. The Truth, however, is what we shall never know.[12]

Like de Man himself, Roudiez creates a mystery where there need be none. His last paragraph is a Shandean barrel of red herrings that provides us with the lesson that de Manian techniques cannot be used to reveal truth. On the contrary, they were designed to do just the opposite, to keep the truth in obscurity. The kind of contextualizing proposed by Roudiez is equivalent to the contextualizing of revisionist historians: for example, we cannot talk about Auschwitz without talking about the Treaty of Versailles, or the Soviet gulag, or Vietnam, just as Tristram Shandy cannot get down to talking about his birth without first talking about his conception, and he cannot talk about his conception without talking about his Uncle Toby, and of course once he starts talking about his Uncle Toby then there is no telling where he is going to wind up. This kind of contextualizing is not to contextualize but to trivialize.

Yet, we can make a judgment on de Man, and we can do so without worrying about what his mother's suicide meant to her, or without worrying whether a relative of an Auschwitz survivor would interpret de Man's anti-Semitic article in the same way as a callow youth who knew nothing about Auschwitz. That is not the context we need to arrive at a judgment about de Man and his work.

We have the context we need in postwar Europe and in de Man's letter to the Harvard Fellows. One must marvel at the ease with which de Man uses language to short-circuit truth. The reader will perhaps recall that when Hamlet urges Guildenstern to play a tune on the recorder, Guildenstern answers that he cannot play a tune because "I know no touch of it, my lord." Whereupon Hamlet replies, "It is as easy as lying." For de Man, as for the vast majority of Europeans, by 1945, lying had become second nature, as easy as breathing. In more ways than one, the letter to the Harvard fellows was the beginning of de Man's career. This tissue of lies, evasions, prevarications, diverticulations, and aporias not only enables de Man to acquire the credentials that will make possible his career in academia, it confirms for him, if he had not already learned it from his Nazi coworkers at *Le Soir* and *Het Vlaamsche Land*, that language is the ultimate vehicle of deception. This is the hermeneutic circle with a vengeance. De Man is clean because the immigration service says he is clean. But the immigration service says he is clean because de Man has told them he is clean. And now he tells the Harvard fellows that if the immigration service says he is clean, he must be clean, etc., etc., etc.

Was de Man an anti-Semite or a Nazi? Probably not. His close friends should know, and they vouch for him. Was he an opportunist? Not even his defenders deny that. Certainly, de Man was not in a class with a Demjanjuk or an Artukovic, sadistic murderous peasants, and it would be the height of folly even to suggest such a thing. Nevertheless, it was intellectuals like de Man who, by their complicity, legitimized the Demjanjuks and made their crimes acceptable. It may well be that Paul de Man was a gentle soul, but we should remember that de Man does not stand by himself. He is a specimen of a postwar European Everyman. He lived on a continent and in cultures ruled by an ideology of perverted Darwinism in which only the strong, the cunning, and the ruthless were deemed worthy to survive. From 1939 to 1945 there had been the Nazi terror. Children were encouraged to betray their own parents. Not even one's closest family could be trusted with certain truths, so lying and concealment and distrust became normality. In the chaos of 1945 and after, it would have been madness not only to tell the truth but even to think it. Before 1945, Jews had to lie about their identity if they were to have even a slight chance to survive. After 1945, it was mainly Nazis and collaborators and Nazi sympathizers who had to lie, often even to themselves, so they could get on with their lives as though nothing had happened. In Europe during the war, and immediately after, people often killed for a scrap of bread. So who cared about lying and truth? Eventually some people lost the ability to distinguish one from the other.

In connection with the de Man affair, there is an interesting letter in the June 4, 1988, issue of *The Nation*, in which Hans Robert Jauss, a former SS member, now a respected reception-aesthetic theorist at the University of Constance in West Germany, writes to "clarify" his relationship to Paul de Man and his own SS past. Jauss acknowledges that he served in the Waffen SS "without interruption from 1939 until 1945 as a soldier, primarily on the Eastern Front." He then goes on to say,

> I was neither a professional soldier nor a member of the General S.S. (infamous for its brutality), nor a member of the Nazi Party. At no time did I serve in a Waffen-S.S. unit when it committed atrocities, although there were other times when atrocities were committed by Waffen S.S. units of which I had been or was to be a member. . . . A tribunal under American auspices formally declared in 1948 that it could find no incriminating evidence against me. . . . I deeply regret my involvement with an organization that was responsible for so much suffering and such unspeakable crimes. It does not console me that I was not fully aware of such events until after the end of the war, for during the war I failed to investigate disturbing rumors and reports or to think through their implications.[13]

Since I discuss Jauss's credibility on this matter at length in chapter 7, I will not dwell on the matter at great length here, but it is inconceivable that a member of the SS could have served on the eastern front from 1941 through 1945 without having committed a single act of cruelty, to say nothing of having spent these years in eastern Poland and the Ukraine and Russia without knowing that a slaughter of innocents was under way. Allan Ryan writes that "Eleven million people were put to death by the Nazi machine."[14] Russians, Poles, Jews, Gypsies, and others were being slaughtered in every nook and cranny of Eastern Europe. *Einsatzgruppen,* mobile killing units of SS troops, ranged across the whole of Eastern Europe committing murder themselves or else supervising others to do it for them. Is it possible that Jauss did not at some point meet a member of one of these units somewhere, on furlough, on R&R, or in the line of duty? Did he never chat with any of these fellow SS troopers, all of whom had at least one thing in common, that they had sworn their lives and souls to Adolf Hitler and to carrying out the Final Solution?

And is it really possible that in five years in Eastern Europe as an

SS member Jauss never saw a transport of Jews packed into cattle cars rolling across the East European countryside? No one who has seen Claude Lanzmann's documentary film *Shoah* would find such a claim credible. Jauss writes that "A tribunal under American auspices formally declared in 1948 that it could find no incriminating evidence against me." Like de Man, Jauss knows in telling truth how not to tell the truth. He does not say that incriminating evidence against him did not exist, only that a tribunal could find none. But in the light of the Klaus Barbie affair we now know how much that means. And Jauss certainly knows how much it means. Let me say, however, that I believe that Jauss believed what he wrote at the instant that he was writing it. Yet must we not conclude that he could believe what he wrote only as a result of self-induced amnesia? This syndrome has been described and analyzed in detail by Alexander and Margarete Mitscherlich, in their sociopsychological study of postwar Germans, *The Inability to Mourn*. "For the German people as a whole," they write, "defense still remains the trump card when confronting feelings of guilt and shame over the Nazi past. . . . Such an attitude means that only certain acceptable fragments of the past are admitted to memory." [15]

Joseph Goebbels founded the Third Reich on the big lie. After the war, another big lie started to take shape, the rumor that nothing special had happened, that it was possible to return to business as usual, that there was only a handful of true Nazis. A double standard began to establish itself: on the one hand, public professions of retribution and swift justice for the criminals, but on the other a desire, even a need, to protect and conceal the war criminals, the collaborators, the Nazi sympathizers. For were they not, in so many cases, friends and relatives, someone's son or father or brother or daughter or sweetheart? I cannot repeat the history here, but anyone interested can read Ryan's book, or Peter Weiss's *The Investigation*, or the literature now emerging on Klaus Barbie, or the story of Pieter Menten, a Dutch Nazi who was responsible for mass murders in Poland, and who accumulated a fortune in stolen art; Menten lived in comfort, shielded by the authorities, until finally tracked down by a relative of some of his victims. [16]

Confronted with a private and collective past too painful to face, the intellectuals of western Europe began an arduous process of inventing elaborate strategies of denial. In all probability Paul de Man was neither a Nazi nor a sadist, but he was a member of an entire generation that had to deny the truth to preserve its self-esteem. The letter to the Harvard Fellows, which worked to perfection, became a turning point. De Man now discovered how skillfully he could use language to pervert the truth. Not surprisingly, he came to believe that language could function in no other way except as a vehicle for subterfuge and untruth. He now dedicated himself to proving that it was language that lied by its very nature, and not the individual who lied by moral choice, for if he proved that, then his own linguistic behavior could in no way be found to be reprehensible. It was never de Man who lied, but language itself.

Thus we may say that de Man's life was consistent and seamless, contrary to Denis Donoghue's uncharacteristically romantic hypothesis of two de Mans. According to Donoghue, it was only the de Man who operated on the level of day-to-day reality that "lied . . . about his wartime years . . . or . . . elided the war from his record. . . ." This mortal de Man, however, had only to enter a phone booth and strip to emerge as Superman freely afloat in the ethereal Sublime. "On the 'higher' level, where the common writ does not run," writes Donoghue, "de Man developed a theory of language and a practice of reading which had as their effect, and I have no doubt their aim, the subversion of every sentiment or prejudice that had made a mess of his early life in Belgium." Yes, indeed, de Man did "develop a theory of language," but not to "subvert" the early "sentiments and prejudices"; he developed the theory, rather, to cover up a past he could not face. Donoghue's bizarre two de Man thesis is contradicted by de Man's silence about his past and by his deliberate cover-up of that past as late as the 1955 letter to the Harvard fellows.[17]

Donoghue, following the lead of Jacques Derrida, does not see it this way. He finds, rather, that "The only way in which we can answer injustice with justice, in relation to de Man, is by reading his entire work." What is the logic of Donoghue's strange sense of "justice?" It is that in the light of de Man's wartime journalism Donoghue now fantasizes "faults" and "hairline fractures" in the totality of de Man's work, where he once thought it monolithic. And what do these imagined "hairline fractures" tell Donoghue? They tell him that the later writings "repudiate" the "early journalism." "Repudiate" is certainly an odd word to describe what de Man did. Repudiation means open, explicit denunciation, an overt articulated revulsion of a named evil. But how can de Man be said to have "repudiated" his wartime writings, when no one, including Derrida and Donoghue, knew what he was talking about until the accidental discovery of his anti-Semitic articles? This notion of "repudiation" of the past is a variant of Derrida's argument that by deconstructing "texts," de Man was actually attacking all forms of totalization. This portrait of de Man as an undercover antiauthoritarian, however, is entirely discredited by de Man's authoritarian posture, as demonstrated in Frank Lentricchia's brilliant chapter in *After the New Criticism*, entitled "Paul de Man: The Rhetoric of Authority." Taking up William Pritchard's figure of the "Yale Mafia," Lentricchia refers to de Man as the Godfather who does not need to "speak often, nor elaborately, because when the don speaks he speaks with total authority, and it is de Man's 'rhetoric of authority' . . . which has distinguished his criticism since its earliest days." [18]

Donoghue ends his essay by McCarthyizing all those who might disagree with him. "But it would answer injustice with injustice," he writes, "if one were to assert that Deconstruction is compromised by de Man's wartime journalism. The current attempt to smear Deconstruction by denouncing de Man is sordid. He didn't invent Deconstruction. . . ." Donoghue can arrive at his conclusion only on the basis of his strained thesis of the two-tiered de Man. But if, as seems more likely, there is only a single de Man, then deconstruction is indeed compromised by de Man's wartime journalism. Though de Man did not invent "deconstruction," for in truth he was not a very inventive critic, he was quick to see its relevance to the life of deception he had been living continuously at least since 1941. For if he was not really a Nazi while he was writing for the Nazi publications *Le Soir* and *Het Vlaamsche Land*, he was living one lie. And if he was a Nazi when he wrote for those publications, then he lived another lie from the postwar period to his death. Always the clever opportunist, de Man brilliantly appropriated deconstructionism to his own needs, and other European literary theorists who were developing their own patterns of denial were not slow to recognize the applicability of his work to their own projects. Whether objectivist or subjectivist, hermeneutic or phenomenological, structuralist or reader-reception, postwar European schools of criticism have one thing in common: they derive, like the revisionist history of Ernst Nolte, from the thinking of Nazi philosopher Martin Heidegger, and they all reflect a desire to efface the recent past. It is clear, then, that so long as we seek to find the true de Man by employing the methods of postmodern criticism, we will never be able to come to any conclusion about de Man's wartime activities or about anyone else's. May we not, then, infer, that this was exactly what de Man intended, that he did indeed spend his professional life devising theories of reading that permitted him to "defer" truth indefinitely? If we can never arrive at the truth about de Man it is truly because de Man and the European intellectuals of his generation were so successful not only in concealing that truth, but in concocting epistemologies and theories of literature and reading that would make truth a meaningless concept.

Donoghue declares, "The current attempt to smear Deconstruction by denouncing de Man is sordid." But is it not very sordid indeed to smear those who have committed no crime worse than disagreeing with Donoghue, and who seek, in good faith, to find the true connection between deconstruction and its sources? Is it not sordid to portray as a victim one who aligned himself with the victimizers? Is it de Man, after all, who must be rescued from "injustice," or those who became victims because of opportunists like de Man? Is it not sordid for Donoghue to turn truth inside out, so that de Man's sordid anti-Semitic writings are rendered nothing worse than a springboard to redemption and salvation, while those who question them are damned to perdition?[19]

The inability of European postmodernist literary theorists and their followers in this country to face the implications of the recent cultural past of Nazism and of a genocide committed on, and in full view of, the European continent, has rendered contemporary criticism incapable of dealing with the human dimension in literature. In its concentration on the ontological status of fictions and on the epistemic status of literature and of literary criticism itself, contemporary literary theory manages to enact a perpetual deferral of human reality. The objectivist and subjectivist extremes of literary theory meet at the edge of the abyss that is the nonexistence of the text, whether that text ceases to exist by virtue of a solipsistic reader-reception aesthetic or by virtue of an annihilating deconstruction. Theory, it is arrogantly claimed, replaces both practical criticism and literature itself because literary texts presumably have nothing to tell us, and therefore "readings" of such texts cannot tell us anything either. "It is as if," Wallace Stevens once said, "we had come to an end of the imagination." Unlike the New Criticism, deconstruction has not paved the way for, nor taught us how to read, hitherto "uncanonized" works, and some of the powerful literature written in the postwar period remains not only unanalyzed and unexamined, but unread.

As an example of this undiscovered (buried, perhaps, would be a better word) literature, consider a little poem that would undoubtedly be considered too simple and too direct to be worthy of the notice of high-powered postmodernist literary theorists in search of aporias or in pursuit of the meaning of literary history, the significance of the reading process, and the origins of Being. Sometime toward the end of 1943 a card was found sewn into the coat of a girl, aged nine at the time of her death, named Elzunia, in the concentration camp at Sachsenhausen. On the blood-stained card were written some words she had composed herself, only the following being legible:

> *Była sobie raz Elżunia*
> *umierała sama*
> *bo jej tatus na Majdanku*
> *w Oświęcimiu mama . . .*
>
> [Once upon a time there was Elzunia
> Dying all alone,
> Because her daddy is in Maidanek
> And in Auschwitz her mommy.][20]

On the bottom of the page the child had added the title of a well-known folk tune to which the words were to be sung.

How, we might ask, would contemporary theory, or de Man's deconstructionist methodology help us to read or understand this poem? Would de Man discover one of his famous aporias in the song? How would Hans Georg Gadamer apply his hermeneutical theories to this poem? Gadamer writes, at one point, that "the essential nature of the historical spirit does not consist in the restoration of the past, but in thoughtful mediation with contemporary life."[21] How, then, would he find the historical spirit of Elzunia's poem by mediating it with contemporary (that is, post-Auschwitz) life? Or better yet, how would Wolfgang Iser and Hans Robert Jauss apply their theory of reception aesthetics to Elzunia's poem? The abyss between the meaning and pathos of Elzunia's poem on the one hand, and the impotence and inapplicability of the high-flying theories on the other, provides a clue to what is wrong with postmodern theorizing. Not only are deconstruction and hermeneutics and reception aesthetics blind and deaf to Elzunia's poem, these theories seek to blind and deafen readers to all that is human.

French Shame and the New Theory

Without questioning the usefulness or validity of the contextualizations of poststructuralism-deconstruction effected in books by J. G. Merquior and by Luc Ferry and Alain Renaut, I should like here to recontextualize the French poststructuralist-deconstructionist-postmodernist phenomenon in the light of what we now know about Heidegger's lifelong attachment to the ideals of Nazism.[1] This new recontextualization may shed some light on deconstruction and postmodernism as intellectual movements and it may also shed some light on the way these imported ideologies forced a turn in American literary criticism and in American academic culture. I should like to start this recontextualization by calling attention to an eerie threefold silence in French literary criticism generally and in the work of the major poststructuralists-deconstructionists in particular. This silence's three aspects are a silencing of the personal past of the deconstructors from 1940 to 1945, a silencing of the historical past of the French nation during the same period, and a silencing of the Holocaust literature that started appearing in France and in the French language as early as 1946.[2]

"Barthes," according to Lentricchia, "says that the capital sin in criticism is not ideology but the silence by which it is masked."[3] But is it only "ideology" that can be masked by silence? What does the silence of the French intellectuals mean? Although Lacan, Barthes, and Foucault lived under, and through, the Nazi occupation, they rarely speak of these years, and when they do it is usually to dismiss them. Yet, these were years of great humiliation and shame for a proud people. In his report on the background and events of the Klaus Barbie trial, Ted Morgan asserts that

Hitler had said, "I will corrupt the countries I occupy," and was as good as his word, for occupation was a degrading experience, a form of colonization, the sort of thing so-called civilized nations had done to so-called backward nations for centuries. You could reason that the vanquished would civilize the victors, as the Greeks had the Romans, and that did happen in a minor way, but what really happened was that the victors degraded the vanquished. The occupation brought out and encouraged what was low and dishonest in people. It changed the national character, and forty years later, the French are still recovering from the shame of that time.[4]

The depth and magnitude of this shame are powerfully expressed in an essay by Vladimir Jankelevitch. The shock for the French resisters and those who were, at the time, concerned with French "honor" was not the defeat itself but the very absence of a sense of defeat among the general populace, where life went on as usual, in total harmony with the Nazi occupiers. The disgrace was not in defeat but in the readiness with which all segments of the French population, including intellectuals, accepted Nazism as a way of life, and the eagerness with which a people with a powerful history of being free adapted to occupation and enslavement.

When in 1917 the Russians capitulated after a defeat incomparably less total and less humiliating than ours, the catastrophe was inscribed on every face; hunger, poverty, and the appearance of the entire society spoke with eloquence of the upheaval which was transforming the infrastructure of Russian society. France did not experience this universal and radical tragedy. . . . Who among us does not remember those Sunday afternoons in the so-called free zone, between 1941–1943, with their public gardens filled with relaxed strollers and the laughter of children.

From time to time an explorer returning from the capital would bring us in our caves a stack of Parisian newspapers, and we learned with stupefaction that Paris had its literary evenings, as is necessary if a great country is to maintain its high status. The republic of letters in 1944 was decidedly a thing of beauty. Because these were good times. A few more years and I can guarantee you that M. Abetz, like every other [state leader], would have had his intellectuals of the left, his metaphysical bistros, and his avant garde reviews. Good times, you say. France carried on beautifully.[5]

Among those who lived through the shame of France were certainly Lacan, Barthes, and Foucault. Let me make clear that I am not striking the heroic pose for myself. I am not intimating that in similar circumstances I would have had the courage to do the honorable thing, to become a resister. As Hemingway well understood, no one can know how he or she will act under pressure until tested under fire. Nor am I saying that the French intellectuals of the sixties through the eighties who were young or mature adults in the forties should have acted more heroically at the time, though that might have proved something. I realize that one cannot demand courage and extraordinary heroism of others. Neither, I should add, am I accusing the transmitters of deconstruction of having been collaborators. My point is merely that as men of great learning and sensitivity, accustomed to reading widely, the intellectuals of the sixties through the eighties could hardly have been ignorant of the "Holocaust" books that were appearing in France, many in the French language. (One prominent example, Elie Wiesel's *Night*, 1960, caused an instant sensation in the United States and may be said to have opened up the field of Holocaust studies in this country. Though the French version, *La Nuit*, was published two years before the English, with a moving foreword by François Mauriac, the book was largely overlooked in France and was certainly ignored by mainstream cultural critics.)[6] As men of feeling with a strong sense of justice and of right and wrong, they must have sensed that they were living in a condition of bad faith. Here they were, advocating a deconstruction of the human form down to a nothingness that would constitute an absolute freedom, but where were they when liberty, equality, and fraternity were being crushed under Nazi jackboots? When they had an opportunity to stand and be counted they did neither, and they must have been conscious of the gap between their ideas and their deeds.[7]

After the war, the French cultivated a myth of total resistance in which every French citizen had been a resister, except for an insignificant number of collaborators who were dealt with as soon as France was liberated. While there were a number of resisters who were undoubtedly extraordinarily noble and courageous souls, it appears that their heroism had to be erased so that the overwhelming majority would not have to face what they perceived as their own dishonor. The gulf between collaborators and resisters, and the small number of the latter, may be inferred from the following passage in a memoir written by a Resistance fighter who was betrayed to the Gestapo and subsequently returned from a German concentration camp:

> The difference between work in the Resistance and service in the so-called regular army had been the freedom in the Resistance, because each person worked independently and on his own initiative. Membership was not imposed but entered into freely. It was Free France in every sense of the word. Each one knew what he had to do: deliver the country from the brutality and the stupidity that was strangling it, preserve its priceless values, and save a threatened people. Everything had been aligned against us: government, family, the social situation, and the mob that brayed, "Marshal Pétain, lead us!"[8]

In creating a comforting myth, the French also created their own version of "a past that will not pass."[9] It was with the arrest of Klaus Barbie and the imminence of a trial that threatened to disinter an ugly past that the myth of total French resistance began to crack. The obvious reluctance to try Barbie and stir up painful memories was a clue to a consciousness of an unsavory past. Just as war criminals remained—and still remain—unfinished business in Germany, so unpunished collaborators remain the unfinished business of postwar France, an unfinished business that makes it difficult for French intellectuals to speak with total candor. As Dominique Moisi, associate director of the French Institute for International Relations, put it in an Op-ed column in the *New York Times* of May 29, 1990,

> Countries cannot move forward without impunity if they are not reconciled with their past and specifically, with their collective responsibility.
> The rise of the extreme right to unprecedented levels in post-World War II France is a case in point. The National Front, the party of Jean-Marie Le Pen, has been using the delicate and popular issue of immigration to hide its hard core ideology: anti-Semitism. It has been allowed to do so for many reasons, but a key one, rarely mentioned, is the existence for too long of a consensus of silence in France about the Vichy years. Some Frenchmen went "beyond the call of duty" in deporting not only the adult Jews demanded by the Nazis but Jewish children as well.[10]

It is in this context of lingering shame, guilt, and an unreconciled past that the French poststructuralists and deconstructionists start to speak to America.[11] And it is in the "consensus of silence" generated by this context that we must consider the French theorists of the sixties, along with the perhaps not wholly coincidental fact that for the scene of American literary criticism their works were mediated by Paul de Man, who wrote literary and cultural essays, some with anti-Semitic content, for collaborationist publications in Belgium in 1941 and 1942.[12] Just as Lentricchia erased the American scene of the fifties and sixties in writing his genealogical history of post-New Critical theoreticism, so the theorists themselves, and by this we can only mean the French theorists, erased the years 1940 to 1945. It hardly seems possible that this silence, this erasure could have been accidental, since three of the intellectuals whose impact on American criticism has been so powerful experienced the trauma personally, as adults or near adults.

Especially intriguing is the silence of Michel Foucault, an advocate of "genealogical" history, a writer more committed to historical investigations than other poststructuralists, who has written at great length about historical instances of oppression and exploitation and about the alleged abuse of power in humanist democracies. It is curious that Foucault should have dedicated himself to so meticulous an analysis of the "panopticon," his paradigm (derived from Jeremy Bentham) of the way in which liberal democracies keep watch over their subjects and thus keep them repressed, while he had nothing to say about the way the Germans kept him and his neighbors in subjection from 1940 to 1944.[13] The thrust of Foucault's analysis is to demonstrate that liberal democracies are more sinister and demonic in their repressive practices than actual police states like Nazi Germany and Stalinist Russia, because the liberal democracies do their repressive work in secret. Certainly Foucault's erasure of his own personal experience under the Nazi occupation constitutes a screaming silence that cannot but undermine the authenticity of his analysis of liberal democracies as repressive states.

In a 1983 interview, Stephen Riggins raises the question of silence, attributing to Foucault the view that there are many silences. Foucault acknowledges that he has thought much about silence and that he learned about different kinds of silence during the war, yet he never mentions his own reluctance to talk about the years of French shame openly and honestly, nor does he explain why he never chose to connect his studies of exploitation and the bureaucratic abuses of power explicitly to the brutal Nazi occupation. Nor can there be any doubt that Foucault's silence about the years of humiliation was deliberate. When Riggins asks specifically whether Foucault has "fond memories of growing up in Poitiers in the 1930s and '40s," he refuses to answer, or rather, he answers evasively, more like a politician than a Diogenes:

Oh yes. My memories are rather, one could not exactly say strange, but what strikes me now when I try to recall those impressions is that nearly all the great emotional memories I have are related to the political situation. I remember very well that I experienced one of my first great frights when Chancellor Dollfuss was assassinated by the Nazis in, I think, 1934. It is something very far from us now. Very few people remember the murder of Dollfuss. I remember very well that I was really scared by that. I think it was my first strong fright about death. I also remember refugees from Spain arriving in Poitiers. I remember fighting in school with my classmates about the Ethiopian War. I think that boys and girls of this generation had their childhood formed by these great historical events. The menace of war was our background, our framework of existence. Then the war arrived. Much more than the activities of family life, it was these events concerning the world which are the substance of our memory.[14]

With this answer, four of the most traumatic years in twentieth-century French history, and one can assume four of the most traumatic in Foucault's personal history, are instantly erased. Foucault says that his "great emotional memories . . . are related to the political situation." Yet we cannot help noticing that in Foucault's memories, France itself must have been without politics, for his recollections have to do only with political matters non-French, and certainly not with the occupation or with the name of "Vichy." He remembers the assassination of Dollfuss, an Austrian, rather than Marshal Pétain or Pierre Laval; he calls to mind refugees from the Spanish Civil War rather than Jewish refugees from Germany who were turned over to the Gestapo by French gendarmes; the Ethiopian War with Italy stands in place of the "phoney" (or virtual non) war between France and Nazi Germany; and—oh yes—as an afterthought, "Then the war arrived." Whereupon Foucault adds that "Our private life was really threatened. Maybe that is the reason why I am fascinated by history and the relationship between personal experience and those events of which we are a part." Certainly this last statement is disingenuous, since what Foucault has done here is precisely to avoid linking his personal experience with the historical events of which he was a part.

But it may be that Foucault's answer to the interviewer's next question will shed some light. The interviewer asks, "What was the origin of your decision to become a philosopher?" Foucault responds that he did not start with the goal of becoming a philosopher, he was at loose ends as a young boy, and adds, "I think that is also something rather typical for people of my generation. We did not know, when I was ten or eleven years old, whether we would become German or remain French." This answer is certainly difficult to understand. Would it, then, have been so easy for Foucault to stop being French and become German? We must remember that to be German in 1940 to 1945 meant something very special. It was not just being German, it was being part of a National Socialist state built on an ideology of anti-Semitism and racism; that is to say, it meant being a loyal subject of a Hitlerist state. Is Foucault telling us that if the occupation had endured he would have had no trouble in adapting to life in a Nazi state?

In 1972, thirty years after the height of the Nazi occupation, Foucault still failed to grasp the true nature of the Hitler state he had lived in during the years 1940 to 1945; an alternative conclusion is that he understood the true nature of the Hitler state and could still admire it in the nineteen-seventies. In the revised version of *The History of Madness* (1972), Foucault continued to celebrate the power of the violent irrational to overcome what he perceived as "the violence of reason." Ferry and Renaut provide a summation of this celebration of the violent irrational as it is set forth in the closing pages of Foucault's work:

When the history of madness is written [by Foucault] from a perspective borrowed from the Nietzschean or Heideggerian deconstruction of the modern *ratio* [as opposed to a Marxist perspective], the "natural" horizon of the topic is an excuse for the irrational, to which the last pages of this work [*Histoire de la folie à l'age classique*, reedited and augmented version of 1972] are unrestrainedly devoted. Passionately describing the great figures of madness (Goya, Sade, Nietzsche), Foucault praises their "sovereign affirmation of subjectivity," their "rejection of natural freedom and equality," their "excessive expression of violence" as "free exercise of sovereignty over and against nature." Through such lightning flashes, the truth of madness returns, a truth reason tries to disguise, the truth of a "power to annihilate" that suddenly rediscovers its own power; with Sade or Goya, "the Western world acquired the possibility of overcoming the violence of reason." Overcoming reason: the horizon of the interpretation is thus clearly traced, and thus is it entirely logical that the book should end with an homage to Nietzsche, in whom the irrationality of madness triumphed over what was believed to have negated it [i.e., Reason].[15]

That Foucault should continue to celebrate "madness" after having lived under the Nazi occupation, and that he should sing praises of the "rejection of natural freedom and equality" and of the "excessive expression of violence" must certainly give us pause in honoring Foucault's writings as a model for liberation. In fact, the "violent irrational" that he celebrates might well constitute a paradigm of the Hitler state Foucault dwelt in from 1940 to 1945.

More than a decade after the publication of the revised version of *The History of Madness*, in his 1983 interview, Foucault evidently still did not understand what it would have meant to have been a German from 1940 to 1944. He might have been more enlightened had he read Jorge Semprun's *Le Grand Voyage*, published in Paris in 1963. Semprun was a Spaniard who fought against Franco, one of those "refugees from the Spanish Civil War" whom Foucault apparently could remember only as a class. Semprun emigrated to France after the Spanish Civil War, joined the French Resistance after the French surrender, was captured by the Gestapo, imprisoned in France, and finally sent to Buchenwald. *The Long Voyage*, a series of meditations on Semprun's experiences as a Resistance fighter and as a captive of the Germans, is organized around the train journey with other captured Resistance fighters from the prison in Auxerre, to the concentration camp, Buchenwald, in Germany. One of these meditations is triggered when the train makes a stop at the station in Trier. A group of Germans gathers on the platform to leer at the prisoners crowded into the cattle car. The onlookers, Semprun tells us, are

talking among themselves, pointing at the train, they're all excited. There's one kid about ten years old, with his parents, directly opposite our car. He listens to his parents, looks in our direction, shakes his head. Then he dashes off. Then he comes running back with a big stone in his hand. Then he comes over toward us and heaves the stone as hard as he can against the opening we're standing beside.[16]

The German boy's hatred of these unknown prisoners on a cattle car, and his murderous intentions toward them inspire the narrator's companion to conclude, "There's nothing very special or mysterious about the krauts, believe me." The narrator, taking a more philosophical view (actually a Marxist view that the "kid's" behavior is socially and historically determined), declines to argue, but goes on thinking:

I say nothing, not wanting to become involved in a discussion. I wonder how many Germans will still have to be killed so that this German kid will have a chance not to become a kraut. That kid's not to blame, and yet he's completely to blame. He's not the one who turned himself into a little Nazi, and yet he is a little Nazi. Maybe there's no longer any way for him not to grow up and become a full-grown Nazi. . . . The only thing to do if this kid is ever to have a chance of not becoming a little Nazi is to destroy the German army. To go on exterminating lots of Germans, so that they can stop being Nazis . . .

Although Foucault would have been fourteen years old when the occupation started and eighteen or nineteen when it ended, he apparently remembered himself, in 1983, as having been a kid of ten or eleven ("We did not know, when I was ten or eleven years old, whether we would become German or remain French."). If the kid of ten or eleven that Foucault remembered himself as being in, let us say, 1941 or 1942, had become a German, would he also have become a "kraut?" This question remains unanswered.

When Foucault seeks to relate "silence" to the war directly, he again seems to remember himself as younger than he actually was, and again his "memory" meanders into the general rather than focusing on the specific. He tells the interviewer, for example, that ". . . any child who has been educated in a Catholic milieu just before or during the Second World War had the experience that there were many different ways of speaking as well as many forms of silence." Foucault next relates an anecdote.

I remember very well that when I met the filmmaker Daniel Schmidt who visited me, I don't know for what purpose, we discovered after a few minutes that we really had nothing to say to each other. So we stayed together from about three o'clock in the afternoon to midnight. We drank or smoked hash, we had dinner. And I don't think we spoke more than twenty minutes during those ten hours. From that moment a rather long friendship started. It was for me the first time that a friendship originated in strictly silent behavior.[17]

Then he goes on: "Yes, you see, I think silence is one of those things that has unfortunately been dropped from our culture."[18]

Another kind of silence is related in Charlotte Delbo's description of herself as an inmate in Auschwitz, watching a truckload of women passing by:

The women pass near us. They cry out. They cry out and we hear nothing. This cold and dry air would be conductive if we were in an ordinary earthly environment. They cry out to us but no sound reaches us. Their mouths cry out, their outstretched arms cry out, and every bit of them cries out. Each body is a cry. So many torches that flame in cries of terror, so many cries that have assumed the bodies of women. Each woman is a materialized cry, a scream that is not heard. The truck moves silently over the snow, passes under a portico, disappears. It carries off the cries.[19]

In 1983, Foucault still seemed to know nothing of this kind of silence, though he had had the chance to learn about it since 1965. For him, the idea of "silence" evokes a set of emotions and memories quite different from those felt by Charlotte Delbo, who, like Semprun, paid the price of resisting Nazism.

Semprun describes the anxiety he experiences after one of the Resistance fighters is captured by the Gestapo. Everything now depends on whether the captured fighter will be able to withstand Gestapo torture:

Alfredo had to hold out, if he didn't we would all be weakened by it. Alfredo had to hold out, so that all of us would be strengthened by his victory. I was thinking of all that, and I knew that Alfredo, as they hit and clubbed him, was thinking of it too. At this minute he's thinking that his silence is not only a personal victory, it's a victory that we shall all share with him. He knows that our truth will don the shining armor of his silence, and that helps him smile in his silence.[20]

This passage is an example of "pathos," a condition that would be dismissed by deconstructionists as belonging to the old "humanism." But Foucault's words here seem trivial in light of Semprun's and Delbo's. This leads one to ask where the deconstructionists were when the French-language version of Delbo's lyrical evocation of the most notorious of the death camps appeared in 1965, or when Semprun published his meditative narrative on German philosophizing and Nazi atrocities in 1963? Would the descriptions of Nazi atrocities and of the courage of those who opposed them have given the deconstructionists pause in their adulation of Heidegger?

I wish to be clear on this point. It is not a question of what the deconstructionists did during the occupation. The duplicity of the deconstructionists lies not in their concealing what they personally did or did not do, nor in their failure to live up to an ideal of heroism they claim not to believe in anyway. Their betrayal lies in their trivializing those who did act with valor and decency and in their helping to carry the intellectual residue of the Vichy shame into the postwar era. As Jankelevitch explains, in order to adapt to the new Nazi order and minimize the trauma of catastrophic defeat, the French people and especially the intellectuals had to invert the normal values that had sustained them for centuries. They had to find a way to turn heroism and self-sacrifice into foolishness and defeat into a virtue: "One can believe," writes Jankelevitch,

that France, a nation of masters with a long and glorious tradition of dominating Europe and of imposing a respect for its [military might] on the world, had long ago lost the knowledge of how to behave in defeat. Alas! the people accustomed to being masters had become the victims of an inconceivable aberration, and self-blinded by a horrible inversion of the value of heroism, they managed to adopt the position, in just a few days, that it might be possible to wrest a "mystique" of "honor" out of being among the vanquished.[21]

Jankelevitch notes, further, that this inversion of values did not disappear with the end of hostilities and the fall of the Vichy regime, but continued to fester in the French psyche throughout the postwar period:

Vichy means ambiguity and confusion. The old German Machiavellianism, which has always specialized in the reversal of contradictions, played extremely skillfully on an ambiguity which cast a pall over the spirit and still weighs heavily on French life and retards the moral restoration of the nation. You will have noticed here the sophism of "double play." Everyone practiced duplicity. There was no scoundrel without an alibi, no collaborator who had not hidden his Jew in a closet, or obtained a false ID card for a Resistance fighter. There is neither guilt nor innocence, and law suits against collaborators fall apart as the moral evidence of the shame and treason fades away. After 1944, the Cross of Lorraine became the favored decoration in fascist buttonholes where the badge of the Legion [the badge of the VLF, a fascist organization] used to flower when it seemed that Vichy would last forever; many pseudo-resisters strolled down the boulevarde eager to contribute to victory at the eleventh hour: because a just cause, when it is triumphant, never lacks friends.[22]

If Jankelevitch and Dominique Moisi are correct, then the French psyche, or conscience, has not yet recovered from a devastating defeat and occupation that required some of the most sensitive of French intellectuals to adopt an inversion of values as a defense mechanism.[23] May it not then be that the French deconstructionists carried the self-deceptions and the moral ambiguities and duplicities of the Nazi occupation over into the post-war period and misled their readers by insisting that their nihilism was the result of rigorous philosophical deliberation instead of the residue of historical exhaustion and moral shame? Was it an accident or a mere oversight that those who were so vocal about the consequences of erasing, marginalizing, and silencing, should have erased, marginalized, and silenced those literary works that depicted the heroism and self-sacrifice of those who bore witness to crimes of such an extraordinary nature that they called out for explanation and for a re-examination of Western values? Was it not by ignoring the testimony of unspeakable crimes against humanity committed in the name of a racist ideology spawned in Germany and supported by German philosophy that it became possible, much later, for a French Heideggerian to announce that "Nazism is a humanism?"[24] Instead of attending to the abundant testimonies that provide ample evidence of the fact that Nazism was not a humanism, but rather the fulfillment and implementation of a hate-driven antihumanist ideology, the deconstructionists honored the man whose dearest hope was to become the official philosopher of that hate-driven ideology.

And just as defeat became a matter for rejoicing and a symbol of honor, so a philosophy that had supported Nazism was re-presented as a philosophy of liberation.

While claiming to be revolutionary, the Heideggerian and Marxist poststructuralists and deconstructionists were promoting not only a highly reactionary philosophy, but an obfuscation of history—a myth that nothing terribly unusual had happened during the occupation years of 1940 to 1945, that the "crisis" of European culture lay in "humanism," in the ideology of constitutional democracy, and in the excesses of capitalism rather than in Heidegger's antihumanism and Nazism.[25] Heidegger and Marx, who were part of the problem and certainly strange bedfellows, were now promoted as solutions to the problem. One of the unfortunate, but perhaps not unintended, consequences of deconstructionist nihilism is the imposition of the dogma that all human acts must remain morally undifferentiated, since *differance* exists only in the language system, only as differences in sounds and concepts, in signifiers and signifieds, so that the only difference between a collaborator and a resister is a difference in sound images.

The leftist French intellectuals who made an impact on literary theory and criticism in the United States were less candid than they seemed, for while they pretended to be stripping away all metaphysical falsehoods, they were propagating their own falsification of history and reality to save face, not only personally but as a culture. Their theories were hostile to "liberal" notions of human rights and freedom of the individual, which they conceived as inventions of bourgeois ideology. Whether they adopted these theories because of their inability to come to terms with their own personal past and with the French and European past, or whether the theories they adopted blinded them, is difficult to say. But we can see how their inability to handle an ugly past crippled them if we consider, again, the testimony of Jorge Semprun. The narrator of *The Long Voyage* relates an incident in which one of the German guards in the prison in Auxerre asks the narrator whether he understands German, and when the narrator says he does, they strike up a conversation. In repeating (or re-creating) his conversation with the guard, the narrator pauses for a moment to reflect:

Hans would be pleased to see the progress I've made in his native language. He loved his native language, Hans von Freiberg zu Freiberg did. Not only can I read Hegel, I can also talk with a German soldier in the Auxerre prison. It's much more difficult to talk with a German soldier than to read Hegel. Especially to talk with him about essentials, about life and death, about the reasons for living and the reasons for dying.[26]

Semprun, a survivor of Nazi brutality and injustice, is one of the few who has left us a record of his attempt to reconcile the rarefied atmosphere of German high culture as represented by Heidegger with the reality of German culture he experienced in a death camp (two others that come to mind are Jean Amery and Primo Levi).[27]

It is more difficult for Semprun's narrator to converse with a German soldier in simple German because what the German soldier has done defies basic traditional ideas of human decency and justice, as well as logic. Hegel, though difficult, can still be understood if one makes the effort; however, the implication is that Semprun may read Hegel without ever having to confront the kinds of "essential" questions raised by the presence of his German guard. Without thinking, and without any clear sense of personal desire, the German soldier has come to France to kill in the name of German ideology. By choice, on the other hand, Semprun's narrator, has put himself in a position to be killed because he believes in the "values" of justice and human integrity that the German soldier has come to eradicate. Contrary to what the deconstructionists would have us believe, the obstacle to understanding is not *solely* the language-system or the inability to make "signifiers and signifieds" coincide, it is, rather, the impenetrability of the mystery that was exemplified by the rapid Nazification of a cultured people and of the whole of Europe, including France.

As the Semprun narrator puts it in concluding his ruminations on his conversations with the German sentinel:

I mention freedom only in passing; what I'm actually concerned with is the story of this voyage. I merely wanted to say that there is only one possible reply to that question asked by the German soldier from Auxerre: *Warum sind Sie verhaftet?* I'm in prison because I'm a free man, because I found it necessary to exercise my freedom, because I accepted this necessity. Similarly, to the question I asked the German sentinel on that October day: *Warum sind Sie hier?*—which happens to be an even more profound question—to this question there is also one possible reply. He is here because he isn't somewhere else, because he did not feel the need to be somewhere else. Because he is not free.[28]

In truth, the conundrums presented by the verbal gymnastics of the deconstructionists are child's play compared to explaining what happened in Buchenwald and on Semprun's long journey to that mysterious destination.

CHAPTER SIX

Collaborators and Deconstructors

At about the same time Semprun was paying the price for resisting Nazism by being transported in a cattle car from a prison in Auxerre, France, to the Buchenwald concentration camp in Germany, a Belgian essayist in occupied Belgium was writing for collaborationist publications in his native land. In March 1941, the Belgian collaborator expressed his deep anguish at the thought that Jewish writers might already have contaminated the purity of European culture. He took comfort, however, from the thought that "despite the Semitic meddling into all aspects of European life, it [i.e., European Aryan culture] has shown that its nature was healthy at the core." This negligible impact of the Jews served as evidence for Paul de Man that "the creation of a Jewish colony isolated from Europe would not lead to deplorable consequences for the literary life of the West." [1]

Not much was heard from de Man after 1942 until he surfaced in 1967 with an essay entitled "The Crisis of Contemporary Criticism." In the essay itself, the term "contemporary" turns out to be interchangeable with the adjective "Continental;" Continental really means French, for the critics de Man talks about, starting with Mallarmé, are all French. Frank Lentricchia, as we have seen, celebrated the arrival of "poststructuralism" in the person of Jacques Derrida: "Sometime in the early 1970s we awoke from the dogmatic slumber of our phenomenological sleep to find that a new presence had taken absolute hold over our avant-garde critical imagination: Jacques Derrida."[2] Lentricchia had no use for de Man, and because he had no use for him, he slighted de Man's contribution to the imposition of poststructuralist ideology on American culture; he also overlooked the fact that de Man and Derrida had become cozy bedfellows. He perceived, correctly, that "What we witness in de Man's critical discourse is a strange discrepancy between a frightfully sobering theory of literary discourse and the actual practice of a critic whose judgments, authoritative in tone and style, betray the theory."[3]

But Lentricchia failed to see the same authoritarianism, and perhaps more important, the same dehumanizing tendencies, in the work of Derrida and Foucault.[4] Nevertheless, it is probably not pure coincidence that if Derrida roused us from the spell of "our dogmatic slumber" in the early seventies, his wake-up call should have come just about the same time that "The Crisis in Contemporary Criticism" was reprinted as the lead essay in *Blindness and Insight* in 1971. Far from coincidence, for it was de Man, through his writings and through the dissemination of his ideas by his graduate students, who mainlined French poststructuralism and deconstruction into the circulatory systems of departments of literature in American universities. Although it is widely agreed that he can not be called one of the original thinkers of poststructuralism or deconstruction, Paul de Man was quick to adopt deconstructionist methods and ideological postures and was instrumental in applying deconstructionist ideology and methods to British literature, thus facilitating the application of deconstructionist ideas and methods to American literature and culture.

As his title indicates, de Man followed the French critical intellectual line by suggesting that Western high culture was experiencing a deep crisis. This crisis, as de Man describes it in 1967, is a

trend in Continental criticism, whether it derives its language from sociology, psychoanalysis, ethnology, linguistics, or even from certain forms of philosophy, [that] can be quickly summarized: it represents a methodologically motivated attack on the notion that a literary or poetic consciousness is in any way a privileged consciousness, whose use of language can pretend to escape, to some degree, from the duplicity, the confusion, the untruth that we take for granted in the everyday use of language.[5]

De Man has slipped several challengeable assumptions into this seemingly innocuous description of an alleged "crisis" in literary criticism. One assumption (though it is effectively concealed with the qualifying phrase, "whether it derives its language from . . .") is that one can pinpoint a monolithic entity called "Continental criticism." But this monolith, like an expressionist painting, is never clearly outlined. Second, de Man assumes that among "Continental critics" there is a "notion that a literary or poetic consciousness is . . . a privileged consciousness," though it is not specified who holds this notion, nor actually what a "privileged consciousness" might be. A third assumption is that we take for granted "duplicity . . . confusion . . . [and] untruth . . . in the everyday use of language." A fourth assumption is that some people (again, we are not told who) believe in the existence of a "privileged poetic consciousness" that "uses" language in such a way as to create the illusion that this language can escape from the alleged mendacity and "duplicity" of the "everyday use of language." This assumption enfolds within itself still another assumption, which is that the language of the "privileged poetic consciousness" is doubly duplicitous because it pretends to escape what it cannot escape, the iron-clad necessity for language to be duplicitous, confusing, and untrue.

It should be added that owing to de Man's deliberately cryptic style, it is difficult to tell, here, who believes what—or, more to the point, what is being presented as what the "Continental critics" believe, what is being presented as what de Man himself believes, and what is being presented as "fact" (that is, as a condition indisputably existing in the world). For example, who is the "we" that "takes for granted" that "everyday language" is [necessarily?] duplicitous, confused, and mendacious? Does the "we" refer to de Man himself, or to de Man and the "Continental critics," or does it mean all human beings? And when de Man says "we" take the mendacity "in the use of everyday language . . . for granted," is he suggesting that this "taking for granted" is "fated," that is, that it is *necessary,* beyond our control, an inevitable "taking for granted" that we cannot avoid? Or why do we take these things for granted if we do not believe that that is the way things are? And does the "taking for granted" indicate that what is "taken for granted" is indeed the case? That is, if "we take duplicity, confusion, and untruth for granted in the everyday use of language," does that mean that everyday language is indeed "duplicitous, confusing, and untrue?" It would, of course, be very difficult to substantiate any of these assumptions and innuendos, either logically or empirically, and de Man makes no attempt to do so.

In converting language into the fated instrument of "untruth," de Man elevated deception to a high art. Lest this seem an exaggeration, consider another assertion de Man makes in the same essay: "The interpretation of everyday language is a Sisyphean task, a task without end and without progress, for the other is always free to make what he wants differ from what he says he wants."[6] Is communication really so inherently laborious and hopeless, is it always such a "Sisyphean task?" We must infer from this deeply despairing assertion that human beings ("the other") are not only "free" to lie, but are likely to lie. Otherwise, why would "the interpretation of everyday language" be such an agonizing, endless, and hopeless task ("without end and without progress")? Although deconstructionist (or antihumanist) dogma holds that there is no human essence, de Man's sense of a "crisis," in this declaration, is rooted precisely in a pessimistic belief in a human essence (that is, the human essence is that a human being is a creature who lies), but this assertion of a human essence is cleverly disguised as a theory of language.[7]

Nevertheless, de Man is either deliberately or unintentionally inconsistent, for he vacillates between locating the problem of the inevitable mendacity of language in the human form, or in language itself. (Finding such inconsistencies in other writers, de Man calls them aporias.) At any rate, in the ensuing sentences, de Man takes the position that it is language itself that lies, necessarily and by its very nature, so that whenever a human being uses speech, that human being cannot help but lie: A "discrepancy exists in everyday language," says de Man, "in the impossibility of making the actual expression coincide with what it signifies. It is the distinctive privilege of language to be able to hide meaning behind a misleading sign, as when we hide rage or hatred behind a smile."[8] Certainly, there are grounds here for confusion. On the one hand, it is human beings who choose to lie by an effort of the will ("the other is always free to make what he wants differ from what he says he wants."), but on the other, it is language that lies by its very nature ("the impossibility of making the actual expression coincide with what it signifies"). On the basis of the diction, we might think that de Man is merely citing a commonplace truism from Saussure's *Course in General Linguistics* (a signifier can never coincide with its signified), but no substantiation from Saussure is given for this bizarre declaration, nor is it likely that one can be found.[9] Just as the French had created a mystique of the honor of defeat after 1940, so the collaborator de Man has created his own mystique of the determinism of the "untruth of language."

But we may say that de Man has also created his own mystique of "memory." In my 1988 reaction to the news of de Man's collaborationist writings, I alluded to his "will to obliterate the past," most evidently exhibited in his essay, "Literary History and Literary Modernity."[10] I pointed out that de Man's actual purpose in an essay that purported to deal with the problem of literary history was to destroy "not only literary history but history itself," as was clearly apparent in the closing sentences of the essay. "To become good literary historians," de Man wrote in 1969, "we must remember that what we usually call literary history has little or nothing to do with literature and that what we call literary interpretation—provided only it is good interpretation—is in fact literary history. If we extend this notion beyond literature, it merely confirms that the bases for historical knowledge are not empirical facts but written texts, even if these texts masquerade in the guise of wars or revolutions."[11] I also drew, at the time, a parallel between de Man's deconstruction of history and the revisionist historiography of Ernst Nolte, another disciple of Heidegger and also a practitioner of Heideggerian hermeneutics.[12] We shall return to what some have taken to be a strained connection between Nolte's revisionist history of the Holocaust and de Man's revisionist theory of "literary history," but before doing so we must take a detour back through the realm of what has been called reception aesthetics, which is, as de Man himself pointed out, more or less interchangeable with what is sometimes referred to as the "science of hermeneutics."[13]

De Man continues the onslaught against the possibility of "history" or, at least, of history as knowledge, in his introduction to Hans Robert Jauss's collection of essays on reception aesthetics. Attributing "the strength of Jauss's method" to "a refinement of the established rules for the historical understanding of literature," de Man goes on to say that

Few historians still believe that a work of the past can be understood by reconstructing, on the basis of recorded evidence, the set of conventions, expectations, and beliefs that existed at the time of its elaboration. What is different and effective in the approach suggested by Jauss are the reasons (implicitly) given for this impossibility: the historical consciousness of a given period can never exist as a set of openly stated or recorded propositions. It exists instead, in Jauss's terminology, as a "horizon of expectation." The term . . . implies that the condition of a consciousness is not available to this consciousness in a conscious mode. . . . [14]

De Man tends to be as careless in his formulations of philosophical problems as he is in his writings on language. What is he saying in the initial sentence? Is it that understanding of a "[literary?] work of the past" cannot be arrived at *only* by reconstructing its literary-artistic-intellectual-cultural-existential context without contemplating the work itself? [15] Of course, such a suggestion is absurd, yet how else are we to understand de Man's assertion? The sentence is much less formidable, however, if we substitute a word like "elucidated" for "understood." One wonders if anyone ever believed that it was possible to "understand" a "work of the past" (presumably a literary work) only by reconstructing its various "creative" contexts, while neglecting to "read" the work. So the phrase, "few historians still believe," is a red herring right off. It is doubtful that any historians ever believed that it was possible to understand any "artifact" of the past without first examining the artifact itself. Nevertheless, one might well say that few historians believe that knowing the various contexts of a work will not help us in some way to reach an understanding of "a work of the past."

Setting aside the arguments for or against the importance that "knowledge" of context plays in contributing to the understanding of "a work of the past," however, we may observe that, in shifting from general beliefs about "context and work" to Jauss's particular way of reading "a work of the past," de Man converts a speculation into a certainty (going from what "few historians believe," to the "impossibility" of understanding "a work of the past"). Jauss's work is "different and effective," de Man tells us, because Jauss provides a set of reasons for "this impossibility." Has de Man demonstrated or proved, then, that it is "impossible" to arrive at an understanding of "a work of the past" by setting it into its fullest possible context? Or is he just saying that it is never possible to understand "a work of the past," regardless of whether we know the context or not? But how would he be able to make such an assertion about any individual's "understanding" of a particular "work of the past" unless de Man believed that he *did* understand that very same "work of the past?" That is, unless de Man believed he understood the work, how could he contest someone else's claim to have understood the work? Moreover, we might ask what de Man's authority is for the assertion that "the historical consciousness of a given period can never exist as a set of openly stated or recorded propositions." Is this the assertion of a presumed truism, that "consciousness can never be converted into language?" If so, that would mean that it would be as impossible to "understand" a "work of the present" as a "work of the past."

Despite this apparent pessimism concerning the possibility of "history as knowledge," de Man does, however, believe that "the historical consciousness of a given period" exists, and that there is a viable verbal configuration for representing its mode of existence, the phrase "horizon of expectation." De Man attempts to elucidate this troubled phrase by comparing it to

the dialogical relationship that develops between the analyst and his interlocutor in psychoanalysis. Neither of the two knows the experience being discussed; they may indeed not even know whether such an experience ever existed. The subject is separated from it by mechanisms of repression, defense, displacement, and the like, whereas to the analyst, it is available only as a dubiously evasive symptom. . . .

[This] analogy with psychoanalysis . . . underscores the epistemological complexity of the historian's task. Both analyst and historian point to a cognition that, for reasons variously identified as psychological, epistemological, or, in the case of Heidegger, ontological, is not available as an actual presence and therefore requires a labor of interpretation or of reading prior even to determining whether it can ever be reached.[16]

For de Man, then, to say that "the historical consciousness of a given period" exists as a "horizon of expectations," is to indicate that it "exists" only as a series of personally predetermined "interpretations" (that is, interpretations that are, by definition, limited by the individual's personal "horizon"; the crux of the entire hermeneutical project is the definition of interpretation, but no satisfactory definition has yet come forth, except to say that what one takes to be the meaning of a text is the interpretation of that text). Moreover, interpretations, in addition to being fenced in by personal limitations, can never be more than a set of verbal formulations of dubious authenticity about nonaccessible experiences that may never have taken place. Reception aesthetics, as represented by de Man in his "clarification" of the "horizon of expectations," is an infinite regress of "interpretations" of linguistic constructs that refer only to each other, and "history" constitutes an unknowable absence that we deceive ourselves into believing can become knowable by way of "interpretation."

Jauss has no quarrel with de Man's representation of his views on reception aesthetics. In an embarrassingly fawning letter to de Man he comments, "I feel understood by you in my intentions and limits, in some positions even 'better than I understand myself.' This is also true for my research group, whose name 'Poetik und Hermeneutik' has never been more accurately commented on than by you." The other point on which de Man has been particularly perspicacious, according to Jauss, is "your truly illuminating explanation of my theory of horizon structure of understanding as a 'complex interplay between knowing and not knowing'; you have brought to light a second similarity between the two groups [the Constance "Poetik und Hermeneutik" and the "Yale hermeneutic mafia"]: the insight into the epistemological ambiguity of historical consciousness and the ensuing 'willingness to give up the illusion of unmediated understanding.' " [17]

In addition to penetrating to the core of the meaning of Jauss's reception aesthetics theory as a "complex interplay between knowing and not knowing," de Man was not slow to notice that the hermeneutic "sophistication" of the reception aesthetics school could be deployed to rewrite general, as well as literary history:

We have come to expect this degree of hermeneutic intricacy from any philosophical or psychological analysis but, surprisingly enough, a similar subtlety is rarely demanded from historians and, among historians, least of all from literary historians—although, according to the logic of the situation with its implied stress on reading rather than knowing, literary history, rather than psychoanalysis or epistemology, should be the privileged example, the model case.[18]

The kind of "sophisticated" literary history that de Man credited the "Poetik und Hermeneutik" group with writing and that he called for from general historians, a history characterized by the "subtlety" of its "hermeneutic intricacy," was, in fact, already being written by another Heidegger acolyte, Ernst Nolte. Although deconstructionists, reception aesthetics critics, hermeneutists, and various other poststructuralist theoreticists bicker with each other about the details of what can and cannot be known and of where to locate the site of knowing, when we put some of their writings and self-positionings side by side, we see that these are mainly family quarrels, and that the thinking of the various groups (deconstructionists, hermeneutists, reader aestheticists) centers on certain clusters of ideas and methodologies that ultimately originate in Heidegger and often, by way of Heidegger, in Nietzsche.[19] For example, in his letter to de Man, Jauss states that ". . . my model [of interpretation] needs the hermeneutical tool of question and answer (a preunderstanding can only be questioned or inquired after, not immediately perceived) . . ." This same "hermeneutical tool of question and answer" is utilized by Nolte in his own "model of interpretation" to arrive at a perception of a "preunderstanding" of Auschwitz:

Did the Nazis, did Hitler only commit an "Asiatic" deed, perhaps, because they thought that they and those like them were potential or real victims of an "Asiatic" deed themselves? Was not the Gulag Archipelago prior in history to Auschwitz? Wasn't "class murder" by the Bolsheviks the logical and real precondition of "race murder" by the Nazis? Are not Hitler's most secret actions to be explained by the fact that he had not forgotten the rat's cage? Did not Auschwitz, perhaps, in its origins come from a past that did not want to pass away?[20]

It is, moreover, worth mentioning that Nolte's style and its effect on readers, as described by Evans, is indistinguishable from that of de Man, Jauss, and the deconstructionists in general. According to

Evans, Nolte has expressed his revisionist view "in a manner that is often obscure, sometimes confused, and occasionally downright contradictory. . . . But in reality, writers are being taken in by Nolte's method. Nolte makes ritual obeisances to current moral orthodoxies, while devoting the larger part of his energies to developing, often by innuendo and suggestion, a series of arguments intended to subvert them and to put forward an alternative view." [21] It may be that these stylistic obfuscations are both more critical and more noticeable in the writing of "history" than they are in the writing of pure theory, since sensible historical writing makes use of evidence and assumes the existence of referents, elusive though they may sometimes be.

It seems to be the Heideggerian Nolte who is also responsible for the promulgation of the bizarre view that the SS were actually victims. In "The Past That Will Not Pass," he writes:

A hasty expression by a member of the Bundestag regarding certain demands by the speakers of Jewish organizations, or a tasteless slip by a local politician are exaggerated into symptoms of "antisemitism," as if every memory of the genuine, and in no sense Nazi antisemitism of the Weimar period had disappeared; at the same time, the moving documentary film *Shoah*, by a Jewish director, was being shown on television, which showed, in several passages, the probability that even the SS guards of the death camps might, in their own way have been victims. . . . [22]

This defensive strategy of taking the offensive by converting perpetrators into victims has also been favored by deconstructionists. Jacques Derrida used it to to cast a cloak of obscurity over the significance of the collaborationist writings of de Man, turning the tables so that the collaborator became the victim, while those who sought to look into the implications of his collaboration became the "exterminators." "To judge, to condemn the work or the man on the basis of what was a brief episode," Derrida wrote, ". . . is to reproduce the exterminating gesture which one accuses de Man of not having armed himself against sooner." [23] But what is at issue is not simply that de Man did not "arm himself . . . against the . . . exterminating gesture," but that he deliberately lied to conceal his own "exterminating gesture," thus rendering himself vulnerable to justifiable feelings of guilt which must have been festering in his psyche all the time he was theorizing about the impossibility of speaking the truth.

CHAPTER SEVEN

Deconstruction
and the SS Connection

In a factual, even-handed biographical sketch of de Man that appeared in the *Nation* after the exposure of de Man's anti-Semitic writings, Jon Wiener called attention to the "matter of de Man's relationship to the German literary critic Hans Robert Jauss. He . . . brought Jauss to Yale as a guest lecturer in the mid-1970s; Jauss is now known to have served in the SS."[1] As has often been the case in disclosures of this kind, Jauss's reaction turned out to be even more revealing than the original discovery. In a letter responding to Wiener, Jauss invoked Nolte's Bitburg defense. He was not, Jauss proclaimed, "a member of the general SS (infamous for its brutality). . . ." Rather, Jauss admitted "only" to having volunteered for the "Waffen SS when I was 17 years old," and to having "served without interruption from 1939 until 1945 as a soldier, primarily on the Eastern Front." Jauss added, "At no time did I serve in a Waffen-SS unit when it committed atrocities, although there were other times when atrocities were committed by Waffen-SS units of which I had been or was to be a member."[2]

The newly created myth of the Waffen SS as a chivalrous, gentle fighting force that was not usually engaged in the commission of atrocities hardly seems tenable. One student of the SS states that the Waffen-SS training and drill produced "an elite consciousness which was in stark contrast with the 'reactionary' army and attracted a new stratum of young . . . leaders: the young Nazis who had been preconditioned in the Hitler Youth movement and had been ideologically trained in the Junkerschools." He adds that the "men of the Waffen-SS" committed their "first major crime, . . . which was to be followed by many others . . . on May 27, 1940: . . . the execution of 100 British prisoners of war."[3] It is also worth noting that the Malmedy Massacre in 1944 was committed by Waffen SS who engaged in a particularly brutal and wanton slaughter of unarmed American prisoners of war.[4] Charles Sydnor, Jr., writes that

The Waffen SS Totenkopfdivision emerged from two significant interrelated forces in the structure of Adolf Hitler's Third Reich. These forces were individual and personal on the one hand, and institutional and ideological on the other. Individually, the SS Totenkopfdivision in a real sense was the personal creation of Theodor Eicke. . . . Ideologically, the SS Totenkopfdivision was the institutional outgrowth of the sinister SS Death's Head Units (SS Totenkopfverbande), the militarized SS formations Eicke recruited, organized, and trained to guard and administer the concentration camps of the Reich.[5]

Jauss's memory also seems to deceive him when he imputes more cruelty to the General SS than the Waffen SS. Sydnor asserts that "Eicke declared that he would transfer to the Allgemeine-SS any member of the SSTV who lacked the necessary spirit of camaraderie and who performed his duties routinely and unenthusiastically."[6] This would seem to suggest that, at least in 1939 and 1940, the General SS was actually a dumping ground for Waffen SS who did not live up to Eicke's standards of cruelty. There is no indication that Jauss was a Kurt Gerstein or an Oskar Schindler; on the face of it his protestations of absolute noncontamination seem highly unlikely. To be as unknowing as Jauss claims to have been throughout the duration of his SS career, he would have had to have spent more than five years hedged in by an impenetrable fence of supernatural angelic innocence while serving for more than five continuous years in Waffen SS units that committed atrocities, but very conveniently only when Jauss happened not to be there.

We must also remember that fighting between armies had ceased in Poland by the end of September of 1939; the German invasion of the Soviet Union did not take place until June 22, 1941. In the interim, the task of setting up the murderous ghettoes and the concentration camps, including Auschwitz, fell to the SS (Waffen or otherwise; all evidence indicates that Waffen-SS units were as much implicated in the extermination process as General SS). R. S. Koehl writes that

> The scheme for the handling of Poland, in whole or in part, once captured, was to turn over police duties to improvised SS (Death's Head) regiments made up of training cadre from the replacement units of the Verfügungs-truppe and the original Totenkopfstandarten, to which were added General SS personnel called up for the emergency. These groups would be spearheaded by Einsatzkommandos (mobile killing units). . . . It was from this early wave of Einsatzkommandos, Self-Defense units, and Death's Head Battalions that the SS occupation tradition took its beginning in wanton cruelty, sadism, and senseless death.[7]

As a member of the Waffen SS, whom was Jauss fighting on the "Eastern Front" during the twenty-one months from October 1939 to June 1941, and what could a Waffen-SS soldier have been doing there if not engaging in terrorist activities against civilians?[8]

We cannot evaluate Jauss's denial of any complicity in SS criminality without pondering the following observation by Hannah Arendt, a student, protégé, and defender of Heidegger, who can hardly be called hostile to German culture:

> Eichmann needed only to recall the past in order to feel assured that he was not lying and that he was not deceiving himself, for the world he lived in had once been in perfect harmony. And that German society of eighty million people had been shielded against reality and factuality by exactly the same means, the same self-deception, lies, and stupidity that had now become ingrained in Eichmann's mentality. . . . The practice of self-deception had become so common, almost a moral prerequisite for survival, that even now, eighteen years after the collapse of the Nazi regime, when most of the specific content of its lies has been forgotten, it is sometimes difficult not to believe that mendacity has become an integral part of the German national character.[9]

But perhaps the most penetrating analysis of forgetting as a form of lying is to be found in Primo Levi's essay on "The Memory of the Offense," where he writes, "An extreme case of the distortion of the memory of a committed guilty act is found in its suppression. Here, too, the borderline between good and bad faith can be vague; behind the 'I don't know' and the 'I do not remember' that one hears in court-rooms there is sometimes the precise intent to lie, but at other times it is a fossilized lie, rigidified in a formula. The rememberer has decided not to remember and has succeeded: by dint of denying its existence, he has expelled the harmful memory as one expels an excretion or a parasite."[10]

In the final analysis, what Jauss did or did not do is now be-tween him and his conscience. Nevertheless, in an age in which liter-ary theory assumes the task of attacking the evils of society at their roots at the same time that it dwells in self-doubt and intense self-examination, the bold confidence of Jauss's summing up of his SS past is astonishing: "There was nothing, and there is nothing, that I have to cover up." To get some sense of the effrontery of this bold denial by a former SS volunteer, who admits to having remained a loyal mem-ber of the cruelest and most savage terrorist organization in history from 1939 to 1945, we must set it against one of those texts that have been so formidably marginalized by contemporary literary theorists (whether by the name postmodernist, poststructuralist, deconstruc-tionist, hermeneutist, reader-reception-aestheticist). We must permit the silenced Jorge Semprun to speak again.[11]

In his narrative, Semprun describes a memory-stimulating event that took place shortly after his liberation. A couple of playful young women have come to have a look at the camp in Buchenwald. At first, he is inclined to spare them the horrors, but after watching their fri-volity and lack of understanding and compassion, he decides to show them the real thing in the hope that he can bring them to the threshold of understanding. The narrator tells how, in the course of the "tour," he pauses

on the large empty square where they had held roll call and the wind was in the beeches and the April sun above the wind and the beeches. There was also, off to the right, the squat crematorium building. To the left, there was also the manege where they executed the officers, the commissars and the Communists of the Red Army. Yesterday, April 12th, I had visited the manege. It was just another manege, like any other, the SS officers used to come there to ride. The SS officers' wives used to come there to ride. But, in the building where one dressed there was also a special shower. A Soviet officer was taken into it, he was given a piece of soap and a bath towel and he waited for the water to flow from the shower. But the water didn't flow. Through a loop-hole concealed in the corner, an SS would send a bullet into the Soviet officer's head. The SS was in an adjoining room, he calmly aimed at the Soviet officer's head, and he sent a bullet into his head. They removed the corpse, they gathered up the soap and the bath towel, and they turned on the shower to erase any trace of blood. When you have understood this simulacrum of the shower and the piece of soap, you will have understood the SS mentality.[12]

The gap between Semprun's portrait of the "SS mentality" and Jauss's presentation of himself as having "nothing to cover up," and of the Waffen-SS as a corps of honorable combat soldiers forces us to start making decisions about whose story we are going to believe. Jauss, like Ernst Nolte and in keeping with postmodernist Heideggerian theories of historical and literary hermeneutics, diminishes the significance of the recent Holocaust past and chisels away at the uniqueness of the SS as an elite brutalized by its ideology; in so doing he distorts history and diminishes the enormity of Nazi crimes. Properly interpreted from the revisionist point of view (whether the revisionism be called "hermeneutic" or "reader-reception," or "deconstructionist" or poststructuralist), the Holocaust becomes an unfortunate but not unique event, and even the SS turn out to be, for the most part, just soldiers doing their job.[13] And just as the SS were just soldiers doing their job in the hermeneutist-revisionist view, so from this same perspective, the ghettos and the death camps were just another instance of human cruelty in just another war, and therefore part of a long history of human cruelty and violence.

In a letter addressed to American readers, Jauss reinforces this view. He exists, reads, studies, thinks, and writes in age-old traditions of European, especially German, philosophy and culture. And why not? He has "nothing to cover up." His conscience is clean. Five years in Hitler's SS have left him miraculously unscarred by racist ideology, and he, like Semprun's sentinel at Auxerre prison, merely did what had to be done, and he was where he was because he was unable to think of any other place to be. But it is exactly that abundance of clean consciences amidst a sea of unspeakable crimes that must have been committed by someone that must give us pause.

It is those ubiquitous clean consciences that are precisely an indication of what Semprun has pinpointed as the "SS mentality." Erich Kahler cites a witness who describes the "practitioners of terror" as "automata" who ". . . admit the most atrocious crimes but show not the slightest sense of guilt." He also speaks of "a peculiar mode of *behavior on the part of the executors* of the Nazi crimes, a novel kind of schizophrenia. . . . These executives, these doctors and university professors—after having done their gruesome work; after having watched, sometimes closely, the ordeal of their camp laborers; . . . after having directed and inspected excruciating experiments on humans—went home to their families, parties, classes, delivered lectures, carried on their research, partook of all the modes and manners of our modern civilization without even the slightest sense of the flagrant contrast between the two aspects of their lives." [14] It was Hannah Arendt's apparent inability to perceive or comprehend this "novel kind of schizophrenia" that led her to characterize Eichmann's monstrous crimes with the phrase, "the banality of evil."

If Jauss has nothing to hide, then it is perhaps unfortunate that so many of his cohort who clearly did have much to hide muddied the waters by also saying, in effect, "There was nothing, and there is nothing, that I have to cover up." Even Rudolf Höss, commandant of Auschwitz from its inception to November of 1943, felt he had nothing to "cover up," and sought to evade responsibility by claiming that he could not control his subordinates, and that "from the very beginning the camp was dominated by theories which were later to produce the most evil and sinister consequences." [15] Jerzy Rawicz comments on Höss's *Autobiography,* "The commandant of Auschwitz was not disturbed by his directing the gassing of millions of people. . . ." [16] Johann Paul Kremer, a physician and Ph.D. who was stationed in Auschwitz for three months in the summer and fall of 1942, kept a diary that included some of his more noteworthy experiences during that period. On September 23, 1942, he made the following entry:

This night was present at the 6th and 7th special actions [i.e., the gassings of two transports, one from Slovakia and one from Drancy, in France]. *Obergruppenfuhrer* Pohl with suite arrived at the *Waffen SS* club-house in the morning. The sentinel at the door presented arms in front of me for the first time. At 8 o'clock in the evening supper in the Home with *Obergruppen-*

fuhrer Pohl, a truly festive meal. We had baked pike, as much of it as we wanted, real coffee, excellent beer and sandwiches.[17]

Kremer was tried, convicted, and imprisoned in Poland, but he, too, felt he had nothing to cover up. He "was a model, even humble, prisoner in the Polish prison, just like other Nazi prisoners, but he changed, as if by magic, as soon as he crossed the frontier of the German Federal Republic. He began to enact the role of a martyr of 'the German cause,' trying to rouse sympathy with his person."[18] Adolf Eichmann also made it clear at his trial that he felt he had "nothing to cover up." As Hannah Arendt put it, "as the months and the years went by, he lost the need to feel anything at all. This was the way things were, this was the new law of the land, based on the Führer's order; whatever he did he did, as far as he could see, as a law-abiding citizen. He did his *duty,* as he told the police and the court over and over again; he not only obeyed *orders,* he also obeyed the *law.*"[19] Of course, there was no reason for Eichmann and the others to feel guilty of anything, or to feel a need to cover anything up, because they did not consider that murdering members of inferior races or enemies of the Hitler state was a crime.

It is incumbent on us not to yield to Jauss's temptation. Kahler writes that Ernst

Junger professes an attitude which he calls "heroic realism," whereby the term "heroic" means much more than sacrifice in military action. Heroism comes to signify a general comprehensive and entirely novel form of self-control and self-denial: not only denial of the individual in the self, but a last and resolute denial of the human being in the self, of the human part in man. We are reminded of Nietzsche's words: "Where are the barbarians of the twentieth century? They will be those capable of the greatest harshness against themselves, those who can guarantee the greatest duration of will power."[20]

One need not read a great many witness accounts to recognize Junger's "heroic realism" as a component of the "SS mentality." We must not forget that Jauss does not present himself to us as he was but as he presumably has become. Although his theory of reception aesthetics, with its concept of the "horizon of expectations," calls for the engagement of the historical and biographical "experience" of the reader in interpreting texts, Jauss's own experience, that is to say his role as an SS occupier in lands where the SS set up thousands of ghettos and concentration and extermination camps, where the SS committed and supervised mass murder and genocide by shooting, beating, torture, injection, forced starvation, and disease, all of this seems to play no role in Jauss's understanding of "the tradition" or in the way he interprets texts. For example, in his letter to de Man, he asserts that if de Man the deconstructionist and Jauss the reader-response aestheticist were to put their differences to an appeal to authority, then "You appeal to the early [Walter] Benjamin . . . and I to the late Benjamin. . . . You prefer the late Heidegger . . . I prefer the early Heidegger. . . . You may enlist Kierkegaard, Nietzsche, and Adorno . . . whereas I can call upon the equally respectable authority of Kant. . . ."[21]

It apparently never intrudes on Jauss's historicist "horizon of expectations" that Benjamin committed suicide in 1940 because he feared falling into the hands of just such an SS man as Jauss himself might have been at that time. Does the question ever enter Jauss's consciousness whether, as one who had taken the SS oath of absolute loyalty and unquestioning obedience to Hitler, he would have beaten and tortured Walter Benjamin for the crime of being Jewish had he been given the command to do so? How would such an awareness, if Jauss were able to achieve it, fuse into a "horizon of expectations" that would modify Jauss's understanding of Benjamin? Does the thought ever enter Jauss's "horizon of expectations," even as a whisper, that there might have been even later Benjamin essays to read, had there not been so many who were ready to follow and take loyalty oaths to a leader crazed with hate? Jauss minimizes the influence that German philosophy exercised on the recent Nazi past, and he also miminizes the importance of his own Nazi past as a commentary on the dialectic between German philosophy and the behavior of certain Germans (including German "philosophers") from 1939 to 1945.[22]

But Semprun provides quite a different perspective. In dramatizing the "SS mentality," his narrative demonstrates that Hitler succeeded in achieving at least one of his goals, that of creating in the world of physical existence his own "interpretation" of what Nietzsche meant by a superman. Did not Hitler prove, Derrida and deconstruction to the contrary, that there is more to language than just an infinitely regressive series of signifiers? And must we not assume that at some point in his life and in his long SS career Jauss must have considered himself to have been a superman? Was not Hitler himself a hermeneutist in this sense? Did he not have an interpretation of what Nietzsche meant by *Ubermensch*, and did he not transform that interpretation of an idea into a reality? And were there not, as in the light of Farias's book cannot be denied, many German philosophers who accepted Hitler's interpretation? Must we not ask whether at least one strain of German philosophy did not become incarnate in the SS (as apparently Heidegger hoped it would) and in the death camps? Was it not the case, as Farias shows, that German philosophers quickly found ways to bring universal philosophy into accord with the new German ideology?[23]

Jauss talks about "a changing horizon of experience." May we not, then, ask how he finds the world has "changed" or what it is that has "changed" for Jauss? How is his "horizon of experience" different from the "horizon of experience" of a pre-1933 or pre-1939 German, or from that of Matthew Arnold? As far as one can tell from reading the essays of Jauss, who voluntarily aligned himself with the victimizers, he identifies few differences between his "horizon of experience" and that of Leo Spitzer or the "late Benjamin" whose work Jauss admires. For Jauss and other postmodern theorists, not much seems to have changed. Even deconstructionists and antihumanists who talk about "rupture" and the "death of man" situate themselves within a philosophical continuum that stretches from the pre-Socratics through Plato and Descartes to Nietzsche and Heidegger and beyond. For them, philosophy may cannibalize itself, but this cannibalizing is uninterrupted by, and has nothing to do with, Auschwitz.

In the narratives told by those victims of Nazi crimes still capable of testifying, we notice a very pronounced difference of perception. While former Nazis, SS soldiers, and war criminals invariably insist that nothing unusual happened, that nothing has changed, and that it is time to look forward and get on with the business of life, the victims say just the opposite, namely that everything has changed and that we cannot get on with business as usual until we have confronted a haunting and unpleasant past honestly and openly. Semprun identifies the "simulacrum of the shower and the piece of soap" as a key to the "SS mentality" and as a symbol of the change wrought by Nazism. What was it about the "simulacrum of the shower and the piece of soap" that provided Semprun with his stunning insight into the essence of the "SS mentality?" Nolte attempts to deny the uniqueness of the Holocaust by recontextualizing the events into a longer continuum of wars, genocides, and acts of cruelty, allowing that the only difference between the Holocaust and other historical atrocities was the "technical procedure of gassing." But Semprun, who was there as a victim, does not permit this evasion. As an inmate of Buchenwald he knew about gassing and about the crematoriums, and he writes about them in his narrative. Yet he focuses on this "simulacrum of the shower and the piece of soap" as the clue to the "SS mentality." In this simulacrum we see a bewildering fluctuation between madness and sanity that characterized the death camps and Nazi behavior in general: the deception; the satanic sense of humor that derives amusement from leading the victim to believe he will engage in a human act of cleansing at the same time that he is being condemned to a bizarre execution; and the obsession with cleanliness in camps that were deliberately organized to become monuments to filth and excrement.[24]

But beneath these "trifles" of cruelty, distressing as they are, lie some more ominous and disturbing elements. In their cruelty and total lack of mercy, in their enjoyment of the pain and suffering of others, in their total contempt for the victims, in their desire to humiliate the victims by forcing them to undress and expose themselves in the "shower"—but above all, perhaps, in the killers' sense of "mastery," in their sense of power over life and death—the SS men assumed the role of gods, and they did so in keeping with their ideology, with the indoctrination they received as members of the elite SS corps.[25]

The inescapable essence of Nazism lies not alone in its methods of mass killing nor in the bureaucratization of mass killing (though such monstrous inventions are not to be overlooked) but in its racist ideology, which led all too many of the German people to believe they were a superrace and the SS to believe they were gods.[26] Dr. Franz Meyer testified at the Eichmann trial that in 1939, after Eichmann had been promoted, he detected a "terrible . . . change" in Eichmann's personality. "I met a man who comported himself as a master of life and death."[27] This may be the reason that the SS had not only to kill their victims but to kill them mercilessly and to strip them of all human dignity before destroying them.[28] Not without cause does Tadeusz Borowski open his story, "This Way for the Gas, Ladies and Gentlemen," with the sentences: "All of us walk around naked. The delousing is finally over, and our striped suits are back from the tanks of Cyclone B solution, an efficient killer of lice in clothing and of men in gas chambers."[29] Or perhaps we should listen once again to one of those French Resistance fighters marginalized equally by deconstruction, poststructuralism, and reader-reception aesthetics, Charlotte Delbo:

> The Dummy. On the far side of the road, there is a field where the SS go to train their dogs. We see them go there with their dogs which they have fastened, two on a leash. The SS who goes first carries a dummy. It is a big doll dressed like us. A faded, dirty striped suit with sleeves that are too long. The SS holds it by one arm. He lets the feet drag and scrape the gravel. They have even put canvas boots on its feet.
>   Do not look. Do not look at this dummy trailing along the ground. Do not look at yourself.[30]

As in Semprun's description of the shower and Borowski's description of the gassing of human beings as though they were lice, we see, in Delbo's evocative poetic vignette, an "SS mentality" that permits the SS to toy with human beings and treat them like puppets, with the SS as the puppeteers. And we cannot miss in Delbo's poetic evocation her underlining the fact that while the "dolls" are grotesque images of the victims, the dogs are grotesque images of the SS, trained to tear apart "dolls" which are, for the SS, interchangeable with human beings, thus confirming the SS men's belief in themselves as gods who not only enjoy the power to decide who will live and who will die, but who can also enjoy toying with their victims. In *King Lear* a despairing Gloucester utters the words, "As flies to wanton boys are we to th' gods, / They kill us for their sport."[31] But Gloucester's gods are restrained and merciful compared to the SS.

Nicholas Berdyaev, who seems to have been a much wiser and certainly a more humane thinker than Heidegger, but who has been silenced by the postmodernists, probably because he expressly affirmed humane Christian values, foresaw the consequences of an acceptance of the Nietzschean announcement of "the death of God" and of a revaluation of values. He also understood what would result from the attempt to convert the Nietzschean revaluation of values into a political reality. Commenting, in the early nineteen twenties, on Dostoyevsky's continuing concern with the human's desire to become a god, Berdyaev wrote that

One consequence [of man's obsession with his own deification] is that there is an end to compassion, there is no more mercy. Compassion is a ray of the truth by which Christianity enlightened the world, and a renouncement of this truth completely changes one's attitude towards one's fellows. In the name of his Magnificence the Superman . . . [discovers] it is henceforth lawful to torture and to kill a man, or any number of men, to transform all being into a means in the service of some exalted object or grand ideal. Everything is allowable when it is a question of the unbounded freedom of the superman. . . . Self-will arrogates to itself the right to decide the value of a human life and to dispose of it. The control of life and the judgment of mankind do not belong to God; man, as the depository of the "idea of the superman," takes them upon himself and his judgments are pitiless, impious and inhuman at the same time.[32]

Berdyaev's imagination failed him only in its incapacity to envisage that when men finally became gods, the absence of mercy and pity would not be limited to one's fellows, but would extend to women and children, even to pregnant women and infants, so that it would not only become "lawful to torture and to kill a man," but just as lawful to torture and kill pregnant women and infants. Sarah Nomberg-Przytyk, who worked in the infirmary in Auschwitz, tells the following story:

Orli [a German political—i.e., communist—prisoner] had told me once how Mengele explained to her why he killed Jewish women together with their children. "When a Jewish child is born, or when a woman comes to the camp with a child already," he had explained, "I don't know what to do with the child. I can't set the child free because there are no longer any Jews who live in freedom. I can't let the child stay in the camp because there are no facilities in the camp that would enable the child to develop normally. It would not be humanitarian to send a child to the ovens without permitting the mother to be there to witness the child's death. That is why I send the mother and the child to the gas ovens together." [33]

Is it surprising that it should have been beyond even Berdyaev's clairvoyance to imagine that when men finally became gods, a father would someday write a lullaby to his son, ending with the words,

> Fall asleep, fall asleep,
> My little man.
> Sleep here,
> On the floor of Hell.
>
> Maybe tomorrow Mr. Mengele
> Won't be poisoning children. [34]

While having been a member of the Waffen-SS is not enough to prove in a court of law that Jauss committed or was implicated in the commission of atrocities, by the same token there is no question that the Waffen-SS was no less implicated in atrocities than the General SS, and it is hardly appropriate for Jauss to cite membership in such an organization as proof that he was not implicated in Nazi criminality. [35] But it is not my intention to "convict" Jauss. Rather, I want to point out that whether he participated in atrocities or not, his letter simply repeats patterns of denial that are all too familiar, all too flimsy. Moreover, his attempt to refute Jon Wiener by setting his relationship to de Man on a personal and purely professional footing totally unconnected to any ideological affinities between them, enables us to close the circle that connects the ideological roots of his reader-response aesthetics to hermeneutics, revisionist (or postmodernist) historiography, postmodernist literary theorizing, and deconstruction.

In bringing up again the myth of Waffen SS innocence, he forces us to reexamine that myth and almost forces us to juxtapose such seemingly anomalous materials as the words of Holocaust victims alongside the words of the victimizers; postmodernist literary theories alongside revisionist historiographical theories; narrative accounts of atrocities alongside historical "evidence" of atrocities committed by Waffen SS units. Nor should this be taken as a matter of guilt by association. It is merely to point out that Jauss has been less than candid in declaring himself innocent by association. Since it was Jauss himself who brought up the issue of the innocence of the Waffen SS, it seemed only fair to pursue the question further, for in addition to declaring his own innocence by virtue of having served in the Waffen SS, the implication of his assertion is that the Waffen SS itself, as an organization, was not as much given to the practice of cruelty as the General SS. Here, the evidence is equivocal at best, and Jauss must know that. While it is true that the SS fought fiercely in military combat to extend and preserve an empire founded on Hitler's racist ideology, it is also true that the same units that distinguished themselves in military engagements sometimes perpetrated the most hideous atrocities against civilians. The Second Waffen SS Panzer Division, *Der Reich*, which fought with distinction on the Russian front, was the same division that locked women, children, and infants in a church in Oradour-sur-Glane and then burned them to a crisp.[36] It is also clear from Dr. Kremer's diary, quoted above, that there were Waffen-SS detachments in Auschwitz.

What is at issue is the ability to face a dishonorable past—and whether it is possible to entrust our spiritual and intellectual well-being to historians and literary theorists who cannot face a very wicked past honestly. We must take seriously Hannah Arendt's observation, quoted earlier, that "The practice of self-deception had become so common, almost a moral prerequisite for survival, that even now, eighteen years after the collapse of the Nazi regime, when most of the specific content of its lies has been forgotten, it is sometimes difficult not to believe that mendacity has become an integral part of the German national character."[37] A. M. Rosenthal has put the matter quite succinctly in questioning the advisability of Vaclav Havel's visit to Kurt Waldheim:

Ever since he took office Mr. Waldheim has been boycotted because he lied about where and how he had served the German Army. He knew that telling the truth would have prevented him from becoming Secretary General of the United Nations.

So Mr. Waldheim lived a lie all the 10 years he was head of the very organization that came out of the German defeat. He was afraid to reveal that he had served in a unit that committed war crimes of murder and torture against partisans from Greece, Yugoslavia and other countries.

Mr. Waldheim knew what was going on in his unit. His lies about his record made him a symbol of all the campaigns of falsehood designed to conceal, minimize or even deny the horrors of Germany's Nazi era.[38]

Jauss argues that his reader-reception aesthetics is a "historicist" theory, and he informs us that he is interested not primarily in the interpretation of a text but in studying the history of interpretations of a text. The theory derives and also diverges from Hans Georg Gadamer's hermeneutics and, through Gadamer, ultimately from Heideggerian "historicism" and hermeneutics. Similarly, Ernst Nolte's revisionist history derives from Heideggerian historicism and hermeneutics. But how can one engage in historicist reception aesthetics or in revisionist history without confronting the special problems of "representation" and "history" raised by the Holocaust past? In a recent essay on the topic, Saul Friedlander has linked the question of "the limits of representation" in literature to "the obstacles to historical interpretation." "The limitations which weigh on the literary and artistic representation of the *Shoah*," Friedlander writes, "reappear in the domain of historical interpretation."[39] Moreover, the questions Friedlander sees facing the historian are similar to those facing the literary theorist:

Does a phenomenon such as the "Final Solution" allow for any kind of "emplotment," does it foreclose certain narrative modalities? Or does it escape the grasp of plausibly persuasive narrative representation altogether?

Second, any discussion of the "Final Solution" must confront the moral issue. Hence, a problem arises with the application of certain new interpretive strategies. Is it possible to embrace such strategies and yet avoid moral relativism?[40]

Friedlander approaches the intertwining of literature and history from more of a humanist and less of a "postmodernist" perspective. From the humanist perspective it appears that just as the writer cannot "represent" a reality so far beyond previous human experience that no reader will be able to respond to it or experience it vicariously, so the historian cannot shape the historical material into a plot that the reader will be able to believe and understand. Events so unique in human experience that they defy the imagination of the novelist and poet equally defy the narrative skills of the historian. As a historian writing a general essay, Friedlander does not dwell on the belletristic problem of the "limits of representation," nor can I do so here. Suffice to say that the problem goes back to the very earliest camp narratives, whose authors often express their recognition that words will never capture the horrors of camp reality. The futility of all attempts at representation was encapsulated in Theodor Adorno's famous dictum (which he later recanted), that it is not possible to write poetry after Auschwitz. His assertion has long been a standard point of reference for those who study the literature of the Holocaust. Basically, Adorno raises the issue that any literary representation of Nazi atrocities would aestheticize, and thus make acceptable, the horrors and cruelty. One would expect this intertwining of these specifically Holocaust problems of historical "emplotment" and literary "representation" to be grist for the Jaussian and Noltean mills. Yet neither shows an inclination to engage such questions.

Having silenced the voices of the victims, how can they? Two decades before Nolte developed his thesis that the "Holocaust" should be conceived as part of a "normal" past, and that there is no difference between Holocaust and other atrocities, Erich Kahler had gone to great pains to demonstrate that the "Holocaust" constituted a new departure in human history. After an elaborate set of comparisons between atrocities of the past and those committed by the Nazis, Kahler raises the question, "What is it, then, that we may regard as new in these happenings?" His answer is, in part, as follows:

The fateful novelty may be seen, I believe, in that accomplished split in the personality, a split reaching deep enough to shatter the identity of the human being. Those persons, Elite Guards, intellectuals, executives, whom we have seen professionally attending to the most gruesome activities, seemed to act only with a certain part of their being, while another part was left behind, remained in the background; in fact, their behavior bears a resemblance to technological procedures and can best be expressed in technological terms.

We could say that different faculties of the human being are switched off or turned on according to requirement; and substantially, these different faculties, or sections of the personality seem entirely disconnected from one another.[41]

The "split" described by Kahler seems to involve, also, an inability by the individual to empathize with an "other." Dr. Kremer, for example, while still in Auschwitz, made the entry, on October 3, 1942: "Today I got quite living-fresh material of human liver, spleen and pancreas. . . ." These specimens, he explained in his trial, were taken from prisoners who had just been executed by phenol injections. Not quite three years later [Aug. 6, 1945], under American occupation, he complained in his diary that: "Today I received from the officiating Senior Mayor Zuhorn the order to work at shovelling. Work begins tomorrow at 7 P.M. in *Servatiiplatz*. One has to put up with things like this because one had been an SS surgeon. No questions are asked whether, as in my case, I have not lost my position through the NSDAP and have not dealt the party one of the heaviest blows in the ideological aspect by publishing my work on the hereditariness of acquired qualities."[42]

The former Waffen-SS surgeon who watched with clinical indifference the torture and gassing of innocent prisoners, and who experimented on living tissue torn from their tortured bodies, nevertheless still feels he is being done an "injustice" in being assigned to a digging detail by the agent of newly arrived American occupation troops. The moral obtuseness and dissociation of sensibility reflected in Kremer's absolute lack of empathy on the one hand, and his righteous self-pity on the other, is indicative, as Kahler puts it, that the Nazi "split in the personality reaches into unfathomable depths, it is total, it is consummate schizophrenia. . . . The part that commits atrocities seems wholly impersonal and, accordingly, in-human in the literal sense of the word; indeed, we should rather call it a-human."[43]

In the late fifties and early sixties, it seemed structuralism would provide a more powerful and less subjective tool for reading literature, but in the hands of readers less learned and less humanistic than Roman Jakobson structuralism, at least as far as literary criticism was concerned, quickly deteriorated into little more than a dehumanized New Criticism. From the standpoint of literary criticism, transformational grammar fluctuated between a sterile positivism and a sterile idealism. Postmodernist literary theory was heralded as an antidote to a moribund New Criticism and, with the leavening of Heideggerian philosophy, was supposed to enrich literature while at the same time avoiding the pitfalls of "logocentric" and Eurocentric transcendentalisms associated with colonialist and imperialist residues. The fact that Heidegger had endorsed Nazi imperialism and saw no inconsistency between his philosophy and the Nazi worldview was conveniently buried.[44]

In 1980 Frank Lentricchia's history of the demise of the New Criticism endorsed a Foucauldian historiography of rupture and discontinuity, though his own narrative of literary theory drew a continuous line that went "progressively" from the New Criticism to structuralism to semiotics, and reached its peak in the most glorious of literary theories, deconstruction. According to Lentricchia, Derrida was the Prince Charming who had come to arouse us from the "dogmatic slumber of our phenomenological sleep." Lentricchia, who balked at the absolutism of Paul de Man, rejoiced in the alleged fact that Derrida ". . . had taken absolute hold over our avant-garde critical imagination."[45] We woke from a "dogmatic slumber" only to find our imaginations in thrall to an absolute monarch who had determined our intellectual fate, leading us to a new intellectual utopia. The characterization of postmodern ways of thinking as an irresistible "progressive" movement has persisted into the eighties. Charles Maier describes the "revisionist accounts of Auschwitz or apologias for the German army" as not a "historiographic postmodernism . . . but as products of a diffused postmodern historical sensibility."[46] This is to suggest that revisionist history and the deconstructionist silencing of Holocaust victims are somehow "in the air," simply a set of undefined ideas that float into the minds of thinkers as an inevitable consequence of contemporary life. "Postmodernism," in this sense, is the crystallization of a world view, independent of any human choice, arrived at through the inevitable conjunction of certain inchoate and undefined philosophical, social, political, and historical forces.

This "postmodern historical sensibility" is less "diffused" than

Maier suggests, and it is, in fact, less a "sensibility" than a deliberately cultivated cluster of ideas with roots in one strain of German philosophy; this cluster of ideas has been nurtured by French intellectuals and has been transplanted to the American academy by Derrida and de Man, to be husbanded there by their followers in the professoriate, and disseminated to undergraduates by legions of devoted graduate student converts. Although the postmodernists claim to be critical of the social ills of contemporary life—runaway technology and technocracy, the power of the state, capitalism, imperialism, colonialism, oppression of the downtrodden (all of which have been targets of respectable pre-postmodern liberal criticism as well)—their ideology carries with it, inevitably, the less desirable tendencies of their patron saint, Heidegger. Their attack on the Cartesian human subject and on reason itself; their contempt for the values of liberalism, of human and individual rights, and of constitutional democracy; their elevation of abstract terminology above affective speech; their cultivation of an obscure vocabulary accessible only to votaries of the movement; their inability to hear voices other than their own; their depreciation of human values (which they prefer to call bourgeois values) and their mocking of any notion of "transcendence," while at the same time elevating their own ideas into a religion with a priesthood and a crucified and resurrected god (Speaking to a gathering of the faithful after the discovery of de Man's anti-Semitic writings, Jacques Derrida, one of the high priests, announced: "He, *himself, he is dead,* and yet . . . he lives *among us.* . . ."[47])—all of these elements of "postmodernism" bespeak, not, as Maier believes, "a historical sensibility" but a deliberate and programmatic antihumanism.[48]

Revisionist history of the Holocaust did not come about because of a vague shift in sensibility, but rather was written as the result a willed effort of intellect that had as its goal changing the way the Holocaust past is perceived; specifically, the aim of revisionist historiography is to replace the point of view of the victims with that of the accused.[49] Similarly, postmodernism in literary theory is not simply an infection transmitted by an airborne virus. It, too, is a willed effort of intellect, one that issues from the same philosophical sources as German revisionist historiography.

This is not to say that "postmodernism" is a conspiracy, but rather that it is a bizarre merging of the agenda of the radical ideological right with that of the radical ideological left, both having in common their enmity to the traditions of liberal democracy. The ostensible targets of the various postmodernisms are pretty much the usual suspects: capitalism; imperialism; colonialism; the integrity of the individual; bourgeois culture and bourgeois values; human rights; constitutional democracy; technocracy, the military-industrial complex; the power structure; and, more exotically, the Logos and metaphysics—the emphasis on specific targets varying with the orientation, left or right, of the critic. The rebelliousness implicit in the various postmodernisms is that of a petulant child, with the U.S., as target, standing *in loco parentis* (the various adjective-nouns, "imperialist," "colonialist," "capitalist," especially when used to modify the noun "power," all become code words for the United States—France, for example, is none of the above).[50]

In mounting their attack on humanism, which they take to be the evil heart of Western culture, the postmodernists unavoidably, and perhaps unintentionally, align themselves with the languages and agendas of the most destructive ideologies of our time. If it is true that "humanism" has not lived up to its promise of freedom, equality, and justice for all human beings, then an antihumanism that arises out of intellectual movements that resulted in such massive destruction of both the concept and the reality of human dignity (whether in the gulag or the KZ-Lager) hardly seems to be an appropriate antidote. It was, after all, the Nazi attack on humanism and its destruction of the ideal of human dignity that fueled the most bestial cruelties of the SS. Ferry and Renaut note that "the Marxist dream of a radiant future" has already collapsed as a viable force among French intellectuals, and they observe that now "it is the neoconservative critique of the Heideggerian type that is in turn being politically compromised." They then pose the following dilemma:

That the two major critiques of modern humanism have proven to be lined with totalitarian adventures is most significant: *Whether conducted in the name of a radiant future or a traditionalist reaction, the total critique of the modern world, because it is necessarily an antihumanism that leads inevitably to seeing in the democratic project, for example, in human rights, the prototype of ideology or of the metaphysical illusion, is structurally incapable of taking up, except insincerely and seemingly in spite of itself, the promises that are also those of modernity.*[51]

Aside from revisionist historians who would persuade us that Auschwitz was not unique, there are deconstructionists and post-modernist thinkers who have adopted the thinking of Heidegger and who would persuade us that Auschwitz did not have roots in German philosophy. But the connection between Heidegger and Auschwitz, which although real is not easy to pin down, is made most tellingly by Amos Funkenstein:

You may object, the possible or even real abuses of a theory (even by its pro-moter) need not be held against it; in part, this has been my own argument. My critique, however, goes deeper than that. The very distinction between authentic and inauthentic existences, not only its possible career, is an in-trinsic assault on the *dignitas hominis*, the integrity and worthiness of each concrete individual life, however lived. The latter attitude, with its difficul-ties and paradoxes, must constitute the absolute center of humanistic ethical theories, even at the cost of subscribing to a one-dimensional, flat philosophi-cal anthropology. At best, Heidegger's distinction diverts from this focus; at the worst, it undermines it. . . . *Mutatis mutandis*, the flaws in the thought of Heidegger are also flaws in those dialectical theologies which speak in Heidegger's idiom.[52]

It is just such an assault on human dignity that has been carried on by the deconstructionist and postmodernist literary theoreticians who could not do otherwise once they had chosen to speak in Hei-degger's idiom. But against this idiom Funkenstein sets the idiom of Primo Levi, another major writer who fails to enter the lucubrations of deconstructionists and postmodernists. "As against the distinction between the begraced and those who lack grace, between authen-tic and inauthentic existences," writes Funkenstein, "the reality of the concentration camps taught Levi other distinctions, distinctions which are purely homocentric, such as the distinction between 'the drowned and the saved.'" After citing a passage from Levi's *Survival in Auschwitz*, Funkenstein concludes: "Out of the experience of the concentration camp, Levi crystallized the building blocks of a true philosophical anthropology, more genuine and accurate than either

Heidegger's or any recent theologian's. The power of his reflections, I repeat, lies in that they are centered around the concrete man, not around a chimera of the authentic self nor around God." [53]

Funkenstein's suggestion that Levi's attempt to reconstruct a meaningful image of the human form out of the shards of Auschwitz constitutes a more profound challenge than Heideggerian philosophy will, in the present academic climate, surely be seen as nothing less than heresy. Yet, what Funkenstein says in a theological context may also be said of postmodernist literary theorists: they are no longer "centered around the concrete man," and as a consequence they have little to say about literature that concerns itself with living human beings. Perhaps something would be learned from examining Heidegger's philosophizing in the context of Levi's writings. And would it be possible to initiate such a dialogue without eventually considering the testimony of Elie Wiesel, whose narrative of a young Jewish mystic abruptly thrust into a hell on earth remains the most widely read and best known witness account, and whose subsequent Jobian wrestling with an inscrutable God remains a constant challenge to both Jewish and Christian thinkers and theologians?

The tendency among contemporary literary theorists, even those, like Merquior and Ferry-Renaut, who are critical of postmodernist clichés, is to treat postmodernist literary theory in isolation from history as a movement grounded (either correctly or mistakenly) in a philosophical continuum stretching, essentially, from Kant through Hegel and Nietzsche to Marx and Heidegger and their followers. In my earlier theoretical essays I have argued that postmodernist literary theory and criticism does not make sense outside the context of what happened at Auschwitz. Literary theory is not likely to get out of the rut of deconstruction until the literary theorists find some way to confront and embrace what has been left out of mainstream literary theorizing for so many years—the Holocaust past in general and the literature of the victims in particular.

Literary theorists must choose between the "philosophical anthropology" of a Primo Levi, which starts from the *experience* of the individual person reduced to a nothingness and is therefore cognizant of the horror of this nothingness, and a Heideggerian philosophical anthropology that constitutes an assault on human dignity and on the integrity and worthiness of each concrete individual life. Purveyors of postmodern ideologies must consider whether it is possible to diminish human beings in theory, without, at the same time, making individual human lives worthless in the real world. And they must decide whether they will continue to neglect the revealing testimony of writers and poets while pursuing obscurantist philosophies that have been implicated in twentieth-century disasters, philosophies that have subsequently shown no capacity to cope with their own complicity in human destructive impulses. To put the question in specific terms, should *literary* theorists expend their energies working to understand the messages from a man-made, twentieth-century hell, transmitted by such emissaries as David Rousset, Jorge Semprun, Charlotte Delbo, Primo Levi, Elie Wiesel, Viktor E. Frankl, and Tadeusz Borowski, among innumerable others? Or should they, rather, spend their energy in laboring to interpret philosophers and theorists like Martin Heidegger, Roland Barthes, Jacques Derrida, Jacques Lacan, among others, who seem to have experienced nothing, and who are therefore condemned to think in a moral vacuum? In short, should *literary* theorists and critics dedicate themselves to interpreting the works of verbal puzzle makers or to understanding the writings of those who have earned the right to tell us what the twentieth century was really about?

I I

Antihumanism and the American University

Marxism, Humanism, and Literature in the University

I have been asked to write about the teaching of Marxism at Brown, but I must admit that it is a matter I know little about. I don't like looking into my colleague's pots, nor do I like them looking into mine. I do, however, want to talk about both Marx and Freud as prophets, and about those who are currently their "true believers," postmodern professors of the humanities.

Marx was a student of economic and political forces who believed he was conducting scientific inquiries into social, political, and economic structures; yet his works, students complain, are not taught at all in the Brown economics and political science departments. Students committed to postmodern ways of thinking discover conspiracy in this phenomenon, but it is more likely that the omission is owing to the fact that professional economists do not respect Marx as an economist. Those who pursue the study of economics as a science do not consider Marx's economic theories sufficiently scientific, and on the basis of what those theories have done to the economies of the Soviet Union and the People's Republic of China, which claim to be Marxist states, who can blame the pros for being skeptical?

A similar situation exists with regard to Freud. Just as Marx is very little taught in political science or economics departments, so Freud is not heralded these days in departments of psychology or psychiatry, and for similar reasons. Though what Freud did in his own time may have passed for science and though he may have considered himself a scientist, he is not a scientist at all by contemporary standards. If Marxist economics has not produced utopias in Marxist states, so, by the same token, Freudian techniques of analysis have not consistently demonstrated their power to cure the most serious (or even the most trivial) psychological disorders.

If Marxist economics is no longer perceived as a tool that can be used to help solve economic problems, and Freudian analytic techniques are no longer applicable in helping to cure patients with mental disorders, what residue of Marxism and Freudianism remains? Once, perhaps, each was a science, at the cutting edge of a certain kind of knowledge, using what were then state-of-the-art empirical techniques to overthrow outworn ideas. But now the discoveries of Marx and Freud have themselves become worn-out ideas, and neither is considered to be at the cutting edge by those who engage in the professional full-time study of the sciences of psychology and economics. There is probably no country on earth, including the Soviet Union and China, whose leaders would apply Marxist economics to help solve the nation's economic problems. Similarly, no responsible mental health professional would try to cure a psychotic or neurotic patient exclusively by trying to talk him or her back to childhood Oedipal origins. Even obsessive-compulsive disorders, once the very heart and soul of Freudian theories of neurosis, are now treated by chemical intervention and behavior modification rather than by Freudian psychoanalysis. Call such disorders guilt-generated "neuroses" if you wish, but contemporary scientists are more interested in the observed datum that the causes of such disorders can be traced to the brain circuits running between the frontal lobes and the basal ganglia than they are in theoretical speculations that obsessive-compulsive neuroses are a result of repression in the anal-retentive stage. Descientized Freudian and Marxian ideas have become the worn clothes that the financially well-to-do pass down to the needy. The threadbare garments of these now pseudoscientific theories have been left by the scientist to his poor academic sibling, the humanist, and specifically, to the postmodernist literary historian.

Though they find an inhospitable climate in the social sciences and in the hard sciences, Marx and Freud have been given a warm home in certain humanities departments committed to postmodern ways of perceiving the world. But they have not found a home there as scientists. They have found a home, rather, as prophets, or perhaps more accurately, as gods. And those who espouse Marxian and Freudian views become the "true believers." The faithlike nature of descientized Marxism and Freudism is attested by the nature of the controversies Marxists and Freudians conduct among themselves. They rarely test the validity of either Marxist or Freudian theories by evaluating them in the physical world, but rather concern themselves with the question of whose interpretation of Marx or Freud is the acceptable one. The issue thus becomes one not of how well does the theory work when applied to the physical world, but of who is the true Marxist, just as for certain religious sects differences in interpretations of central documents invariably turn into quarrels about who is the true believer.

But what happens to Marxist and Freudian ideas when they lose their empirical grounding and their power to explain events in the physical world? Free-floating Marxist and Freudian ideas have been fused to establish at least one of the foundations of postmodernist literary theory and to promulgate an image of the human form as a robot controlled by "ideology." This term, which has become an article of faith for the Marxist deconstructionist, was coined by Marx and Engels; adapted, modified, and promulgated by a discredited French wife-killer; and then popularized by an American postmodern Marxist academic who proves his own belief in the evils of wealth, unequal distribution, and commodification by living on a handsome salary provided by the generous overflow of a tobacco fortune.[1] Nevertheless, though their entire system of belief hinges on the concept of "ideology," Marxians cannot agree on what Marx and Engels meant by the concept, so they often argue violently among themselves to determine who has the only right interpretation of the term, for though postmodernist Marxists babble about indeterminacy of meaning, they do not wish to leave the meaning of what *they* consider central in an indeterminate state.

One recent Marxist deconstruction theorist delivers in a voice of authority a definition of "ideology" that is at least both succinct and relatively clear, if not universally accepted. "Ideology," this theorist writes, "signifies not a set of explicit political ideas but a 'lived relation to the real' determined by a matrix of psychosexual and social investments. . . . Because ideology works most effectively through its *unconscious* hold on subjects, it resists being made conscious or explicit. An ideology structures 'seeing' and 'feeling' before it structures 'thinking,' and appears to have no historical or social specificity but to be simply the *natural* way of perceiving reality."[2] This is a neat polemical trick, for by virtue of this definition the more you deny the existence of "ideology" the more you prove you are hopelessly caught in its clutches. Ideology thus becomes the postmodernist's version of what the Puritan called "original sin." Just as an individual's denial of "original sin" might prove to a Puritan divine that the denier was in the grasp of the Devil, so the individual's denial of ideology may prove to the Marxist deconstructionist that the denier is in the grasp of the capitalist-imperialist-racist-sexist cultural vise. And as the Puritan sinner could only be saved by grace, so the capitalist-imperialist-racist-sexist slob can be saved only by Marxist theory as tendered by the new priesthood, those who are the purveyors of Marxist truth. By an impressive bit of sleight of hand, those who accept an ideology, that is—to define the term as Marx and Engels intended it—those who accept a consciously held cohesive set of beliefs, declare themselves ideology-free, while portraying those who have no ideology (those who do not adhere to an explicitly articulated body of doctrine) as ideologists (or ideologues).

Other residues of descientized Marx and Freud are "the class struggle" and "sublimation." But the class struggle as Marx conceived it never really took root in American culture. The kind of rigid hierarchy that Marx grew up with in central Europe never had an opportunity to become established in the constitutional republic created by the Founding Fathers. Even now, empirical sociologists have difficulty in defining what constitutes a "class" in American culture, and in determining where one class ends and another begins. It is well known that the vast majority of Americans define themselves as middle class, which then makes it necessary for sociologists interested in arriving at finer distinctions to divide the middle class itself into upper, middle, and lower, and so on. What this means for postmodernist Marxists who want to turn their guns on American culture is that the Marxian model they inherited from *Das Kapital* and other Marxist writings forces them to construct a fictive reality that is out of synch with the empirical reality of American culture itself (though postmodernist Marxists who see all verbal structures as narratives do not recognize a distinction between "fiction" and "reality"). Looking at American culture through Marx-tinted glasses, they see the world that Marx taught them they ought to see rather than the world that is actually there. In other words, the postmodern Marxists have to build hovels in the air. In order to superimpose onto the American scene the model they have inherited from Marx, and in order to retain the myth of the primacy of class conflict in human affairs (for Marxism thrives on myths of conflict and domination, just as Christianity thrives on myths of nonresistance and redemption), the postmodernist Marxists must create classes that do not exist. In fact, the postmodern Marxists have been more inventive in this regard than nineteenth-century American writers of fiction, who complained that they were unable to write novels on the European model precisely because in America there were no classes—no royalty, no nobility—and therefore fewer opportunities for representing "Clarissa"-type dramatic conflicts in "mimetic" fictional narratives. For that reason the great nineteenth-century American novels focused on the conflict between human beings and natural forces, and not on the conflicts between lower-class servant girls and boys trying to seduce and marry their upper-class masters and mistresses.

Postmodern Freudians are forced into similar absurdities. Freud based his theory of sublimation (neurosis-as-the-price-of-culture) on the very rigid Austro-German family, constituted by a strict, punishing, disciplinarian father, a submissive mother, an obedient son, and a subservient daughter. But if this paradigm of the family ever did exist in the United States, it had virtually disappeared before the turn of the twentieth century. Anyone who has read extensively in nineteenth-century American literature cannot help but notice how far the American family had departed from the Freudian-

German model by the 1880s. Since American culture was revolutionary, antiauthoritarian, and antihierarchical from its origins in eighteenth-century Enlightenment ideas, it never developed the Germanic authoritarian structure that Freud grew up in. Marx and Freud analyzed Austro-German culture and thought they were analyzing the universe. For them Austro-German culture was universal culture, as it consequently becomes for believing Marxists and Freudians.

Postmodernists, then, would have us believe that while we imagine we are free, we are actually in bondage to an "ideology" that controls us through the [Freudian] unconscious. Such absurdity is a form of postmodern aphasia. Postmodernists confuse metaphorical and non-metaphorical language, asserting dogmatically that *all* language is metaphorical. However, one need only read books like Adam Michnik's *Letters From Prison* or Alexander Wat's *My Century* to see the mendacity of such claims. Wat was a Jew, a Marxist, and a Pole, not necessarily in that order. When the Germans and the Soviets divided Poland between them in 1939, Wat fled east, to the Soviet zone, where he was promptly imprisoned by the Marxist regime as "a Trotskyite, a Zionist, and an agent of the Vatican."[3] He spent several years in a Marxist prison system where beatings were the rule, where starvation was not unusual, where disease and death were commonplace. For defying a Marxist government, Michnik, a leader of the Solidarity movement, served two and a half years in prison. Michnik's experience led him to his own postmodernism, a postmodernism quite different from that which dominates humanities departments in American universities. In one of his letters, Michnik explains why he has refused to purchase his release from prison for the seemingly negligible price of signing a pledge of loyalty to the Marxist regime. "It is very easy, indeed," he writes,

to exchange the barred window, with its clear outline of a barbed wire fence behind it, for "freedom." The steel gates of Bialoleka will open up before you, and instead of the prison yards you will see the streets of your hometown, filled with strolling army patrols and rolling tanks. You will see people being asked for identification cards, cars being stopped to have their trunks inspected. . . .[4]

The Marxist deconstructionist expresses his opposition to liberal humanism with a metaphor. The average person, he maintains, is "inscribed by the culture" and is the "prisoner of an ideology." Thus the Marxist deconstructionist portrays the individual in a liberal humanist culture as a robot, lacking freedom of will, whose behavior is "determined by a matrix of psychosexual and social investments"; without the individual's realizing it, he operates as the prisoner of an "ideology [that] works most effectively through its *unconscious* hold on [its] subjects. . . ." The Marxist deconstructionist, be it noted, does not seem to apply this determinism to himself. This "prisoner," however, who is oblivious to his condition, acts as if he is free. He walks the streets; he does not live behind barred windows and barbed wire fences and steel gates, limited to strolls in a prison yard. It might be said that in the imagination of the Marxist deconstructionist he dwells as a prisoner, but in his own imagination he is a free man. Or, to put it differently, the Marxist deconstructionist relativizes the words "prison" and "prisoner."

For Michnik the case is reversed. "Prisoner" is not the relativized and ambiguous word, but "freedom." "A few strokes of the pen on a loyalty oath will suffice," Michnik explains to the addressee of his letter. With those few strokes he will put himself in a position once again to "see the streets of [his] hometown, filled with strolling army patrols and rolling tanks . . . [and] people being asked for identification cards, cars being stopped to have their trunks inspected. . . ." So for Michnik, in a Marxist culture, being freed from prison paradoxically does not mean being free. Living in a Marxist state, for him to be imprisoned by an ideology is not a metaphor. It is a reality. And even the condition of being a prisoner after release from prison is not a metaphor but a reality. For living "outside of prison" merely means that the bars and the barbed wire have been erected on a grander spatial scale, that is, from border to border.

One reason for Michnik's refusal to sign the loyalty oath is that he refuses to metaphorize the word "freedom." He will not exchange the comforting reality of knowing he is in prison for the unsettling illusion of freedom. But there is a more important reason for his not signing; he realizes that signing would be an act of collaboration, and that the price of achieving the illusion of freedom is high, nothing less than his human dignity: "But you know already—your instincts are telling you—that to forsake your dignity is not a price worth paying to have the prison gates opened for you." But Michnik goes still further in describing what it would mean to pledge loyalty to the postmodern Marxist state:

Your loyalty declaration will transform itself into your pact with the devil. This is why you should not give these police inquisitors even the tip of your finger: because they will instantly grab your whole arm. Surely you must know someone whose life has been shattered by one moment of moral in-attention or weakness of spirit, someone who has been pursued by phone calls, whose home and office are regularly invaded by the police, who is black mailed every time he or she goes abroad. Such people pay for one moment of unwisdom with years of degradation and fear.[5]

Anyone living in the climate of Western postmodernism must be struck immediately by what would appear to be the quaintness not only of Michnik's diction, but of his ideas. In the climate of post-modernist deconstructionism, Michnik's statement makes no sense. The postmodern deconstructionist would not be able to accept the reality of a "pact with the devil" and would be nonplussed by the notion of "moral inattention"; "weakness of spirit" would be nothing more than a floating signifier. Since postmodern Marxists claim not to believe in the integrity of the individual or the legitimacy of indi-vidual acts of "conscience," they would have to consider Michnik's assertions of human dignity and of the integrity of the individual to be either madness or mere "fictions of the self," part of the ideology with which all the benighted "souls" living in liberal democracies are "inscribed."

Yet one wonders how Adam Michnik, raised in a Marxist society, came to be inscribed with the most sublime ideas of liberal democ-racy and individual conscience. Michnik sounds like no one so much as our own Henry David Thoreau. Was it not Thoreau who said, in 1849, that "Under a government that imprisons any unjustly, the true place for a just man is also a prison"? and "This American govern-ment . . . has not the force and vitality of a single living man . . ."? and "Can there not be a government in which the majorities do not virtually decide right and wrong, but conscience?" Marxist decon-structionists deny the existence of "truth," of "universals" of "right and wrong," of "determinacy of meaning," yet they seem to accept their own beliefs as universal truths that have a determinate meaning and that are right rather than wrong. They make claims to greater self-awareness than the rest of us, but they have yet to come to terms with the fact that their own ideology has been developed out of the metaphysics of a Nazi philosopher and has been most widely promulgated by a literary critic who was a Nazi collaborator and who lived his entire adult life under false pretenses.

POSTSCRIPT

I wrote this essay in January 1989 at the invitation of an enterprising Brown undergraduate, and it was first published in April 1989 in a collection of writings on Marxism by Brown faculty and students, entitled *Imbroglio*. Since I wrote the essay, Marxism has been rejected en masse in eastern Europe. Owen Harries, coeditor of *The National Interest*, wrote in a *New York Times* Op-Ed piece, October 29, 1989, that "Whatever happens in the Communist world, the days of Marxism-Leninism as an ideology capable of competing seriously with liberal democracy are over." In the terminology coined by French Marxist theorist Louis Althusser, this is to say that the people of eastern Europe prefer living under an "ideological state apparatus" to living under a "repressive state apparatus." Only British and American Marxist deconstructionist academics who have not caught up to the times, it seems, prefer the repressive state apparatus to liberal democracy.

For whatever reason, wherever a Marxist state has been established, it has been accompanied by the ruthless annihilation of all opposition and by the suppression of civil and human rights. The Marxist believer explains this in two ways. The first line of defense is to argue that the present repressive Marxist state is not yet the ultimate Marxist state. It is only a stage toward the "dictatorship of the proletariat." The second line of argument is to disparage human and civil rights as mere deceptions, fictions devised by the ruling class in a capitalist society to facilitate the oppression of the poor. Even a relatively civilized Marxist like Terry Eagleton can write of

Northrop Frye that he "stands in the liberal humanist tradition of Arnold, desiring, as he says, 'society as free, classless and urbane.' What he means by 'classless,' like Arnold before him, is in effect a society which universally subscribes to his own middle-class liberal values." [6] Eagleton does not deem it worth mentioning that at least one twentieth-century alternative to "middle-class liberal values" has been the Marxist gulag. Perhaps that is why so many of those living under Marxist regimes are eager to give up their present utopian existence to assume the "yoke" of those very values that academic Marxists denigrate with such utter contempt.

CHAPTER NINE

And What Are You, Reader?

The humanities are in flux. Liberal democracy, on which the humanities rely for sustenance and which they in turn sustain, is under attack by "humanists"; literary criticism has not only become politicized, but politicized against the values of liberal humanism. I should like to discuss two books that seem to me to be symptomatic of the directions literary criticism has taken in the eighties: George Dekker's *The American Historical Romance*, and Robert Shulman's *Social Criticism & Nineteenth-Century American Fiction*.[1] In different degrees and in different ways they reflect the latest politicization of academic literary criticism, yet are old-fashioned in their methodology. That is to say, while the authors bow to the "new" politics, they are New Critical rather than deconstructionist in their reading strategies.

Yet these books cannot be said to constitute a turn away from deconstruction and toward a new historicism, either. Though both books announce their support of the need for canon revision, they defer the task of accomplishing that revision to others. Dekker, for example, announces that "My decision to concentrate almost exclusively on the elite figures in the historical romance tradition was not taken lightly" (p. 4). Nevertheless, lightly or not, the decision was made not to revise the canon. Similarly, Shulman writes, "I concentrate on mainstream writers not because I am indifferent to the need to rethink the established canon but because I want to assume and not have to demonstrate the value of the works I consider" (p. x). But is it not precisely the point of "canon revision" and the new "new historicism" that we must not "assume . . . the value of works," but prove the value of each work constantly? One gets the uneasy sense not so much of a genuine belief in the need for a revisionist historicism but of the hegemony of the canon-revision police, who demand that every critic pay tribute to their agenda, even when he or she does not intend to follow it.

Having joined these books together, however, I must hasten to set their actual politics asunder. Robert Shulman openly embraces a Marxist position, adopting the Gramscian-Raymond Williamsian notion that literature is one of the means by which "a dominant class" maintains its "hegemony" over the "oppressed classes"; George Dekker adopts the values of liberal democracy, but he is defensive in assuring the reader that his commitment to these values is not merely the result of ignorance and insensitivity: "To examine Scott's American legacy in any depth," he tells us, "means paying close attention to matters which are of the first importance to Marxist criticism: social revolution, colonialism, and the relationship between literary-generic and socio-economic change" (p. 9), as if it is only "Marxist criticism" that is interested in such matters.

I should say immediately that Dekker and Shulman are ripened scholars, rich in learning and experience. Both books give evidence of their author's wide reading, dedicated research, scholarly discipline, creative spirit, and sincere commitment to rethinking the possibilities of American literature. Both authors are to be admired for bringing the literature back to its historical-contextual roots; nevertheless, their books are unleavened breads in which the yeast is either missing or has failed to ferment. Both books leave us disappointed, but for opposite reasons: Dekker's because the thesis is too dense and multifaceted, Shulman's because the thesis is too simplistic.

If it is true that the most elegant theory is simple and at the same time explains the widest range of phenomena, then Dekker's thesis is certainly very far from such elegance; it is convoluted and multitiered, and the range of phenomena it explains is relatively narrow. It is as if Dekker kept discovering new theses as he proceeded in his research and, being loath to give up any one of them, finally decided to include them all. The main thesis, embodied in the title, *American Historical Romance*, is itself three-tiered (one tier for each term) and requires a full chapter to define the three terms; the second thesis, which also requires a full chapter of exposition, is the influence of Walter Scott and the "*Waverley*-model" on American "romances"; and the third is the alleged pervasive presence in American "romances" of "the stadialist model of progress," which also requires a full chapter to develop. So it takes three of the nine chapters in the book just to establish the thesis.

Though none of the three terms in the title is adequately defined, I must limit my discussion here to Dekker's problems in handling the second two. "For a fiction to qualify as 'historical,'" Dekker writes, "what more can be required than that the leading or . . . determinative social and psychological traits it represents clearly belong to a period historically distinct from our own?" This definition would seem to include everything but the immediately contemporary as "historical," and, at the same time, would seem to require a belief in historical determinism. Dekker also finds that none "of the characters need to have been actual historical personages," and he questions whether characters based on "actual historical personages" have any more "authenticating force [as history] than the ebbing sea of shaggy red prairie grass in *My Antonia*" (p. 14). If so, however, then why has he not included *Moby-Dick* as an American historical romance? Does not Melville's "insular city of the Manhattoes, belted round by wharves . . . [and] commerce" have this same "authenticating force" in *Moby-Dick*?

Still less satisfactory is Dekker's definition of the "romance." Having opened this can of worms, he attempts to close it peremptorily. The problem is that the question of defining the genre of American romance has been under debate ever since the appearance of Richard Chase's *The American Novel and Its Tradition* (1956). Since then, the question has been treated in innumerable books and essays. But Dekker sidesteps the problem disingenuously:

Mainly following James or Hawthorne, that other American master practitioner/theorist of romance, academic critics have employed the distinction [between novel and romance] to get at the special character of the American novel or have hotly denied its "reality of interest." Rather than rehearsing

their arguments, I propose to come back to James by way of some earlier figures with the aim of saying only as much about the novel/romance debate as
is necessary to explain what I mean by the oxymoron "historical romance."
(p. 16)

This offhanded evasion is accompanied by an omnibus footnote that
lists a small portion of the literature on the American romance and
novel. If the question of "American [historical] romance" were merely
incidental to Dekker's thesis, his refusal to become involved in the
intricacies of the debate would be understandable and excusable. But
since the term "romance" is in the title of Dekker's book and at the
core of his thesis, his offhandedness is hardly appropriate, and is,
in fact, somewhat irresponsible. Moreover, he derives his principal
support for the notion of American "romance" from Henry James's
preface to the New York Edition of *The American*, which is also one
of the main documents used by Chase in developing his argument.
Hence, Dekker's refusal to meet the issue minimizes his ability to
move the argument forward.

Dekker's secondary thesis, the Scott influence on American fiction, works best for Cooper, for the obvious reason that the influence
is direct, documentable, and one that every reader can "feel." The
Scott thesis works less well for Hawthorne, and is practically useless
when applied to Melville and the twentieth-century American novel-
ists. The third thesis, the pervasive presence in American "romances"
of "the stadialist model of progress," raises some interesting questions, but is relatively far-fetched and not worth the time and effort it
obviously took for Dekker to develop it. What is perhaps most damaging to the multifaceted thesis in all its complexity is that it does
not really "enable" Dekker's insights into individual works and is all
too often dragged in as an afterthought. For example, commenting
on the prefatory note to "The May-Pole of Merry Mount," Dekker
writes that "Hawthorne has telescoped, rearranged, omitted, and invented such 'facts' as he needed to make a 'philosophic romance' in
miniature—one in which the binary oppositions are basically those
of the *Waverly*-model, enriched and modified by ones drawn from
Spenser, Milton, and their Romantic imitators" (p. 154). Aside from
the fact that the "*Waverly*-model" must share prominence with no

less than "Spenser, Milton, and their Romantic imitators," it is common knowledge that Hawthorne's mind was permeated with the Puritan mind-set of "binary oppositions," so that no intermediary influences need be invoked to explain their presence in a tale focusing on the imposition of stern Puritan morality and discipline on a licentious Dionysian community.

The most serious deficiency in Dekker's thesis, however, is that it is powerless to touch that most puzzling and challenging of nineteenth-century literary phenomena, *Moby-Dick*, considered by some the single greatest instance of the "American Romance" (and a work which may be considered in many ways no less "historical" than books Dekker does write about, such as *The Prairie* and *My Antonia*, among others). Nor can the absence of any extended discussion of *Moby-Dick* be dismissed as a negligible oversight, or as a matter of an author's having the privilege of writing the book he wants to write, for how useful can a thesis be, after all, that does not account for the most central, the most challenging, and the most puzzling phenomenon in the world it purports to explain?

The omission is all the more puzzling in the light of Dekker's assertion that "For Scott and most of his younger contemporaries, the historical romance was, above all, a modern version of the epic, hence a heroic and masculine genre preoccupied with the fate of entire societies. . . ." (p. 28). What nineteenth-century work of fiction, British or American, comes closer to that description than *Moby-Dick*? Moreover, an entire section of the second chapter ("The *Waverly*-model"), dedicated to the "historical romance as epic," seems to cry out for the inclusion of Melville's great romance-epic. In describing what " 'epic' has meant to the authors of historical romances, [Dekker] distinguish[es] four pertinent meanings of epic: (1) an Aristotelian model of narrative form and mimetic fidelity to nature; (2) the proper narrative (but sometimes dramatic) vehicle for treating 'heroic' matter; (3) the product and portrait of a "whole" community; (4) the most inclusive form, capable of containing romance" (p. 55). Clearly, one would be hard pressed to find a "historical epic romance" that comes closer to embodying all four of these "pertinent meanings" than *Moby-Dick*. Nor has any book come closer to fulfilling what Dekker describes as the aim of "Scott's American followers . . . to incarnate epic form in the age and new world of democracy." If one asks how Dekker could have been so blind to the centrality of *Moby-Dick* to his own thesis, the answer must be that his ideology has forced him to swerve away from putting a biblical epic—written in biblical language and saturated with biblical ideas—where it belongs, at the center of his thesis.

Unlike Dekker's ideas, Shulman's do not develop as the book progresses. Like Adam and Eve in the Garden, once his eyes are opened to "the basic processes of commodification or reification" (p. viii) and to an "understanding" of "the crosscurrents of the hegemonic process" (p. vii), his direction is set for eternity. As he puts it: "Successive chapters do not develop a deductive argument or a nineteenth-century narrative" (p. x). What the successive chapters *do* is to find the "hegemonic process" everywhere, and they use it to explain all the ills of humanity. What "original sin" was for the Puritan, "hegemonic process" is for the Marxist.

Though Dekker's book and Shulman's both deal principally with mainstream nineteenth- and twentieth-century American authors and fiction in developing their political agendas, they rarely deal with the same works, which suggests that canon is really not much of an issue, after all. For example, Dekker discusses *Pudd'nhead Wilson*, while Shulman discusses *The Adventures of Huckleberry Finn* and *A Connecticut Yankee*; Dekker does *The Age of Innocence*, while Shulman does *The House of Mirth*; and while Dekker deals with Cooper and Dreiser, Shulman focuses on Franklin and Faulkner. Nevertheless, the books do intersect directly at three points: Hawthorne's "My Kinsman, Major Molineux" and *The Scarlet Letter*, and Melville's *Billy Budd*. A comparison of their readings of *Billy Budd* may, I believe, reveal something not only about the inevitable pitfalls of a thesis-bound critical method, but about the coercive nature of the new orthodoxy that is settling into the academy.

I should start by saying that on the whole Dekker gives the more balanced assessment of the novel and of Melville's thinking. He locates Melville's writing of the book in the context of the centenary of the French revolution, in 1888, finding significance in the fact that

"Melville began writing [the book] with loud public praises of universal Progress echoing in his ears and a quiet conviction . . . that very much had been lost" (p. 208). In Dekker's view, "Nelson, Billy, and even Vere reincarnate the heroic ideal . . ." (p. 209). He also concludes that

Melville quite openly takes sides in *Billy Budd*—with angelic Billy against diabolic Claggart; with Nelson's panegyrists against his detractors. . . . Confronted with a choice between highly imperfect socio-political systems, Melville now preferred the one that most frankly recognized the imperfection of man and the inequality of talents. The rule of "custom or convention" or better of "founded law and freedom defined" was precisely what citified man required. He also required what the English system was capable of producing in time of need, heroic leaders like Nelson, patriarchal leaders like Vere. The latter . . . was more complete as a man and a better governor for all seasons, working good out of the evil of Cain's city. . . . If the evils [of war, atheism, greed] are universal and even more than commonly active in England at the time of the action of *Billy Budd*, their crusading legions are the "conquering and proselyting armies of the French." (pp. 211, 212, 213)

On the whole this seems to be a fair representation of what Melville came to believe in the years before his death, a tragic view of the human condition, in which human beings are left to choose from among relative evils. But it is a reading that is in agreement with many earlier readings of the novella, and one that Dekker could therefore have arrived at, and probably did arrive at, without the help of his thesis.

What I find somewhat alarming, however, is that Dekker feels a need to placate the new academic left with a disclaimer: "It may appear that even today I do [Melville] a disservice by foregrounding what can be ignored easily enough by readers of a different political persuasion. It is true that his questionings of progress and democracy and his caricature of the French Revolution can be shrugged off as mere reactionary crotchets of an isolated old man; or they can be turned on their head as the ironies of a venerable liberal *manqué*" (p. 213). Can one, then, do a writer a disservice by telling what one believes to be true about the way in which that writer came to perceive the world and the human condition? And is the view attributed to Melville here (a view that Melville arrived at only after having experienced most devastating tragedies in his own life), that "evil" is rooted in the human imagination, one that must be apologized for? Is Melville to be cast into outer darkness for having believed that the brutal excesses of the French Revolution were not an unmitigated good? And does it make any sense at all for a well-paid, tenured academic ensconced in an elitist establishment university to apologize for the "conservative politics" of the risk-taking, conscience-tormented, nay-saying, eternal "outsider," Melville? Is it that Dekker fails to see the ludicrousness of such an apology, or is he afraid that Melville will have to be booted out of the humanities course at Stanford if he is perceived as anything other than a Guevarist revolutionary?

Not to worry. Robert Shulman redeems Melville's reputation for the new orthodoxy by reading *Billy Budd* (and every other work he analyzes) as a critique of capitalism and of America as a "Market Society." Whereas Dekker tends to absorb previous readings into his own silently, as it were, without acknowledging that the meaning of the novel has been bitterly contested since the 1950s, Shulman disparages earlier readings, asserting that "the theological and psychoanalytical emphasis of the 1940s and 1950s succeeded in abstracting the story from its American social roots" (p. 67) (as though "the theological" itself were not part of "American social roots"). The "prevailing assumptions," he avers, "emerge in the way Wendell Glick detaches *Billy Budd* from American history and society and gives the readers of PMLA a lesson in 1950s accommodation . . ." (p. 67). However, what Shulman takes to be Glick's shameful "lesson in accommodation" is basically a sober-minded reading of the novel that anticipates Dekker by some thirty-five years (a reading accomplished, needless to say, without the benefit of either "the stadialist model of progress" or the model of "hegemonic process"). Glick makes the point that by the 1880s Melville had arrived at the belief that "an ordered society at least guaranteed the preservation of *some* rights; and though this fell far short of the ideal of the preservation of *all,* it was far better than the sort of 'society' which in the idealistic attempt to guarantee all rights, degenerated into chaos and so permitted their complete and total destruction" (p. 67).

Instead of treating the differences between himself and Glick as honest differences in interpretation, Shulman disparages "1950s accommodation" as though the thinking of the 1950s is not only hopelessly time-bound but corrupt. At the same time, he finds universal and eternal truth and purity in the theory of "hegemonic process" that he has adopted from Antonio Gramsci. Yet, as Dekker's reiteration of the Glick position some thirty-five years later indicates, Glick's interpretation is not necessarily a matter of mere 1950s accommodation, and may still have as much appeal and validity for a reader in the 1980s as Shulman's Marxist-Gramscian reading of the book. One side takes Melville to be saying that given the human condition, a sane society must accept compromise, as represented by Vere, even if the cost is (paradoxically and tragically) the sacrifice of absolute good. The other takes Melville to be saying that a society willing to sacrifice the absolute good, as represented by Billy, is itself a paramount evil. Perhaps the heated acrimony with which the antagonists debate the issue should tell us that the greatness of *Billy Budd* as a work of art is its ability to make this dilemma come passionately alive for generation after generation of readers. And perhaps the inability of readers to agree is testimony to Melville's own "negative capability," his genius for presenting the human dilemma in terms that are always challenging and ever irresolvable.

But Marxist readers are not known for their tolerance of negative capability, and Shulman is no exception to this rule. Shulman's Marxist rigidity is not without its irony, since it is precisely Vere's rigidity, or what he takes to be Melville's portrayal of Vere's rigidity, that lies at the heart of his interpretation of Melville's story. In Vere, Shulman states,

Melville dramatizes the inadequacies of an administrative outlook that is too rigid, too committed to order, regularity, and the state, all at the expense of human values, compassion, humanity. Vere represents a habit of mind that divides things into neat, mutually exclusive categories. The result is that he dehumanizes himself and kills Billy Budd. . . . He has made himself into an impersonal instrument of the state. To further his view of order and the true welfare of mankind, Vere fragments himself internally. (pp. 69–70)

Shulman's characterization, an extremely harsh extension of the "ironic" readings of Vere generated by Phil Withim, is possible only if one disregards the last meeting between Vere and Billy in which, the narrator tells us,

> The austere devotee of military duty, letting himself melt back into what remains primeval in our formalized humanity, may in the end have caught Billy to his heart, even as Abraham may have caught young Isaac on the brink of resolutely offering him up in obedience to the exacting behest. But there is no telling the sacrament, seldom if in any case revealed to the gadding world, wherever under circumstances at all akin to those here attempted to be set forth two of great Nature's nobler order embrace. There is privacy at the time, inviolable to the survivor; and holy oblivion, the sequel to each diviner magnanimity, providentially covers all at last. (chapter 22, *Billy Budd*)

Significantly, when Shulman lists "the world-ranging host of associations . . . that Melville gives Billy" (p. 71), the one he does not include is the association of Billy with the biblical Isaac. This would be the blindness of insight if it were accompanied by insight, but in reality it is the blindness of ideology. Writing from the perspective of dialectical materialism, Shulman cannot enter into the innermost depths of Melville's religious consciousness. Neither can Dekker, who writes from the perspective of an unnecessarily narrowed secular liberalism. Though Dekker at least takes note of the meeting, he can understand it only in secular, sociopolitical terms: "In the Abraham-Isaac relationship between Saxon Budd and Norman Vere," he writes, "we perhaps glimpse a representation in miniature of the English socio-political system as an ideal patriarchy . . ." (p. 212).

But while Melville was surely a child of the Enlightenment, who bridled at (and in his youth resisted) authority and denounced the oppression of the weak by the strong wherever he found it, he was also a child of the Puritans who, by the time he wrote *Billy Budd*, had come to contemplate his own tragic past in the light of biblical tragedy— and mystery—the "mystery of iniquity" (*Billy Budd*, p. 76), as Melville's narrator puts it. Having experienced the loss of his two sons (one a possible suicide at the age of eighteen, and the second in 1886, approximately the time he started writing *Billy Budd*), Melville now undertook the writing of his own meditation on the religious paradox that Kierkegaard called "the teleological suspension of the ethical." This is not to deny, as Dekker points out, that Melville was probably aware of the centenary of the French Revolution, nor to deny, as Shulman notes, that he was probably familiar with newspaper accounts of the Haymarket riots. But his gaze was now more than ever (and when was it not?) fixed on eternity. If Melville conceived Vere as an unmitigated bureaucratic villain who had abandoned "human values, compassion, humanity" to become "an impersonal instrument of the state," then why would he have joined him to Billy in the phrase "two of great Nature's nobler order embrace?"

Nor can it be argued that Melville intended that phrase as ironic. Not only would the tone of the passage itself be enough to render such a suggestion absurd, but it would mean that Melville was mocking Billy as well as Vere. Moreover, Melville diminishes the possibility of an ironic interpretation with the narrator's authoritative description of the immediate aftermath of the meeting between Vere and Billy:

> The first to encounter Captain Vere in act of leaving the compartment was the senior lieutenant. The face he beheld, for the moment one expressive of the agony of the strong, was to that officer, though a man of fifty, a startling revelation. That the condemned one suffered less than he who mainly had effected the condemnation was apparently indicated by the former's exclamation in the scene soon perforce to be touched upon. (chapter 22, *Billy Budd*)

Shulman is strikingly correct when he writes, "As I see *Billy Budd*, Melville illuminates the self under the pressure of the emerging centralized military state and the threat of revolutionary crisis. . . . Melville anticipates the twentieth-century war world in which the state has increasingly centralized its control of the police and the military" (p. 68). Melville was, indeed, a prophetic genius in anticipating the rise and proliferation of military-police states in the twentieth century. But blinded by his ideology, Shulman fantasizes the military state aboard the *Bellipotent* as America, completely ignoring the twentieth-century reality of Hitlerist Germany, Stalinist Russia, and the many actual police states existing in the world right now that are founded on Marxist ideology.

This willful blindness is most apparent in the absence of any full-length discussion of *Walden*. Just as the absence of *Moby-Dick* is the black hole in Dekker's thesis, so the absence of any extended consideration of *Walden* is the black hole in Shulman's. Though *Walden* gets a paragraph in the chapter on "Bartleby," it does not play a major (in fact, not even a minor) role in a book entitled *Social Criticism & Nineteenth-Century American Fictions*. How is this possible? Is there any single work in any language or any culture that is a more trenchant piece of "social criticism," that articulates a more devastating denunciation of an acquisitive, materialistic "market society" than *Walden*? Just as Dekker's omission of *Moby-Dick* is no accident, neither is Shulman's failure to include *Walden*—and as an unavoidable concomitant, "Civil Disobedience"—for these two works, honestly presented, would have blown Shulman's Gramscian thesis out of the water.

The Marxist-Gramscian thesis depends on a conspiracy theory according to which the "dominant classes" exert their influence over the "subordinate classes" covertly by means of educational, religious, and other institutions, and "ruling groups pre-empt the high ground of universal morality and truth" (p. vii). Because the dominant classes dominate the oppressed classes in secrecy, by means of social institutions, the artist must respond to this dominance with symbolic representations. Let one example suffice. In a chapter entitled "The Artist in the Slammer: Hawthorne, Melville, Poe, and the Prison of Their Times," Shulman writes that "Hawthorne, Melville, and Poe were motivated to exploit the mode of symbolic indirection that was theirs for the taking. In their version of the style of the inmate, the techniques of symbolic indirection and symbolic intensification allowed them to communicate and conceal, to satisfy the demands of their vision and commitments and also to disguise them from unsympathetic readers." And he concludes, after an extended discussion of *The Scarlet Letter*, that "Based on his complex experience and finally on his experience as an artist in America, in *The Scarlet Letter*, Hawthorne, too, came to see America as a prison" (pp. 176–77, 195). It is true that Hawthorne, Melville, and Poe were writers who looked at the world through a glass darkly. It is also true that their preferred methods of representation, thanks to their saturation in biblical literature, were allegory and symbolism. It is also true that Melville, at least, loved to "hoodwink the reader," as he put it. But there is no reason to infer from this that it was because of the "hegemonic process" that all American writers were forced to utter hidden truths about the dominant classes in obscure symbols and allegories. In fact, the symbolic representations often had little to do with the "hegemonic process."

But more important, when American writers wanted to attack the dominant classes they did not have to do so in allegories. And that is why Shulman would prefer not to talk about Thoreau. Thoreau is such an outspoken critic of the society that any lengthy consideration of his writings would wipe out the "ruling-class-conspiracy-hence-need-to-write-in-symbols" theory. How is it possible to sustain the argument for covert domination by means of sacrosanct institutions, when Thoreau openly denounces those institutions and declares in no uncertain terms that they are not sacrosanct at all? And how can it be argued that "ruling groups [secretly] pre-empt the high ground of universal morality and truth" when Thoreau ringingly dissociates himself from any "ruling groups," and proclaims precisely that the ruling class having abandoned the high ground, each individual must now seek "morality and truth" for him and herself? Furthermore, why should Shulman write about the artist imagining himself (and the rest of the society) in a *metaphorical* "slammer," when Thoreau wrote from a *real* slammer, that "Under a government that imprisons any unjustly, the true place for a just man is also a prison?" Is it really necessary for an American writing about oppression in American culture to seek guidance from Marx and Gramsci, when we can find such strong and open advocacy of resistance, antiauthoritarianism, and even anarchism in our own tradition?

I ask myself why I am not more pleased with these books. If the authors want to write about literature as a way of asserting their disdain for oppression, racism, authoritarianism, and exploitation and, at the same time, affirm their belief in the values of liberty, fraternity, equality, community, peace, love, justice for all, and renunciation of violence, I should commend them wholeheartedly, for these are values I believe in too. Perhaps, then, we differ only on the means by which these values can be achieved. Yet that is not the whole story either. The politicizing of literature has turned the act of reading literary criticism into a sortie through a mine field. These books do not simply want to educate me, they want to make a claim on my deepest being. Both books, the humanist and the Marxist, seem to want to diminish, if not negate, my selfhood.

In "Loose-Fish, Fast-Fish" (chapter 89) in *Moby-Dick*, Melville ridiculed Anglo-American property law as an exercise of raw power. A Fast-Fish on the high seas, it turns out, belongs to anyone who can keep it. But the same thing is true of a Loose-Fish. It, too, is the property of anyone who can hold onto it. Melville then expands the doctrine of "Loose-Fish, Fast-Fish" to encompass not only property rights, but political freedom and ultimately freedom of the will. He ends the chapter on one of those magnificent metaphysical flights so typical of his *Moby-Dick* style:

What are the Rights of Man and the Liberties of the World but Loose-Fish? What all men's minds and opinions but Loose-Fish? What is the principle of religious belief in them but a Loose-Fish? What to the ostentatious smuggling verbalists are the thoughts of thinkers but Loose-Fish? What is the great globe itself but a Loose-Fish? And what are you, reader, but a Loose-Fish and a Fast-Fish, too?

Melville recognized that the powerful are wont to consider the property of others a Loose-Fish (that is something to be taken by whoever has the power to take it). But he also realized that while materialists take our property as a Loose Fish, it is our souls that are Loose Fish to "the ostentatious smuggling verbalists." To the writers of politicized literary criticism, what are we all, readers, but Loose Fish?

CHAPTER TEN

Metaphors and Structures

In *Reflections on Language*, Noam Chomsky, the patriarch of transformational grammar, expresses his dismay at the fact that readers have interpreted the word *deep*, in the phrase "deep structures," to mean "deep" in its fullest (including metaphorical) sense. "The term 'deep structure' has, unfortunately, proved to be very misleading," Chomsky observes. "It has led a number of people to suppose that it is the deep structures and their properties that are truly 'deep' in the nontechnical sense of the word. . . . This was never intended." If it is not "the deep structures and their properties that are truly 'deep,'" then what is? And is it really the readers who are at fault for not having perceived Chomsky's intention, for not knowing that when he said "deep structure," he did not really mean "*deep* structure?" Nevertheless, Chomsky never does tell the reader what "deep" means in the technical sense of the word. What Chomsky would like to do, apparently, is to cut the word "deep" off from any possible metaphorical meanings, an impossible task. How is it, we may ask, that from first to last, the metaphorical implications of his own phrase have eluded the famous grammarian?

The answer lies, at least in part, in Chomsky's splitting off form from meaning in grammatical structures. In *Syntactic Structures* (1957), he had announced that "the notion 'grammatical' cannot be identified with 'meaningful' or 'significant' in any semantic sense," and that "any search for a semantically based definition of 'grammaticalness' will be futile." Despite later gestures toward semantics, and despite the heroic efforts of Fodor and Katz, transformational grammar remains saddled with its sterile origins, and transformational grammarians continue to seek syntactic explanations for ambiguous utterances such as "The lamb was too hot to eat."

So electrifying was the initial impact of transformational grammar that for a time it was thought Chomskyan linguistics could be utilized effectively in analyzing literary texts. But because of its severance of form from content and a consequent inability to deal with the qualitative aspects of metaphorical language, transformational grammar has turned out to be practically useless in getting at the core of a literary work. Richard Ohmann, one of the early believers in Chomsky, attempted to provide a paradigm Chomskyan analysis, later widely anthologized, of a clause in a sentence from James Joyce's short story, "Araby." Ohmann's analysis of this clause has been criticized elsewhere; I return to his reading here not to flog a dead horse, but to focus on the limitations of transformational grammar as a literary-critical tool, and to demonstrate that the large claims Ohmann makes for the application of transformational grammar to literary criticism are not likely to be fulfilled.[1]

The clause, which is taken from the concluding paragraph of Joyce's story, reads as follows: "Gazing up into the darkness I saw myself as a creature driven and derided by vanity. . . ."[2] Ohmann first describes the surface structure of this clause, and then proceeds to analyze its deep structure. Since Ohmann's analysis of this beautiful and moving sentence is so tightly knit and so closely argued I must, I fear, quote at length in order to do his analysis justice:

In the deep structure . . . the matrix sentence . . . has embedded in it one sentence with an intransitive verb and an adverb of location—"I gazed up into the darkness"—and two additional sentences with transitive verbs and direct objects—"Vanity drove the creature," and "Vanity derided the creature." Since darkness and vanity are derived nouns, the embedded sentences must in turn contain embeddings, of say "(Something) is dark" and "(Someone) is vain." Thus the word "vanity," object of a preposition in the surface structure, is subject of two verbs in the deep, and its root is a predicate adjective. The word "creature," object of a preposition in the surface structure also has a triple function in the deep structure: verbal complement, direct object of "drive," and direct object of "deride." Several transformations (including the passive) deform the six basic sentences, and several other relate them to each other. The complexity goes much farther, but this is enough to suggest that a number of grammatical processes are required to generate the initial sentence and that its structure is moderately involved. Moreover, a reader will not understand the sentence unless he grasps the relation marked in the deep structure. As it draws on a variety of syntactic resources, the sentence also activates a variety of semantic processes and modes of comprehension, yet in brief compass and in a surface *form* that radically permutes *content*.

I choose these terms wilfully: that there are interesting grounds here for a form-content division seems to me quite certain. Joyce might have written, "I gazed up into the darkness. I saw myself as a creature. The creature was driven by vanity. The creature was derided by vanity". Or, "Vanity drove and derided the creature I saw myself as, gazer up, gazer into the darkness". Content remains roughly the same, for the basic sentences are unchanged. But the style is different. And each revision structures and screens the content differently. The original sentence acquires part of its meaning and part of its unique character by resonating against these unwritten alternatives. It is at the level of sentences, I would argue, that the distinction between form and content comes clear, and that the intuition of style has its formal equivalent.[3]

Let me, now, summarize my understanding of Ohmann's procedure. Using the methods of transformational linguistics, he maps out the surface structure and then the deep structure of Joyce's sentence. He next expresses the deep structure by converting Joyce's rather elegant syntax into a number of more elemental grammatical patterns. These patterns, in turn, yield a nucleus of meaning that cannot be reduced any further. And from this nucleus it then becomes possible to generate any number of sentences without significantly changing the meaning of Joyce's original sentence. Ohmann infers from this procedure that he has demonstrated the way in which content can be separated from form ("the distinction between form and content comes clear").

It strikes me, however, that Ohmann's deep-structural description and the inference drawn from it raise a number of questions. First, is the description accurate? Second, is it adequate? Third, is the inference drawn from the description justified—that is, has Ohmann's analysis of the sentence demonstrated for all time that at the level of sentences, as he says, "the distinction between form and content comes clear"?

As to the accuracy of the description, since it involves nothing more than Ohmann's ability to use a specialized set of symbols without violating the rules governing their use, let me say immediately that accuracy in that sense does not seem very meaningful to me. What Ohmann has given us may very well be an accurate description of the deep structure of Joyce's sentence from the point of view of transformational linguistics. If it is, however, then it appears that deep structure is not likely to provide very many new insights into the way in which artists create meaning through style. Indeed, I would have to conclude that the meanings discovered in the deep structure may lead us to meanings that are startlingly distant from literary meanings.

Putting aside the question of "accuracy," then, I shall focus on adequacy; I mean by that term the extent to which the linguistic description gives us all the meanings that inhere in the sentence and no meanings that are not in the sentence. Let me start by recapitulating the six basic sentences comprising the nucleus of meaning that according to Ohmann are embedded in Joyce's one sentence:

1. I gazed up into the darkness
2. Vanity drove the creature
3. Vanity derided the creature
4. Something is dark
5. Someone is vain
6. I saw myself as a creature.

That the sentences are not beautiful goes without saying. But that is not the worst. The fact is that every one of these so-called basic sentences is in some way misleading or erroneous as a description of what Joyce says in the story.

"I gazed up into the darkness" for "gazing up into the darkness" is misleading because it distorts one of the basic elements in the sentence, its communication of an ongoing process. The transformations "Vanity drove the creature" and "Vanity derided the creature" are simply misrepresentations of the information that is communicated by Joyce's sentence. The narrator of Joyce's story does not state that a "creature" *is* driven and derided by vanity but that in one passing moment he *sees* himself *as* a "creature driven and derided by vanity". The difference, I submit, is significant. In Ohmann's deep-structural transformation the focus is on an outer phenomenon, while the sentence written by Joyce does not focus on the outer phenomenon; rather, it focuses on the narrator's mental state. To put the matter slightly differently, the phenomenon under consideration in Joyce's sentence is the mental state of the narrator, whereas the phenomenon under consideration in the basic sentence is the outer condition of the narrator.

The matter of *darkness* and *vanity* as derived nouns that imply the embedded sentences "(Something) is dark" and "(Someone) is vain" is one, it seems to me, that goes beyond linguistics and borders on metaphysics. Suppose, for instance, it is agreed that nouns of this kind always contain embedded sentences, how does such knowledge benefit us? For example, would it make sense to say that the sentence "Vanity of vanities, all is vanity" contains the sentence "(Someone) is vain" repeated three times, once with a plural subject and predicate? Or, on the question of darkness, how meaningful is it to say that the derived noun contains the sentence "(Something) is dark"? In the case at hand, what is the "something" that we shall say is dark? Is it the sky? Is it the air? Is it the atmosphere? Do we indeed always mean to say "(Something) is dark" when we utter the word darkness? If so, then why not change the basic sentence to "I gazed up into the dark sky?" Finally, we have the basic sentence "I saw myself as a creature." Insofar as this basic sentence repeats Joyce's actual language and syntax it is difficult to find fault with it. What makes it misleading, however, is the wrenching of it out of its original setting. In this setting, as we shall see presently, it becomes metaphorical, deriving shades of meaning from its modifiers.

It may be argued, at this point, that though none of the six basic sentences is adequate in itself, nevertheless, when they are all put together they still add up to the proper sum. I think this is not the case, but in order to demonstrate that, it will be necessary for me to express a number of meanings that do not show up in Ohmann's representation of the deep structure.

To begin with, in the clause "Gazing up into the darkness I saw

myself as a creature driven and derided by vanity" Joyce conveys one
of those epiphanic moments that are so familiar in, and so crucial to,
his fiction. And the essence of this particular epiphany, which can be
immediately apprehended in the surface structure of the sentence, is
its momentary nature. The narrator has a revelation of something that
takes place within time, and the surface structure, by balancing the
present participle *gazing* against the abstract noun *vanity*, conveys
the sense of a narrator who experiences simultaneously the vast tracts
of eternity and the urgency of time's chariot drawing near. Hence, to
change the present participle which communicates the idea of movement and process to the reader is indeed to effect a major change in
what Joyce is telling us: not that this sensitive young boy gazed up
into the darkness but that in the act of gazing up into the darkness
something important happened to him. Joyce, of course, might, as
Ohmann asserts, have written "I gazed up into the darkness," but the
fact that he did not should say something—to linguists as well as to
critics.

The separation of the clause "I saw myself as a creature" from the
modifying phrases that precede and follow it causes another change in
meaning. Presented as separate sentences, "I gazed up into the darkness" and "I saw myself as a creature" are unrelated or are distantly
related at best. But when the two clauses are joined by subordinating
the first, a number of implications make themselves felt. In Joyce's
syntax, the darkness becomes a kind of mirror. The image created by
the linked clauses is that of someone standing somewhere midway
between the heavenly and the earthly, between the world of the senses
and the world of the spirit. As he looks up, the narrator encounters darkness, the absence of light (and not something dark), without
which the perception of earthly objects is impossible. Encountering
the unyielding outer darkness ("Nothingness" would not be an exaggeration), his gaze is forced inward, and what he then sees in the
darkness is a reflection of his own soul, or perhaps a projection of
his own soul imposed on the universe. This movement from outer to
inner, incidentally, is characteristic of the Romantic meditative lyric.

The overall impact of the sentence, which is, after all, also a part
of its meaning, derives from the manner in which the syntax of the

sentence reflects the image of a speaker poised somewhere between heaven and earth, between spirit and flesh. The syntax of Joyce's sentence, which is characterized by a stunning symmetry and counterpoint, is a perfect embodiment of the balance between the temporal and the eternal. A subordinate clause begins the sentence and a subordinate clause ends the sentence. Linking these subordinate clauses together is an independent clause modifying both. Each subordinate clause contains five words. The operative word in the initial clause is the first word in the clause (*gazing*), and the operative word in the third clause is the last (*vanity*). These happen to be, also, the first and last words of the whole clause. The whole clause begins on a note of perception (gazing) and ends on a note of real or imagined self-knowledge (vanity). Moreover, while the beginning of the sentence describes a voluntary movement upward ("gazing up"), the concluding clause describes an involuntary attraction downward ("driven and derided by vanity"). The contrapuntal perfection of the sentence is augmented by Joyce's starting it with a word denoting a physical activity (*gazing*) and ending it with a word denoting a moral condition (*vanity*), and of course it is the balancing of a word describing a physical movement with one denoting a moral condition that makes the sentence metaphorical and intones the symbolic resonances. Finally, there is the suggested irony that the physical act of gazing upward may in itself be one more manifestation of the moral condition of vanity, real or imagined, that is pulling the speaker downward.

The fulcrum on which these two weighted ends are balanced is the independent middle clause. Containing six words (as to five for each of the two subordinate clauses), the independent clause bristles with nominals (I, myself, creature). This heavy concentration of verbal manifestations of the self in a centrally located, grammatically self-sustaining unit indicates both the centrality of the narrator's inner being and the shift from ignorance (*darkness* again) to recognition (*vanity*). It also helps to locate the speaker squarely between the darkness above the emptiness below.

If we return, now, to Ohmann's own summation of six basic sentences into one basic sentence that contains the nucleus of the content of Joyce's sentence, out of which any number of sentences equivalent in meaning may be generated, then the full extent of the inadequacy of the transformational-generative method becomes readily apparent. Thus reads the Ohmann sentence: "Vanity drove and derided the creature I saw myself as, gazer up, gazer into the darkness". Aside from its awkwardness, Ohmann's sentence succeeds in adding one more dislocation of meaning to those already noted. The syntax of Ohmann's sentence suggests not that the speaker of the sentence, gazing up into the darkness, sees himself as a creature driven and derided by vanity, but that a creature driven and derided by vanity sees himself as a gazer up, a gazer into darkness.

Equally important is the loss of symmetry and counterpoint, which in themselves convey so much of Joyce's meaning. The tension between the upward movement and the downward pull is gone. The balance between a physical action at one end of the sentence and a moral condition at the other is gone. The movement from perception to real or imagined self-knowledge is gone. The powerful nuclear independent clause is gone. The image of a speaker torn between two worlds is gone. The momentary but momentous epiphany has declined into a flat description of a phenomenon that is in no way distinguished or distinguishable from any number of other phenomena. A metaphorical utterance has been converted into a prose statement.

Inevitably, the question arises whether Ohmann's failure to locate the pulse of the Joycean epiphany is merely an instance of one isolated specific failure in the application of a method, or whether it reflects a failure in the method itself. I shall propose that the latter is the case. To generalize on the basis of one instance is no doubt unwise, but what leads me to believe that the failure may be in the method itself is the disturbing disparity between what Ohmann's analysis actually does and what he thinks it does. Ohmann feels that in identifying the deep structure of Joyce's clause, he has established a clear distinction between the form of the clause (the surface structure) and the meaning of the clause, which is apparently to be found in the deep structure. Gordon Messing pointed out that "The Joycean test case is scarcely convincing. It is most certainly NOT primarily a clear-cut demonstration of any implied contrast between surface and deep structure."[4] But I should say it is not only a matter of "surface and deep structure," since semantics are implicated throughout Ohmann's analysis.

Ohmann seems to imply an equation between "deep structure" and "deep meaning." He says that as the clause "draws on a variety of syntactic resources, the sentence also activates a variety of semantic processes and modes of comprehension. . . ." But the "meanings" that emerge from his deep-structural analysis are no "deeper" than "meanings" that can be gleaned from a casual reading of the sentence. For example, to know that the sentence embedded in "Gazing up into the darkness . . ." is "I gazed up into the darkness" would not be very significant knowledge even if it were accurate, which, unfortunately, it is not. All that Ohmann has done in extracting the "embedded sentence" is to convert a dependent participle into a finite verb in the past tense. In doing so, he has changed the meaning of the phrase "gazing up into the darkness" but he has not revealed anything about its "deep structure." The change in meaning is perhaps not too noticeable in English, a relatively uninflected language, but in a highly inflected language the change would be striking and immediately apparent. The same questionable procedure that I have described here is followed by Ohmann in establishing all the "embedded sentences" that he disinters.

The conclusion that may be drawn from Ohmann's procedure, I believe, is that the usefulness of transformational grammar in analyzing poetic utterances is circumscribed by the limitations of its positivist orientation. Transformational grammar asks limited questions in the hope of discovering limited answers. Insofar as the transformational grammarian has any dealings with meaning at all, it is propositional meaning that concerns him—meaning that can be "verified" by recourse to the phenomenal world.[5]

But Joyce's sentence strives to break out of the finite and the limited. Messing finds, I believe rightly, that the "most obvious contrast" in Joyce's sentence lies not in the difference between surface structure and deep structure but "in the striking act of *gazing up into the darkness,* the result of which is usually to see nothing, while nonetheless, contrary to the logic of such a process, I saw; still another surprise awaits us when we learn that the object seen, despite the darkness, is the viewer himself, as if the darkness had become a mirror.[6] What the deep structure of the sentence has failed to reveal to Ohmann is that in the surface structure the word *saw* is used metaphorically, and that it is by using the word metaphorically that Joyce creates his "epiphany." As is usually the case with successful metaphorical expressions, the word *saw* carries its literal meaning, which can perhaps be approximated in the words "I considered myself." The metaphorical structure in which *darkness* becomes a mirror and *seeing* becomes an act of spiritual perception constitutes for Joyce a bridge between the world of quotidian reality on the one hand and a world beyond everyday reality on the other.

Misunderstanding the semantic properties of Joyce's sentence, as well as the surface structure, Ohmann fails to catch the significance of the verbal symmetry set up by Joyce, and also the significance of the way in which the symmetry creates an antiphonal harmony between the words *saw* and *vanity*. The former has long been associated in Western consciousness not only with the biological function of perceiving physical objects but with the spiritual act of intuiting transphysical phenomena: hence the currency in "religious" language of such terms as *seer, vision, visionary*. The word *vanity* also has a long tradition of religious usage, indicating "the fruitlessness, emptiness, and transitoriness of all that happens upon the earth." It is the brilliance of Joyce's syntax that sets all the multiple connotations of both words reverberating against each other.

Is it possible to conclude, as Ohmann does, that we have here "interesting grounds . . . for a form-content division"? Or can one agree with Ohmann's assessment of his rewriting of Joyce's sentence that "content remains roughly the same," while it is only the style of Ohmann's sentence that is different? I think not. The fact is that no other arrangement of Joyce's words (or substitutes for them) could possibly communicate the same content, for Joyce's sentence marks one of those luminous moments in which the writer has risen to sublime heights of inspiration and craft. This is not to say that form and content can never be separated. It seems likely that in our everyday utterances we communicate meanings in one form that could as easily have been communicated in another. But the language of poetry is different. It communicates cognitive and emotive meanings in a special way. If it is great poetry, it communicates in unique forms, forms that cannot be reduced to anything more basic than themselves.

Vexing as metaphor has been to grammarians, it has been no less so to philosophers. The philosophical literature on the subject yields six basic definitions of metaphor, which divide into two sets: the first set is comparison, substitution, interaction; the second is deviance, lexical selectivity, split reference. All attempts to explain the phenomenon of metaphor are variants of these basic definitions.

The operative definition of metaphor as comparison is Aristotelian: "A perception of the similarity in dissimilars." Metaphors of comparison are sometimes considered variants of simile and analogy (compressed, or elliptical, simile). Substitution, like comparison, depends on the presence of two terms; it is best described as the saying of one thing in terms of another. The relationship between metaphor-as-comparison and metaphor-as-substitution is succinctly stated by Max Black in *Models and Metaphors*:

The chief difference between a substitution view . . . and the special form of it that I have called a comparison view may be illustrated by the stock example of "Richard is a lion." On the first view, the sentence means approximately the same as "Richard is brave"; on the second, approximately the same as "Richard is like a lion (in being brave)," the added words in brackets being understood but not explicitly stated. In the second translation, as in the first, the metaphorical statement is taken to be standing in place of some literal equivalent.[7]

Black's summary is not without its problems: the most troublesome is the question, What is a "literal equivalent"? Clearly Black does not commit himself to the view that "Richard is brave" is indeed a literal equivalent of "Richard is a lion." But what does Black mean to say by the assertion that "Richard is a lion" [the metaphorical statement] is "taken to be standing in place of some literal equivalent," such as "Richard is brave?" Does Black mean to say that "Richard is brave" is comprehensible, while "Richard is a lion" is not? Or is it that the former is correct while the latter is not? Or does the former satisfy certain "truth conditions" that the latter does not, etc.? As Black knows, he uses metaphor in speaking about metaphor, for what is "standing in place of," if not a metaphor itself, and what does the phrase tell us about the way metaphor functions? Does a sentence actually "stand"? Does it actually occupy the space that was formerly occupied by a "literal equivalent," or that should have been occupied by a "literal equivalent?" To avoid the naive equivalence, " 'Richard is a lion' means 'Richard is brave,' " Black makes use of the saving metaphor, "stands in place of."

Black's purpose in looking into the workings of metaphor from a language-analysis philosopher's point of view was to demonstrate that metaphorical language was not merely decorative. He wanted to show that using metaphorical language was a way of thinking. The essence of metaphor, Black believed, was to be found in I. A. Richards's observation that metaphorical use of language forced the reader to "connect two ideas." "In this 'connection,' " Black writes, "resides the secret and the mystery of metaphor. To speak of the 'interaction' of two thoughts 'active' together . . . is to use a metaphor emphasizing the dynamic aspects of a good reader's response to a nontrivial metaphor."[8] Yet, while Black bases his "interaction" theory of metaphor in the connection of ideas, the theory still depends on a belief in the referentiality of language. As long as it is assumed that the words "refer to" objects in the physical world, and that it is the physical entities that are being compared, or that physical entities are being substituted for abstract concepts, the comparison/substitution and interaction theories make sense. Under the pressure of deconstructionist deployments of Saussurean linguistics as a denial of referentiality, these theories begin to crumble. If language is thought of as no more than a system of signs, and words do not necessarily "refer to things," then it becomes almost impossible to determine what is being compared ("signs," "sounds," "concepts," "images"), or whether, indeed, anything is being compared.

Black's "interaction theory," which was intended to replace comparison and substitution theories, is actually an elaborate variant of them; it, too, depends on the presence of two elements. In the 1962 essay Black had called these two elements "a 'principal' subject and a 'subsidiary' one." In reconsidering, some seventeen years later, he preferred the terms primary and secondary.[9] Black's theory also depends on the assumption that words "refer to things," but for Black, "these subjects are often best regarded as 'systems of things' rather than 'things.'" Avoiding the terminology of comparison and substitution in the early essay, Black nevertheless maintains that "systems of things" are juxtaposed. Instead of saying that in the metaphor *A* is compared to *B*, he says that "the metaphor works by applying to the principal subject a system of 'associated implications' characteristic of the subsidiary subject."[10] Black's terms (whether principal and subsidiary, or primary and secondary) are already inherently comparative. This comparative element in the interaction theory is more clearly stated in the later essay, when Black explains that "the duality of reference is *marked by the contrast* [italics mine] between the metaphorical statement's focus (the word or words used nonliterally) [that is, the subsidiary subject] and the surrounding literal frame [the principal subject]."[11] Black's contribution is principally to caution us that in the terms of the comparison, it is not the totalities of the "things" that are being compared, but only certain aspects of the things ("associated commonplaces").

Theories of "deviance," "lexical selectivity" (which is closely akin to Black's "associated commonplaces"), and "split reference" tend to be more insistent in raising such questions as the relationship between metaphor and "truth conditions," metaphor and "reality," and metaphor and "world." "Deviance" theories suffer from a fusion of "systemics" (language as a "system" of related signs) and "pragmatics" (language as a "pointer" to a "world-out-there"). Metaphors are described as "linguistically deviant expressions," in contrast to "well-formed sentences," the implication being that these are well-defined categories. But "deviance" theorists can provide no clear criterion of what constitutes a "well-formed sentence." There is no way of determining whether notions of "deviance" and "well-formed" are based on semantics or syntax. A deviance theorist's example of a deviant sentence is "the stone died." Syntactically the sentence seems to be well-formed, with a subject and a predicate. We do not, however, normally think of inanimate objects as being subject to dying. Does that constitute a syntactic or a strictly semantic problem, or neither of the above? Is the sentence deviant or merely unusual, or, again, neither of the above? The way in which proponents of deviance get around such questions is to posit the notion of "construal," which introduces a hearer or speaker into the linguistic equation. Presumably metaphors as deviant expressions require construal, and the theorists then claim, as a consequence, that this need for construal distinguishes metaphorical from literal utterances. But the meaning of construal is vague, and it can be (and has been) argued that all linguistic exchanges, not just metaphors, involve "construal." The need for construal as a criterion removes the facade of "objectivity," for what one reader may find in need of construal another may find perfectly obvious and instantly comprehensible.

"Lexical selectivity" theories are related to notions of interaction and deviance. In order to construe a deviant utterance, the hearer or reader selects certain lexical features of the secondary subject and applies them to the primary subject. According to Black's much-traveled example, the sentence, "Man is a wolf" "evoke[s] the wolf-system of related commonplaces,"[12] whereby the hearer understands that the sentence is referring to man as "something fierce, carnivorous, treacherous, and so on." The underlying assumption here is that the hearer "knows" something (has in his mind a set of related commonplaces) about *man* and *wolf*, and chooses accordingly those features of wolf that can be applied to man. Conversely the hearer presumably screens out such features as hairy, four-legged, incapable of uttering sentences, inclined to howl, etc. But when the sentence is reversed, i.e., "Wolf is a man," the lexical selectivity and screening break down. This formulation displays a distressing circularity. Black starts with the assumption that a seemingly nonsensical utterance may be meaningful, and then describes the process by which the conversion from nonsense to meaning is effected.

As is perhaps to be expected in a climate in which language is assumed to occupy a central position in the acquisition and promulgation of knowledge, metaphor has become a subject of study for social scientists and theorists of science as well as for literary critics, linguists, and philosophers. In the collection entitled *Metaphor and Thought*, several authors discuss metaphor from the perspective of linguistics, psychology, sociology, and language-analysis philosophy. The collection includes sections headed, "Metaphor and . . . Linguistic Theory, Pragmatics, Psychology, Society, Science, Education." Of special interest is the keynote essay of the section called "Metaphor and Pragmatics." Written by the speech-act philosopher John Searle, the essay combines the notions of "deviance," "lexical selectivity," and "substitution" (saying one thing but meaning another— or, one utterance "standing in place of" another). Searle hypothesizes a distinction between speaker's utterance meaning (what the speaker actually means) and word or sentence meaning (what the speaker actually utters). When the two coincide, they constitute a literal statement; when they do not coincide, then the speaker's utterance meaning is metaphorical. In this formulation, "speaker's utterance meaning" seems to be another way of saying "intention."

According to Searle, "Many writers . . . think there are two kinds of sentence meaning, literal and metaphorical. However, sentences and words have only the meanings that they have." [13] The assertion seems to be tautological, and it does not explain why, if sentences and words have only the meanings they have, skilled readers often disagree about the meanings even of "literal" words and sentences. Moreover, the distinction between an "utterance meaning" and a "sentence meaning" seems unwarranted, since the examples Searle uses appear to us only in the form of sentences. In one of his examples, Searle writes that a person who "hears the utterance, 'Sam is a pig' . . . knows that cannot be literally true, that the utterance, if he tries to take it literally, is radically defective." [14] But it seems the utterance may indeed be "literally true," since people often give animals proper names. Therefore, the sentence, "Sam is a pig" may be "literally true." But even if there were not a pig named Sam, it is not clear why the utterance would be "radically defective." On the basis of this assumption of what happens when a hypothetical listener hears this sentence, Searle arrives at a strategy for identifying metaphor: "Where the utterance is defective if taken literally, look for an utterance meaning that differs from sentence meaning." [15] In Searle's view, the speaker's "utterance meaning" is something like "Sam is a glutton," or "Sam is sloppy," or "Sam eats too much," which is to say he takes the "substitution" view of metaphor. By way of illustrating this method of recognizing metaphor, Searle cites his experience of Keats's "Ode on a Grecian Urn": "If I hear a figure on a Grecian Urn being addressed as a 'still unravished bride of quietness,' I know I had better look for alternative meanings." [16] But in Keats's poem, the speaker seems to be addressing not a figure on the urn but the urn itself. Moreover, would the utterance cease being metaphorical if it were addressed to a living person? And when Searle looks for "alternative meanings," will it not be the alternative meanings of certain words that he will be seeking, rather than a vague entity called a "speaker's utterance meaning?"

Let one more instance of the inadequacy of speech-act philosophy in encompassing metaphor suffice. Searle writes, "Thus, if the hearer is told, 'Sam's car is a pig,' he will interpret that metaphor differently from the utterance, 'Sam is a pig.' The former, he might take to mean that Sam's car consumes gas the way pigs consume food, or that Sam's car is shaped like a pig." [17] Are we to assume here that Searle's utterance meaning is different from the sentence meaning? For surely it cannot be literally true that he would interpret the sentence "Sam's car is a pig" to mean that "Sam's car consumes gas the way pigs consume food," for that would mean that he believes that cars have snouts and mouths and that they crowd into a trough with each other to gobble up comestibles. Clearly, the essence of metaphor is not easily mastered, even by a distinguished thinker.

If philosophical analyses have not been able to tame metaphor, sociological and psychological analyses have not done much better. Sociologists point out, rightly, that the metaphors we use govern our perception of the (social) world, and therefore affect the kinds of problems we perceive and the ways in which we try to solve them. [18] But of course, exactly the same thing may be said of the nonmetaphors we use. Social psychologists (and apparently educationists as well) become involved in what is a basic methodological flaw—the illusion that subjective responses may be transformed into "objective knowledge" by being quantified. Bruce Fraser, for example, exposes groups of students to such statements as "He is a termite," "She is a termite," and finds (proves) by his experiments that interpretations of zero-context metaphors are highly inconsistent. That is, students trying to interpret the kind of statement cited above display a wide range of interpretations, such as "He is a pest, is destructive, eats a lot," etc., and "She is nosey, is always eating," etc.[19] This is another case of documenting the obvious: the skimpier the context, the greater the number of possible interpretations.

Essays on science and metaphor all tend to work from ideas broached by Max Black and Thomas S. Kuhn. All revolve around the questions of metaphorical language as a mode of thinking and an instrument of scientific discovery. Perhaps the most striking element in sociological and analytic discussions of metaphor is that there seems to be more agreement on how to define metaphor than on how to define literal meaning. This phenomenon is underscored in a provocative essay by Michael Reddy, who attacks the problem of the unavoidability of using metaphor to talk about metaphor. (Consider Max Black's need to substitute the phrase, "stand in place of" for the word, "mean.") Some of the theorists are more cognizant of this problem than others, but Reddy deals with it directly: How is the measuring rod to measure itself?[20]

This is not to say that Reddy has all the answers, or even that the answers he gives are always satisfying. But he does not lose sight of the central question. He is on the right track in identifying what he calls the "conduit metaphor of communication." The term *conduit* presents difficulties of its own, but setting those aside for the moment, I will use Reddy's deployment of that term as a way of identifying some of the problems of "literal meaning." Reddy's initial description of the conduit metaphor may serve as a starting point.

What do speakers of English say when communication fails or goes astray? Let us consider (1) through (3), some very typical examples,

(1) Try to get your *thoughts across* better
(2) None of Mary's *feelings came through to me* with any clarity
(3) You still haven't *given me* any *idea* of what you mean,

and . . . take them as problem-setting stories, as descriptions of "what is wrong and what needs fixing." Are there metaphors in the examples? Do these metaphors set the directions for possible problem-solving techniques?

Although (1) through (3) contain no fresh metaphors, there is in each case a dead metaphor. After all, we do not literally "get thoughts across" when we talk, do we? This sounds like mental telepathy or clairvoyance, and suggests that communication transfers thought processes somehow bodily.[21]

A reader must be struck immediately by the abundance of metaphor in Reddy's attempt to distinguish metaphorical from literal meaning. For example, the assertion that "communication . . . goes astray" is a metaphor, is it not? Dead metaphor, a phrase much favored by contemporary linguists, is itself a metaphor, and so, one might add, is the phrase fresh metaphor. Reddy goes on to speculate: "We do not literally 'get thoughts across' when we talk, do we?" That depends on what he means by literally. Getting thoughts across (presumably by making utterances) sounds to Reddy like mental telepathy. Is "mental telepathy" a metaphor, too, and if so, is it one in the same way as "getting thoughts across"? Reddy says, later in the essay, that "if there are dead metaphors in (1) through (3), then they all seem to involve the figurative assertion that language transfers human thoughts and feelings"; and again that the English language encourages speakers to assume "that human communication achieves the physical transfer of thoughts and feelings."

If there were physical objects connected to the words *transfer* and *get across*, then Reddy would have no problem. If, instead of thoughts and feelings, we spoke of transferring bricks and sacks of potatoes, and if, instead of talking about language, we talked about wagons, then there would also be no question of metaphor. If we said only that "a wagon transfers bricks and potatoes," that presumably would be a "literal" statement.

By a dead metaphor, then, Reddy (and he is not alone in this usage) means a metaphorical expression long in use that is not perceived as a metaphor. But what does he mean by literal? He finds sentences (1) through (3) metaphorical, and he apparently objects to the notion "transfer of thoughts and feelings" because the sentences and the notion both mix nonphysical entities such as thoughts and feelings with the verb transfer. It would seem, then, that when transfer is used with words "pointing to" nonphysical entities, the result must always be metaphor. A further cluster of questions then arises. Are literal statements involving the nouns *thought* and *feeling* limited to a highly restricted set of specialized verbs? And, if so, what are the verbs that can provide "literal predication" for these nouns? Are all statements involving the nouns *thought* and *feeling* metaphorical? Is any statement that mixes a "physical verb" with a "nonphysical noun" automatically metaphorical? If literal language is language that makes statements about (points to) the physical world, and if language itself is a nonphysical entity, does that not mean that all language about language is metaphorical? Is a dead metaphor actually no longer a metaphor? For example, if what we mean by a dead person is the nonexistence of that person, then is a dead metaphor one that has ceased to exist as that metaphor? And does that then mean that we can say "transfer thoughts" without being metaphorical? Must the word transfer be linked only to physical objects to remain "literal?"

Reddy argues, perhaps rightly, that the way we conceptualize language is a consequence of the conduit metaphor. But it can be argued with equal force that the popularity of the conduit metaphor results from the way we conceptualize language. Reddy claims to be objecting to the metaphor itself rather than to the ideas generated by the metaphor:

Actually, no one receives anyone else's thoughts directly in their minds when they are using language. Mary's feelings, in example (2), can be perceived directly only by Mary; they do not really "come through to us" when she talks. Nor can anyone literally "give you an idea"—since these are locked within the skull and life process of each of us. Surely, then, none of these three expressions is to be taken completely at face value. Language seems rather to help one person to construct out of his own stock of mental stuff something like a replica, or copy, of someone else's thoughts—a replica which can be more or less accurate, depending on many factors. If we could indeed send thoughts to one another, we would have little need for a communications system.[22]

Is it the metaphor that bothers Reddy, or is it the ideas, or is it that Reddy does not accept his own hypothetical sentences (1) to (3) as an accurate reflection of "the way things are"? Again his own formulations of the way language works are abundantly metaphorical. He complains that no one can literally give you an idea. But does he believe, then, that ideas are literally "locked" in the skull? If we cannot take expressions (1) to (3) at face value, then neither can we take Reddy's description at face value. But what is "face value" if not another metaphor? Are descriptions, after all, money or bonds? Is "stock of mental stuff" not a metaphor (actually the conduit metaphor, since it implies that the mind is a warehouse filled with goods)? Is "a replica" of someone else's thoughts less metaphorical than someone's "receiving thoughts directly"? Or is the former a more accurate metaphor than the latter? I am not objecting to Reddy's use of these metaphors, or even to the particular metaphors he is using. Instead I am intrigued that Reddy, like the conduit-metaphor user, seems to think that he has freed himself from the shackles of metaphor. Having pointed out that hearers do not "literally" receive ideas, he then goes on to say that expressions do or do not have a "face value," and that hearers create "a replica . . . of someone else's thoughts." In other words, though Reddy rightly takes note of the pervasiveness of the conduit metaphor, he too seems to confuse literal and metaphorical statements.

One of the problems we have in defining such terms as *literal utterance, literal predication, literal meaning, literal language,* etc., is that they are all either metaphorical or redundant, since literal literally means "according to the letter" (which is to say according to the character used to represent a speech sound) and, by extension, "according to the word." This redundancy is neatly built into Searle's characterization: "in literal utterance the speaker means what he says." Andrew Ortony converts the letter according to itself into the scientist's precision: "Science is supposed to be characterized by precision and the absence of ambiguity, and the language of science is often thought to be correspondingly *precise and unambiguous*—in short, literal" [italics mine]. If literal means "precise and unambiguous," then must we say that all vague and imprecise utterances are metaphors?

Zenon Pylyshyn tries to grasp the literal by distinguishing literal from metaphorical description:

My own tentative feeling is that the difference between literal and metaphorical description lies primarily in such pragmatic considerations as (a) the stability, referential specificity, and general acceptance of terms; and (b) the perception, shared by those who use the terms, that the resulting description characterizes the world as it really is, rather than being a convenient way of talking about it, or a way of capturing superficial resemblances. . . .

Whereas metaphor induces a (partial) equivalence between two known phenomena, a literal account describes the phenomenon in the authentic terms in which it is "seen." [23]

Pylyshyn's account provides a convenient synthesis of widely held notions. Literal Language is precise, unambiguious, nonproblematic; it is descriptive and represents ("characterizes") an accurate reflection of the physical world. But in his last sentence Pylyshyn fudges. Does "literal" language present the world "as it really is" (Pylyshyn's first formulation) or "in the authentic terms in which it is 'seen' "? If the latter, then may we not say that poets "see" the world in metaphor, and that for the poet the utterance, "the morn in russet mantle clad" is as authentic and direct as the utterance "Day is dawning"?

Even Max Black is evasive when it comes to defining literal. In the sentence "The chairman plowed through the discussion," the word *plowed*, according to Black, is used metaphorically, while "at least one of the remaining words is being used literally," by which he seems to mean "normally" or "conventionally," or perhaps even "referentially." [24] But in the stanza by Emily Dickinson,

> I dwell in Possibility—
> A fairer house than Prose—
> More numerous of Windows—
> Superior—for Doors [25]

such sharp distinctions are obliterated. No single term can be pinned down to a "conventional" meaning or narrowly referential usage.

If we were to try to paraphrase (translate) the stanza into contemporary English prose we would have no basis for separating a "focus" word from a "literal frame." We should say, I suppose, that Emily Dickinson is meditating on (I hesitate to say "making an assertion about") human freedom and limitations, and about the beauty of a world filtered through imagination, as opposed to the drabness of a world perceived without imagination.

If we can think of "The chairman plowed . . ." as a "low-energy" metaphor and "I dwell in Possibility" as a "high-energy" metaphor, we may get a clue to the weakness of most of the philosophical, scientific, and linguistic formulations about metaphor. With very few exceptions, such formulations limit themselves to the analysis of low-energy metaphors of the "chairman plowed" variety. Philosophers and social scientists tend to steer clear of the complex metaphors actually found in poems. But the mystery of metaphor is not likely to be solved by avoiding analysis of the utterances of poets.

Here again Reddy makes an important contribution to our further thinking about metaphor. As an alternative to the conduit metaphor he presents an elaborate "toolmakers paradigm" that I do not have space to replicate or even summarize. Suffice it to say that Reddy finds that

The toolmakers paradigm is very much in accord with the long postulated connection between information, in the mathematical sense, and the entropy expression of the second law of thermo-dynamics. . . . The second law states that if left to their own devices, all forms of organization always decrease in time. Successful human communication involves an increase in organization, which cannot happen spontaneously or of its own accord. Thus, the shift in viewpoint of the toolmakers paradigm merely seems to bring the model of human communication into line with a previously extant paradigm from the physical sciences. But even though, mathematically, information is expressed as negative entropy, debate and confusion have always surrounded this connection. And it may be that this confusion springs, in part at least, from the dominant position occupied by the conduit metaphor in our language. For the conduit metaphor is definitely in conflict with the second law.[26]

Although I would not use it in exactly the way Reddy does, the notion of entropy seems promising. Great metaphors generate energy, and the more powerful the metaphor, the longer it takes for the energy to run down. The majestic opening of Psalm 19—"The heavens are telling the glory of God, the firmament declares the work of his hands; day unto day utters speech, and night unto night reveals knowledge"—has retained its high-energy charge for thousands of years, but "The chairman plowed through the meeting" loses its energy almost immediately. This metaphor is not so much dead as stillborn. The exploding metaphor-chain of the psalm is a potential stimulus to thinking about the human condition and about the possibilities of human dignity and humility and humanity's place in the universal scheme of Being.

Paul Ricoeur has written subtly and profoundly about metaphor and literal meaning because he has not forgotten that metaphors are made by poets as a way of thinking "beyond" the physical world. Ricoeur seeks to demonstrate that though both poets and philosophers use metaphor, a difference exists between "the speculative" and "the poetic"; more specifically, he wants to show that "speculative thought" (that is, philosophy) takes precedence over poetry.

Ricoeur combines hermeneutic theory with a "split reference" theory of metaphor: "Poetic discourse," he writes, "is that in which the epoché of ordinary references is the negative condition allowing a second-order reference to unfold." [27] This is a variation of the "deviance" theory, stated, however, with greater subtlety. It is also an echo of Keats's famous "Negative Capability," that is, the condition in which "a man is capable of being in uncertainties, Mysteries, doubts, without any irritable reaching after fact and reason." The difference is that Ricoeur himself does not refrain from that "irritable reaching after fact and reason." For him words in discourse may have more than one meaning: when the "literal," or "ordinary," or "proper" meaning does not "make sense," or is not in accord with "our ordinary concept of reality," the reader seeks a "metaphorical meaning." Such "split reference" usages may be found in philosophy as well as poetry. While this creates the danger that speculative discourse may merge with poetry, that threat is averted because "speculative thought employs the metaphorical resources of language in order to create meaning and answers thus to the call of the 'thing' to be said with a semantic innovation." [28] Philosophy resolves the poet's Negative Capability by asserting reason over mystery.

The contribution of "poetic discourse" is to bring "to language a pre-objective world in which we find ourselves already rooted, but in which we also project our innermost possibilities. We must thus dismantle the reign of objects in order to let be, and to allow to be uttered, our primordial belonging to a world which we inhabit." [29] Ricouer sees "poetic discourse" as man's way of placing (identifying) himself as a total being (feeling, thinking, perceiving) within the totality of "reality" (or perhaps otherness). Poetry is a way for man to overthrow the tyranny of the "objective."

But though Ricoeur puts a high value on poetry, philosophy still has the last word:

> Speculative thought, on the other hand, bases its work upon the dynamism of metaphorical utterance, which it construes according to its own sphere of meaning. Speculative discourse can respond in this way only because the distanciation, which constitutes the critical moment, is contemporaneous with the experience of belonging that is opened or recovered by poetic discourse, and because poetic discourse, as text and as work, prefigures the distanciation that speculative thought carries to its highest point of reflection.[30]

Ricoeur meets the challenge of the infiltration of philosophy by metaphor. To the question, "How will speculative discourse [i.e., philosophy] reply, given its resources, to the semantic aim of poetic discourse?" he answers: "Through an ontological clarification of the postulate of [split] reference." Ricoeur believes that philosophy can construe, and therefore rule, metaphor. Though speculative discourse cannot purge itself of metaphor, nevertheless to the extent that such discourse is self-reflective it is capable, Ricoeur believes, of arriving at an ontological clarification of the order of split reference characteristic of poetic discourse (metaphor), and of "work[ing] out the critical scope of the notions of secondary reference and redescription in order to insert them into speculative discourse." So while poetry humanizes the world by "dismantling the reign of objects," philosophy embraces poetry and man's sense of the empirical by assuming what may be called a position of higher objectivity from which it is possible to decide on what constitutes the "truth value" in the poet's forays into imagination.

The key to the philosopher's mastery over poetry lies in Ricoeur's concept of hermeneutics: speculative thought construes metaphorical utterance according to its own sphere of meaning. But what is the nature of this higher hermeneutics, and in what way does it place the philosopher not only above the literary critic but above the poet himself? In an appendix, "From Existentialism to the Philosophy of Language," Ricoeur spells out his notion of hermeneutics:

The kind of hermeneutics which I now favour starts from the recognition of the objective meaning of the text as distinct form the subjective intention of the author. This objective meaning is not something hidden behind the text. Rather it is a requirement addressed to the reader. The interpretation accordingly is a kind of obedience to this injunction starting from the text. The concept of "hermeneutical circle" is not ruled out by this shift within hermeneutics. Instead it is formulated in new terms. It does not proceed so much from an intersubjective relation linking the subjectivity of the author and the subjectivity of the reader as from a connection between two discourses, the discourse of the text and the discourse of the interpretation. This connection means that what has to be interpreted in a text is what it says and what it speaks about, i.e., the kind of world which it opens up or discloses; and the final act of "appropriation" is less the projection of one's own prejudices into the text than the "fusion of horizons"—to speak like Hans-Georg Gadamer—which occurs when the world of the reader and the world of the text merge into one another.[31]

Unfortunately, Ricoeur has chosen to solve the problem of metaphor and meaning by falling into the mystifications of Heideggerian hermeneutics, which lead only to further mystification and which nullify the poet's attempt to humanize the world by seeking out the parameters of the I-thou encounter. Following Heideggerian hermeneutics, Ricouer rejects the authorial subject, thus undermining poetry as the interaction between human and human. The biblical I-thou is replaced by the "connection between . . . discourse of the text and the discourse of the interpretation." As Ricoeur notes, for Heidegger, "the key word . . . *es gibt* . . . carries the mark of a determined ontology, in which the neutral is more expressive than the personal and in which the granting of being at the same time assumes the form of something destined. This ontology proceeds from a listening turned more attentively to the Greeks than to the Hebrews. . . ."[32] But the Heideggerian attentive listening to the Greeks and the hermeneutical "fusion of horizons" never "opens up or discloses" the world of Auschwitz, where, as Jean Amery testifies, the fusion of horizons did not disclose the key word, *es gibt*. Rather,

existence *as such* . . . became definitively a totally abstract and thus empty concept. To reach out beyond reality with words became before our very eyes a game that was not only worthless and an impermissible luxury but also mocking and evil. Hourly, the physical world delivered proof that its insufferableness could be coped with only through means inherent in that world. In other words: nowhere else in the world did reality have as much effective power as in the camp, nowhere else was reality so real.[33]

The final clause in Ricoeur's paragraph is a heartwarming annunciation, but to what purpose? To proclaim that "the final act of 'appropriation' is less the projection of one's own prejudices into the text than it is a 'fusion of horizons' " is to contract billions of individual, inscrutable, and unexaminable acts of reading into a single untestable, unprovable, and untenable ex cathedra pronouncement. The image of fusion itself may be a description of the process of reading, or of what happens when a "text" is read successfully, or it may be a stipulative definition of interpretation. Or perhaps the image of fusion is in its own right a metaphor of sorts, from which we can take some consolation. But as a characterization of interpretive acts, the "fusion of horizons" and the connectedness of disembodied discourses ignores the testimony of twentieth-century history and overlooks the question of how a post-Auschwitz consciousness can fuse horizons with representations of a pre-Auschwitz world.

"Man," the psalmist says, "is like a breath," and "his days are like a passing shadow." Is there not more truth in this simple metaphorical expression than in all the efforts of hermeneutists to establish ironclad principles of interpretation, for what the hermeneutists do is to convert a problem into a mystery. Is it to be expected that a creature dwelling in the uncertainty captured in the psalmist's metaphors could rest content with a language of precision, a language devoid of ambiguity? Is the mystery of metaphor perhaps the mystery of humanity itself? And may it not be accurate to say that metaphor, far from being deviant, anomalous, or a subservient object of philosophical discourse, is the most accurate reflection we have of human reality?

CHAPTER ELEVEN

Speech Acts and the Language of Literature

From time to time, philosophers have been good enough to shed the light of their wisdom on literary texts and on the process of literary criticism. I shall venture to be so bold as to turn the tables here by trying my hand at analyzing a philosophical text. This boldness I shall justify on two grounds. The first is that the text in question centers on problems of language, the element that is the *sine qua non* of literature and literary criticism as well as a vital element in philosophy. The second ground on which I justify my temerity is the belief that literary fictions, which are the critic's normal diet, share with philosophical treatises the tendency to make hypothetical statements about "reality" and about language itself. Hence, it may be possible to approach certain philosophical texts in the same way that one would approach "literary fictions." As a literary critic, I will tend to concentrate on metaphorical language, analogies, and, on occasion, narrative technique. My ultimate purpose will not be frivolous. By explicating certain passages in John Searle's *Speech Acts: An Essay in the Philosophy of Language*[1] I hope to be able to show that his basic hypothesis, "that speaking a language is engaging in a rule-governed form of behavior," is a fiction that does not correspond to the total language-reality.

To be sure, Searle's hypothesis is both more complicated and more restrictive than the above assertion indicates, and I would like, in order to do Searle justice, to quote in full:

The hypothesis of this book is that speaking a language is performing acts according to rules. The form this hypothesis will take is that the semantic structure of a language may be regarded as a conventional realization of a series of sets of underlying constitutive rules, and that speech acts are acts characteristically performed by uttering expressions in accordance with these sets of constitutive rules. (pp. 36–37)

For the present, I wish to point out only that in Searle's hypothesis it is not simply "rules" that govern the behavior called speaking a language, but "constitutive rules." Moreover, Searle must show that the "semantic structure" of a language is in some way "a conventional realization" of these "constitutive rules." As he says elsewhere, the question that is "crucial" to his "enterprise" is "Are conventions realizations of rules?" It will be noticed that an element of confusion creeps in here between the two formulations, the first indicating that "semantic structure" is "a conventional realization" of "constitutive rules," and the second suggesting that the "conventions" themselves are "realizations of rules." The confusion is in no way diminished by the vagueness and indeterminacy of the word "realization."

Confusion aside, however, it is clear that much hinges on the concept of "constitutive rules," and much will hinge, therefore, on the way in which the concept is defined. To preserve the continuity and integrity of Searle's argument, I shall quote at length part of two paragraphs. In the first quotation, Searle distinguishes between "regulative" and "constitutive rules," defining the two different kinds of rules on the basis of the way in which they function. In the second quotation, Searle shifts from definition by function to definition by guidelines, providing us with guidelines for recognizing regulative and constitutive rules, guidelines that depend on the language in which the rules are cast. The statements are as follows:

As a start, we might say that regulative rules regulate antecedently or independently existing forms of behavior; for example, many rules of etiquette regulate inter-personal relationships which exist independently of the rules. But constitutive rules do not merely regulate, they create or define new forms of behavior. The rules of football or chess, for example, do not merely regulate playing football or chess, but as it were they create the very possibility of playing such games. The activities of playing football or chess are constituted by acting in accordance with (at least a large subset of) the appropriate rules. Regulative rules regulate a pre-existing activity, an activity whose existence is logically independent of the rules. Constitutive rules constitute (and also regulate) an activity the existence of which is logically dependent on the rules. (pp. 33–34)

Problems crop up immediately. It seems that the categories are not mutually exclusive, since constitutive rules both constitute and regulate. Moreover, because regulative rules regulate and do not constitute, while constitutive rules both constitute and regulate, regulative rules seem to be a subcategory of constitutive rules. There are hints of circularity: regulative rules regulate; constitutive rules constitute. Terms are used loosely, particularly such terms as "forms of behavior" and "activity." The nature of the problems will be dealt with later, in an analysis of Searle's discussion of constitutive rules.[2]

For the moment, however, I would like to preserve the continuity of Searle's argument. "Regulative rules," he asserts,

characteristically take the form of or can be paraphrased as imperatives, e.g., "When cutting food, hold the knife in the right hand," or "Officers must wear ties at dinner." Some constitutive rules take quite a different form, e.g., "A checkmate is made when the king is attacked in such a way that no move will leave it unattacked," "A touch-down is scored when a player has possession of the ball in the opponents' end zone while a play is in progress." (p. 34)

Immediately startling is Searle's assertion that regulative rules "characteristically take the form of or can be paraphrased," or that "some" constitutive rules "take quite a different form." The sense conveyed by such phrases is that the articulation of both regulative and constitutive rules is largely arbitrary. It is therefore difficult to see how the form in which the rules are expressed can be a definitive or a distinguishing condition. For example, let us look at the first regulative rule presented by Searle: "When cutting food, hold the knife in the right hand." I must confess that I do not see what makes this sentence necessarily any kind of a rule at all. On the basis of pure analysis of the language of the sentence, I would take the sentence to be a suggestion rather than a rule. Or perhaps I might take the sentence as a command, but commands are not always rules (For example, "Open the door!" is a command, but hardly a rule.). What can be said, I think, is that only a person who has prior knowledge of the contours of American etiquette would take this statement for a "rule." But aside from this confusion, it requires little ingenuity to rephrase this "rule" so as to remove the imperative element altogether. One can say, "It is not considered polite to cut food while holding the knife in the left hand." Or better, "It is considered polite (or proper) to hold one's knife in the right hand while cutting food."

The regulative rule about officers wearing ties can also be stated in nonimperative terms: "Proper dinner attire for officers will consist of a tie, dress shirt, etc." Or else, "Officers who are not wearing ties will not be admitted to mess hall during the dinner hours." Or, "An officer who does not wear a tie at dinner will be considered to be improperly dressed." Or, "An officer is considered properly dressed for dinner when wearing a tie with his class A uniform."

On the other hand, one can reverse the procedure and state constitutive rules imperatively: "In order to score a touch-down, a player must have possession of the ball in the opponents' end zone while a play is in progress." The same thing, of course, is true of chess rules: "The king must be moved only one square at a time, in any direction," "The rook must not be moved diagonally," etc. One could continue along this line indefinitely.

Let us move on, however, to what is certainly a more crucial phrase of Searle's argument, his presentation of the two formulae he uses to characterize constitutive rules. Again, it is necessary to quote at some length in order to preserve the texture of Searle's argument.

The distinction as I have tried to sketch it is still rather vague, and I shall try to clarify it by commenting on the two formulae I have used to characterize constitutive rules: "The creation of constitutive rules, as it were, creates the possibility of new forms of behavior," and "constitutive rules often have the form: X counts as Y in context C."

"New forms of behavior": there is a trivial sense in which the creation of any rule creates the possibility of new forms of behavior, namely, behavior done as in accordance with the rule. That is not the sense in which my remark is intended. What I mean can perhaps be best put in the formal mode. Where

the rule is purely regulative, behavior which is in accordance with the rule could be given the same description or specification (the same answer to the question "What did he do?") whether or not the rule existed, provided the description or specification makes no explicit reference to the rule. But where the rule (or system of rules) is constitutive, behavior which is in accordance with the rule can receive specifications or descriptions which it could not receive if the rule or rules did not exist. I shall illustrate this with examples.

Suppose that in my social circle it is a rule of etiquette that invitations to parties must be sent out at least two weeks in advance. The specification of the action, "He sent out the invitations at least two weeks in advance," can be given whether or not that rule exists. Suppose, also, that in my athletic circle football is a game played according to such and such rules. Now, the specification, "They played football," cannot be given if there were no such rules. It is possible that twenty-two men might go through the same physical movements as are gone through by two teams at a football game, but if there were no rules of football, that is, no antecedently existing game of football, there is no sense in which their behavior could be described as playing football. (p. 35)

I shall postpone, for a moment, commenting on the second paragraph quoted and start with Searle's examples, which are deficient with respect to symmetry. By drawing the examples of etiquette and football asymmetrically, Searle not only invites but breeds confusion. I think I can best describe the asymmetry I am thinking of by resorting to simple algebraic proportion of the kind, $A:B = B:C$. If we were to convert Searle's formulation about sending invitations and playing football into this kind of equivalence, the result would come out something like this: "This act of sending invitations two weeks in advance" is to "etiquette" as "the rules of football" are to "football." It is obvious that this is a false equation. Sending-invitations-two-weeks-in-advance is only one of the rules of what we might call the game of "etiquette," or perhaps the game of inviting, whereas "rules of football" apparently means all the rules of the game.

When the equation is properly balanced ("the rules of the game of inviting" are to the game *inviting* as "the rules of football" are to the game *football*), then what we say of one side of the equation we can also say of the other. Hence, if we say that football would cease to exist if there were no rules of football, so, in the same way, we might say that inviting-two-weeks-in-advance would cease to exist if there were no rules of inviting. Similarly, if we can say that the act-of sending-invitations-two-weeks-in-advance would continue to exist even if there were not a particular rule specifying that invitations must be sent two weeks in advance, so, in the same way, we might say that the act of throwing a football might continue to take place even if there were not a particular rule of forward passing in the game of football that specified that a man must throw the ball only in such and such a way and under such and such conditions.

It will perhaps be argued, at this point, that if there were no rules of football there could be no footballs to throw, but it seems to me that such a conclusion does not necessarily follow. There is no logical reason why someone cannot make "an inflated oval with a bladder contained in a leather casing" without there being an officially defined "game of football." Indeed, I think it is more likely that there would not be invitations without rules of inviting than that there would not be footballs without a game of football. A close look reveals that *inviting* is like *promising,* which Searle takes to be the prime example of an activity governed by constitutive rules. Just as "the utterance of such and such expressions under certain conditions counts as the making of a promise" (p. 37), so "the utterance of such and such expressions under certain conditions counts as the sending of an invitation."

Let us now reexamine Searle's "principle of specification." Searle asserts that "The specification of the action, 'He sent out the invitations at least two weeks in advance,' can be given whether or not the rule exists," and that "the specification, 'They played football,' cannot be given if there were no such rules." But if we amend the situation in such a way as to bring the two sides of the equation into balance, then Searle's assertions are clearly seen to be invalid, and it becomes apparent that the principle of specification will not work. The specification "He sent out the invitations at least two weeks in advance" cannot be given "if there were no rules of inviting," any more than the specification "They played football" can be given "if there were no rules of football."

It will be argued that even if my analysis is correct so far, I have done no more than show that inviting is the same kind of activity as playing and promising; it, too, happens to be a form of behavior governed by constitutive rules, and that in itself would not invalidate the distinction between regulative and constitutive rules. It would only mean that Searle has chosen an unfortunate example. I will answer that Searle has not only chosen an unfortunate example, he has created difficulties by his method of presentation.

I shall attempt to show what I mean by testing the assertion that "the creation of constitutive rules, as it were, creates the possibility of new forms of behavior." What does this mean? Shall we say that without the rules of football it would not be possible for twenty-two men to run around, to bump into each other, to throw a ball, to kick a ball, etc.? Searle himself would not say so, since he grants that "It is possible that twenty-two men might go through the same physical movements as are gone through by two teams at a football game" even if there were no rules of football. He does not deny the possibility of the behavior without the constitutive rules. He denies only that we would be able to specify of this behavior that "They played football." It seems, then, that the initial assertion would have to be amended to say that "the creation of constitutive rules *brings into being* new forms of behavior" rather than "*creates the possibility* of the new forms of behavior." I think we would have to grant that the "possibility of the new forms of behavior" was latent in man, and that the constitutive rules were created only because the possibility existed that men would be capable of engaging in such and such a form of behavior. Who, for example, would create a game with a set of rules calling for behavior that exceeded the bounds of possible human activity? One would not be likely to make a game with a rule saying that "a touch-down is scored when a player swallows an inflated football." So what Searle really wants to say here is that certain possible forms of human behavior are verbalized, channelized, and regularized when constitutive rules are created. When one or more people act in the ways that the rules call for, then those possible forms of human behavior become actualized.

What I am getting at is that Searle's faulty parallels are not merely a case of an unfortunate choice of examples. The language that Searle uses to set up his examples and parallels pushes the reader (and Searle himself) into unwarranted and undesirable conclusions by creating two kinds of confusion. The first is the confusion between rules and behavior and the second is the confusion between rules and behavior on the one hand and the way in which they are spoken about on the other. Let me try to illustrate the first kind of confusion by returning to the statement, "It is possible that twenty-two men might go through the same physical movements as are gone through by two teams at a football game, but if there were not rules of football, that is, no antecedently existing game of football, there is no sense in which their behavior could be described as playing football."

Suppose, now, we add to this assertion the condition that these twenty-two men went through these physical movements, not just once, but every Monday night, even though there were no written or verbal representation describing, delimiting, or in any way governing these activities. Would we then say that these men are acting according to rules, or not? If the answer is that they are still not going through physical movements governed by rules, and that their behavior cannot be "described as playing football," then I would infer that rules can mean only that which is verbally expressed, and not that upon which there has been some kind of nonverbal understanding or agreement. This would agree with Searle's position that speaking a language is not acting by means of a series of randomly arrived-at conventions but a rule governed activity in which conventions are the "realization of underlying rules." A question still remains, though: What set of terms *would* we use to describe or characterize the behavior of these twenty-two men? If they are not "playing football," what *are* they doing?

I shall leave this question in suspension momentarily, in the hope that I can shed some light by discussing another one of Searle's creative analogies. In attempting to show that promising is an "illocutionary act" performed under certain conditions that are necessary and sufficient, Searle sets up the following situation:

If we get such a set of conditions we can extract from them a set of rules for the use of the illocutionary force indicating device. The method here is analogous to discovering the rules of chess by asking oneself what are the necessary and sufficient conditions under which one can be said to have correctly moved a knight or castled or checkmated a player, etc. We are in the position of someone who has learned to play chess without ever having the rules formulated and who wants such a formulation. We learned how to play the game of illocutionary acts, but in general it was done without an explicit formulation of the rules, and the first step in getting such a formulation is to set out the conditions for the performance of a particular illocutionary act. Our inquiry will therefore serve a double philosophical purpose. By stating a set of conditions for the performance of a particular illocutionary act we shall have offered an explication of that notion and shall also have paved the way for the second step, the formulation of rules. (pp. 54–55)

Now, let me ask, isn't this person who has learned to play chess without ever having the rules formulated in the same position as the twenty-two men who go through the motions of football without playing football? Must we not say, to remain consistent, that this person is going through the same physical movements as are gone through by a chess player, but there is no sense in which this behavior can be described as playing chess?

Put the question in a different way. How is it possible to learn to play chess without having the rules formulated in some way or other? Let us consider some ways in which one can learn to play chess. Probably the most common way is to be taught by another person. In the normal course of teaching, the instructor will say things like, "A pawn moves forward one square at a time, like this," and then the instructor will in all likelihood give a physical demonstration of a pawn move. "Except," the instructor will continue, "on the pawn's first move, you can move it two squares if you want to." In this instance, rules are certainly being formulated. Another way of learning to play chess is to read a book on the subject, and in such a case the rules are certainly formulated for the learner. There remains, now, the possibility of pure imitation. One watches others play and then without a word being said, the watcher imitates what he has seen.

My question is this: Is moving the chessmen according to the way one has seen them moved by others a way of formulating the rules of chess, or does "formulation of the rules of chess" mean that the rules must be given some form of verbal expression? If we formulate the rules by moving the pieces "correctly," then it seems to follow that we create the rules of chess by enacting the rules (without knowing them?),[3] and then it would seem that our twenty-two men by making the correct moves of football would be creating the rules of football, which would also mean that we could specify that they "played football." On the other hand, if the answer to my question is that formulated rules are rules that have been given verbal expression, then what seems to follow is that Searle's chess player would be using the actual playing of the game of chess to arrive at the very rules without which no actual playing of the game of chess would be possible.

If we turn from chess to "promising," we can see that the same problems apply to the "promising" half of the analogy. If moving the chessmen according to the rules of chess is a way of formulating the rules of chess, then that implies about promising that we create the conditions of promising by making a promise. On the other hand, if formulated rules are rules that have been given some form of verbal expression, then, again, Searle is setting out to do the logically impossible. Let me try to clarify the nature of the dilemma with a series of linguistic characterizations:

1. Human speakers would not be able to make promises if there were not a set of rules governing promising.
2. Rules means rules that have been expressed in language.
3. The rules underlying promising had never been expressed in language before Searle expressed them.
4. Nevertheless, Searle will analyze the act of making a promise in such a way as to arrive at a way of expressing the rules of making a promise.

Given sentences 1, 2, and 3 above, sentence 4 should be impossible. Let me put the matter another way. Searle's problem seems to be the arrow of time. If, as he claims is the case in chess, the rules must exist before there can be a game of chess, then it would seem to be impossible to start with a game of chess and work back to "discover" the rules. Similarly, in the case of promising, if rules of promising must exist before someone can make a promise, then it would seem to be a logical impossibility to start with the way we make a promise and then work backward to "discover" the rules of promising. One is put in mind, here, of the would-be plumber who can't get a job until he joins the union and who cannot join the union until he gets a job.

At this point, someone might be inclined to bring up the notion of "internalized rules." Such a notion, however, does not release us from the logical dilemma. If we mean by an "internalized rule" a rule that has somewhere and at some time been expressed in language and is then obeyed, without any external coercion, by someone who has absorbed the rule into his consciousness, that seems to me to make sense, but in no way supports the notion that one acts according to rules that have not been formulated. On the other hand, if an "internalized rule" is inferred from one's ability to observe patterns of behavior that do not derive from any known expressed formulation, then I must deny that such an inference is justified. For example, a patient suffering from a compulsive neurosis may carry on an activity that is repeated constantly, always in exactly the same way, yet, we do not say that such a person is carrying on an orderly rule-governed activity.

There is one highly significant flaw in the chess/promising analogy that I still have not mentioned. That is, Searle does not indicate whether the person who learned to play chess without having the rules formulated is definitely aware that there are "rules of chess." If he is, then he is different from the man analyzing promising, who can only hypothesize that there are rules of promising. I shall try to show how this lapse in the analogy is significant by discussing Searle's attempt to deal with "apparent counter-examples" to his necessary condition of promising, number 4: "H would prefer S's doing A to his not doing A, and S believes H would prefer his doing A to his not doing A." "Suppose," Searle writes,

I say to a lazy student, "If you don't hand in your paper on time I promise you I will give you a failing grade in the course." Is this utterance a promise? I am inclined to think not; we would more naturally describe it as a warning or possibly even a threat. But why, then is it possible to use the locution "I promise" in such a case? I think we use it here because "I promise" and "I hereby promise" are among the strongest illocutionary force indicating devices for *commitment* provided by the English language. For that reason we often use these expressions in the performance of speech acts which are not strictly speaking promises, but in which we wish to emphasize the degree of our commitment. To illustrate this, consider another apparent counter-example to the analysis along different lines. Sometimes one hears people say "I promise" when making an emphatic assertion. Suppose, for example, I accuse you of having stolen the money. I say, "You stole the money, didn't you?" You reply, "No, I didn't, I promise you I didn't." Did you make a promise in this case? I find it very unnatural to describe your utterances as a promise. This utterance would be more aptly described as emphatic denial, and we can explain the occurrence of the illocutionary force indicating device "I promise" as derivative from genuine promises and serving here as an expression adding emphasis to your denial. (p. 58)

I would say that Searle is incorrect and somewhat insensitive to English usage when he says that " 'I promise' and 'I hereby promise' are among the strongest illocutionary force indicating devices for commitment." I believe that in the above context, "I promise" is actually a euphemism for more potent, more portentous, and more dangerous expressions, expressions so powerful that a teacher hesitates to use them to students for fear of damaging his credibility with the class. The expressions I have in mind are "I swear to you," "I give you my word," "My word of honor," "I vow to you," etc. These expressions, I believe, would have the effect of overcommitting the user, and as a consequence, a teacher, who knows that no matter how powerfully he threatens to punish those who submit late papers, still, in the nature of things, some papers will be late, such a teacher wisely leaves himself a way out. Instead of using the strongest possible force indicator, he uses one that can be reneged on without too much loss of honor.

Second, just imagine how this example would work if we were to return to the analogy with chess. That is, suppose deriving the constitutive rules for promising is like deriving a formulation of the rules of chess on the basis of playing chess without having formulated the rules. Now what would happen if our chess player who had learned to play without having the rules formulated for him (and who did not "know" the rules) noticed that every once in a while, a player moved a pawn backward, that is moved a pawn from a point in the center of the board or on the opponent's side of the board, toward its starting position. Would the chess player who had learned by imitating formulate a rule saying that "backward" movement of a pawn is illegal, or would he try to find a rule that would accommodate cases of pawns moving in just such a way? I believe that an honest answer to this question is that the imitating chess-learner would do the latter. And what I would like to know, following the analogy, is why Searle does not do the same. That is, instead of creating a rule that makes a nonutterance of what people do actually utter, why does he not try to find a rule that will encompass all uses of the word "promise"? The same applies to the second counterexample, of promising that one did not do something. An adequate set of the rules of chess would have to account for all observed moves, and a rule of promising should account for all recorded instances of the use of the word "promise." If speakers use "promise" to indicate what Searle calls "emphatic denial," then does that not mean that the rules should be capable of accounting for all instances of "promising" which are emphatic denials?

In fact, it seems to me that it is possible to question whether Searle is actually providing a set of constitutive rules of promising at all. I shall not attempt to analyze each of the nine conditions for promising that Searle sets forth.[4] Rather, I shall examine his basic constitutive rule of promising, the rule without which, he believes, there could be no such entity as promising: "The utterance of Pr counts as the undertaking of an obligation to do A. I call this the *essential rule*." To begin with, I am afraid that I must question the validity of the "X counts as Y in context C" formula, principally on the basis that the phrase "counts as" is vague and misleading. I do not find the phrase listed in any dictionary. But say one interprets the phrase to mean something like "is equivalent to" or "fulfills the requirement for." If we apply a test of substitution, such as (to use one of Searle's own examples) "acting in accordance with all or a sufficiently large subset of the rules (is the equivalent of) or (fulfills the requirements for) playing basketball," then it is immediately apparent that the rule "X counts as Y in context C" sets up a false equivalence where there should be not equivalence but identity. That is, it is not that "Acting in accordance with all or a sufficiently large subset of the rules *counts* as playing basketball," but that acting in accordance with all or a sufficiently large subset of the rules *is* playing basketball. In a similar way, the "counts as" has no value in the promising rule.

The rule that "the utterance of Pr counts as the undertaking of an obligation to do A" may just as well be stated, "the utterance of Pr *is* the undertaking of an obligation to do A." In fact, Searle actually does drop the "counts as" obfuscation and makes the assertion elsewhere in the book: "the constitutive rule that to make a promise is to undertake an obligation" (p. 185). Once the "counts as" obfuscation is dropped, we see that two problems arise immediately. The first takes the form of the question, "In what way is this equivalence of phrases different from an ordinary synonymy?" That is, is this not simply a case of replacing one set of words ("make a promise") with another set of words ("undertake an obligation"), without leaving us any the wiser?

The second question is, what does Searle mean by the phrase "to undertake an obligation"? The answer, I suppose, is that "to undertake an obligation" is "to commit oneself to some specific behavior to be carried out at some specific time in the future." But how is committing oneself in this particular way different from saying, "I shall do such and such at such and such a time?" What is the difference semantically and in terms of commitment between saying, "I promise to take you to the circus" and "I shall take you to the circus"? Searle would say, no doubt, that "promise" is a force indicator, but if I apply Searle's sincerity rule ("S intends to do A") and his "normal input and output condition" (the criterion of "saying something literally and seriously"), to the assertion "I shall take you to the circus," then semantically I am equally committed by both statements. Perhaps Searle will argue that in using ordinary future tense I am not bound by any sincerity rules or by the standard of "serious and literal," but if this is the case, then it seems to make a mockery of all human communication. It would imply that I need mean what I say only when I promise, and that in utterances that are not promises I am free not to mean what I say, or not to intend to do what I say I shall.[5]

To convey some sense of how we arrived at this peculiar position, I would like to give an example of my own. Suppose I borrow money from a friend. I tell him "I shall repay you in six months." Applying the criteria of intention and serious and literal statement, I have made a commitment. I meant what I said. I intended to repay. I expected to be able to repay. My friend believed me. Now suppose I said, "I promise to repay you in six months." Applying the same criteria, I seem to have made the same commitment. In both instances I meant what I said and my friend believed that I meant what I said. In either case, if I do not repay I can be accused of being a liar or of having failed to keep my word. What is the difference?

I suggest that the difference may lie in the device of "coercion," a device that Searle casts aside too casually with the remark that "not all constitutive rules have penalties" (p. 41). It may be that the difference between an assertion cast in the future tense and a "promise" is that the latter may expose me to some form of physical or social coercion, and I would suppose that the difference between saying "I shall" and "I promise" is not very great if no coercion is involved. To the question, then, "What is undertaking an obligation?" my answer is that "undertaking an obligation" is making oneself liable to some kind of penalty or some form of outside force.

Consider another example. I lend someone ten thousand dollars. On taking the money he makes a promise to repay me in two years. In two years' time, I show up at the borrower's office, asking for my ten thousand dollars. He tells me he does not have the money, cannot repay me, and would not repay me even if he were able to. What do I do in this case? Do I show him a copy of *Speech Acts* and say, "You see, when you promised to repay in two years you committed yourself semantically by virtue of the constitutive rule of promising, which holds that if you say 'I promise to repay,' that counts as 'undertaking an obligation' to repay?" At this point, the borrower has a good laugh and throws me out of his office, telling me not to waste his time. I call Searle and tell him what happened, and his answer, no doubt, is that the borrower had made an insincere promise.

That, of course, is little consolation to me, and furthermore, the assessment of insincerity may not even be accurate. It may be that when the borrower promised to repay in two years he was being sincere, but that at the time payment was due, he had changed his mind.

The problem is that there are really two ends to "promising," which are "making a promise" and "keeping a promise." And there is, after all, a way for me to see to it that the second part follows from the first. I can request that the borrower sign a promissory note under conditions that are legally binding. Or I can ask him to leave in my possession something worth more to him (and to me) than the ten thousand dollars. Then I do not have to rely on any so-called constitutive rule of promising, and I do not have to rely on the borrower's intention, seriousness, literalness, or sincerity. Indeed, on the basis of experience, one would have to say that sincerity usually is not assumed of promisors. If it were, then there were no need for legal devices that force borrowers to repay. And it would not be necessary for lenders to require collateral. All these devices that assure that obligations are indeed created tend to indicate that neither promisors or promisees rely on intention or sincerity.

Neither does it seem to be a rule or condition of promising, as Searle indicates, that the fulfillment of the promise would not have been carried out in the normal course of events (condition 5: "It is not obvious to both S and H that S will do A in the normal course of events"). How, after all, can an action that has not yet taken place be either "obvious" or "not obvious"? But let us say that Searle means that "Neither S nor H expects that S will do A in the normal course of events." Yet it is clear that in practice promisors do indeed promise to do what they would be expected to do in the normal course of events. They promise to repay what they borrowed even though it may be expected that in the normal course of events they would repay what they borrowed.

It should be obvious that when Searle says that "the serious utterances of the words commit one in ways which are determined by the meaning of the words" (p. 189), he is indulging in a bit of Panglossian logic. The notion that a "constitutive rule" of language is more binding than an enforced "obligation" is absurd, as we can see from the example of the man who refused to pay me back my ten thousand dollars.[6]

What I have tried to indicate with these examples is that the linguistic characterization, "making a promise counts as undertaking an obligation" is not a constitutive rule but a linking of two synonymous expressions, and that the only way to break out of the circularity inherent in the synonymies "making a promise" is "undertaking an obligation" is "committing oneself to," etc., is by bringing in the idea of coercion. Because physical coercion coming from some outside force is most readily apprehended, I spoke of that first. I clearly "undertake an obligation" when I submit knowingly to having my possessions taken from me, getting beat up, going to jail, being put in the stocks, etc., if I fail to perform, at a designated time in the future, some action that I had indicated I would perform.

But coercion that stems from threats of physical violence or deprivation imposed by outside forces stronger than oneself is not the only kind of coercion. There is also what we might call inner, or moral, coercion. That is, I may be taught that if I do not keep a promise a demon will descend on me. Or it may be that I become convinced that there is a nonphysical force greater than myself that commands a person to keep his promise, and that will punish him in a world to come if he does not. Or perhaps I am persuaded that there is an "ethical law" that calls for a person to be sincere. Under certain conditions, such forms of inner coercion may be stronger than threats of physical harm, as we can easily learn by reading a book of martyrs. If we look at such "inner" coercion from a nonskeptical viewpoint, "morality" might be an apt term to describe its function.[7] It may be, for example, that I am taught about promising in just such a manner, that when I "make a promise" and do not keep it, I am, in my own view, "guilty of moral transgression." After all, there is no more logical necessity in the assertion, "making a promise is undertaking an obligation" than there is in the assertion "keeping a promise is fulfilling a moral precept," just as there is no more logic in the assertion "A touchdown counts as six points" than there is in the assertion "A touchdown counts as ten points."

It is because Searle ignores this element of "inner" coercion that he is able to divorce "making a promise" from morality altogether, as he does in the following declaration:

I think, incidentally, that the obligation to keep a promise probably has no necessary connection with morality. It is often claimed that the obligation to keep a promise is a paradigm case of moral obligation. But consider the following very common sort of example. I promise to come to your party. On the night in question, however, I just don't feel like going. Of course I ought to go, after all, I promised and I have no good excuse for not going. But I just don't go. Am I *immoral*? Remiss, no doubt. If it were somehow very important that I go, then it might be immoral of me to stay home. But then the immorality would derive from the importance of my going, and not simply for the obligation undertaken in promising. (p. 188)

I believe that all readers will quickly perceive, now, that Searle has cheated on us. The cheating comes in his use of the word "obligation." We may say, so to speak, that when Searle uses the word "obligation" he is undertaking an obligation to mean *obligation,* but it is clear that Searle is not really talking about an "obligation" at all, and what one may infer from his example is that he never did mean "obligation" at any point in his book. Because what he is telling us here is that having made a promise (that is, having undertaken an obligation), he is still *not* under any *obligation* whatsoever. There is clearly no inner or outer need for him to fulfill his "promise." He has, by his own admission, made a promise, but, as one would expect, a purely semantical "constitutive rule" has no binding power at all; such a rule has not the power of creating any sense of obligation in Searle, so that if he "just doesn't feel like going" to my party, he can find nothing that would, in fact, obligate him to go. He is behaving just like the character who refuses to pay me my ten thousand dollars. That is to say he is acting exactly as if he did not believe that "the utterance of Pr counts as the undertaking of an obligation to do A." We may gather that his essential rule is, to quote Hamlet, "more honor'd in the breach than the observance."

"Am I immoral?" Searle then asks, as if this were a rhetorical question calling for an unequivocally negative answer. "Remiss, no doubt," he says, thereby displaying again an astonishing disregard for the way in which language works. For if Searle has truly meant all along that "the utterance of Pr counts as the undertaking of an obligation to do A," then he could not possibly be so casual about breaking his promise to go to my party, and he would not assume so easily a negative answer to the question "Am I immoral?" For our own edification, I shall quote the definition of "obligation" provided in the *American Heritage Dictionary*. Other dictionaries define the word in pretty much the same terms, but the *AHD* happens to state the definition with exemplary crispness. The first two definitions are as follows:

1. The act of binding oneself by a social, legal, or moral tie. 2.a. A duty, contract, promise, or any other social, moral, or legal requirement that compels one to follow or avoid a certain course of action.

Two elements should stand out in these definitions: a sense of compulsion or binding, and a built-in implication of "moral" reference. A little further probing in an etymological dictionary reveals the suggestion that through the Latin root *ligare*, the word "obligation" is "certainly very closely akin to L. *religare* (s. relig-), to bind again, hence int(ensive), to bind strongly, is *religio* (s. relig-), a binding back, or very strongly, sc to one's faith or ethic . . ."

I hope that my objections to Searle's presentation of promising as a form of rule-governed behavior will not be taken to mean that I do not believe in the potency of language. On the contrary, I do indeed believe that language shapes human beings in every conceivable way, but not in the simple "X counts as Y," therefore "uttering X commits one to do Y" formula worked out by Searle. For example, I believe that there are people who when they utter the words "I promise" or "I swear" or "I vow" consider that they have "undertaken an obligation." But that is because they see all of these verbal configurations as putting them under some kind of "moral constraint." That is, they believe that "breaking a commitment" is a "transgression," or a "sin," or a "trespass." I do not deny that such conceptions as "sin," "trespass," "moral duty" would be impossible without language. What I am arguing, I suppose, is that language enters into and determines the texture of human thought and the contours of the human form in a much more complex way than Searle suggests. I also believe that these complexities are much more a matter of conventions and of the arbitrariness of language than a matter of "constitutive rules."

I shall try to demonstrate what I mean by giving a literary critic's analysis of one of Searle's more creative examples. To complete his answer to one of the questions he raises ("are illocutionary acts rule governed?") and "to begin to answer" another ("Is language rule governed?"), Searle introduces "two imaginary cases for the purpose of illustrating certain relations between rules, acts, and conventions." Searle's witty and entertaining presentation of the imaginary cases runs as follows:

First, imagine that chess is played in different countries according to different conventions. Imagine, e.g., that in one country the king is represented by a big piece, in another the king is smaller than the rook. In one country the game is played on a board as we do it, in another the board is represented by a sequence of numbers, one of which is assigned to any piece that "moves" to that number. Of these different countries, we could say that they play the same game of chess according to different conventional forms. Notice, also, that the rules must be realized in some form in order that the game be playable. Something, even if it is not a material object, must represent what we call the king or the board.

Secondly, imagine a society of sadists who like to cause each other pain by making loud noises in each others' ears. Suppose that for convenience they adopt the convention of always making the noise BANG to achieve this purpose. Of this case, like the chess case, we can say that it is a practice involving a convention. But unlike the chess case, the convention is not a realization of any underlying constitutive rules. Unlike the chess case, the conventional device is a device to achieve a natural effect. There is no rule to the effect that saying BANG counts as causing pain; one can feel the pain whether or not one knows the conventions. (p. 39)

Since we are dealing here with "fictions," what Searle calls "imaginary cases," we may assume that there is no "truth claim" involved, and that it may be useful to introduce alternative fictions to test the contention that we have a case here in which chess "is played in different countries according to different conventions." Let us, then, imagine a single chess enthusiast who delights in collecting sets of chessmen and chess boards, who then arranges a chess tournament to be held in one of the great rooms of his mansion, with the stipulation that no two matches can be played with the same pieces, and in which some games are even conducted according to a number system rather than by moving actual pieces. Naturally, all of these matches can take place in the same room, and it does not seem that there would be any question of "different conventions." The reason that such a tournament would be possible and the reason that "different conventions" would not enter in at all is that the rules of chess do not make any specifications about the size or shape of the pieces. In this case, we would not say that "they play the same game of chess according to different conventional forms," actually a nonsensical statement, but that "they play the game of chess with a variety of pieces and boards." Imagine, for a moment, Arthur Rubinstein playing a Beethoven concerto with his usual aplomb on a Steinway that is standard in every way except that the keys are red and green instead of black and white. Would we say that Rubinstein is playing the same concerto according to different conventional forms? I think not. The color of the keys has nothing to do with the sound of the music, just as the size and shape of the pieces, with one possible exception, has nothing to do with the rules of chess. The one exception, I would think, is that whatever the size and shape of the pieces, one would not want to play with thirty-two identical discs.

If we ask how Searle was able to arrive at the notion that his players were playing "the same game of chess according to different conventional forms," the answer is that he set up his fiction in such a way as to make such an assertion seem plausible by introducing the persuasive, but not necessary, condition that using chess pieces of different size and shape in different countries is an example of playing "according to different conventions."

In moving to the society of "sadists" who say BANG in each others' ears we move to a totally new narrative stance. Whereas in the chess-with-different-pieces fiction, the narrator was a limited observer unconcerned with motivation, in the BANG fiction the narrator sees into the motives of his character with greater penetration. But imagine, now, that we tell the BANG story from the same limited point of view as the chess narrator. What we observe, then, is a situation in which people make the noise BANG in each others' ears. The persons who make the BANG, let us say, laugh, while those at whom the BANG is made wince. We do not have any special information to the effect that the society is one of "sadists," nor that the people in the society "like to cause each other pain," and we do not know that they make the noise BANG only for this purpose. Further, we do not have the privileged information that "the convention is not a realization of any underlying constitutive rules." As a matter of fact, let us imagine that the question, "Is this convention a realization of underlying constitutive rules?" is one to which we are seeking an answer.

How do we know, in this situation, whether or not there are underlying constitutive rules? Imagine that we do not know anything about motivation or ultimate purpose. We proceed to investigate this strange society and find out eventually that there is a game of "punking," with the rule "Punking is achieved when you say BANG in someone's ear." That the banger may feel pleasure and the bangee pain is entirely beside the point. We may then conclude that in this Bang society there are "underlying constitutive rules" involved, and that saying BANG counts as punking.

On the other hand, imagine that we exchange narrators, and narrate the chess-in-different-countries tale from the vantage point of omniscience. We imagine a secret international society of hedonists who take great pleasure in moving pieces of different sizes and shapes around on boards of various designs and colors. When the pieces are in certain positions relative to each other, these people experience the greatest pleasure. Then we would be able to say about chess as Searle does about BANG that "the conventional device(s) (are) device(s) to achieve a natural effect. There is no rule to the effect that moving the pieces counts as causing pleasure; one can feel the pleasure whether or not one knows the conventions." In other words, the difference between chess and BANG is not the existence or nonexistence of "constitutive rules" or that one is a conventional activity and the other something else. The difference lies in the telling of the tale. In one case the narrator sets the condition that "chess is played in different countries according to different conventions," and in the other he sets the condition of a "society of sadists who like to cause each other pain." Change the narrative voice and you change the conclusions to be inferred.

Of course, I am playing a game, and so is Searle. I don't mind playing games. Indeed, I enjoy it. My objection to Searle, though, is that he underestimates the complexity of the game he is playing. Take the analogy between chess and language as constitutive-rule governed activities. There is a fundamental complication involved in this analogy that Searle overlooks completely. Think, for a moment, of the position of a chess player vis-à-vis the game of chess. If he is a genuine chess player, he knows at any given moment that there are rules of chess; he knows what these rules are; he has the mental capacity to retain all the rules and also any given game of chess he is playing in his mind at one instant. Or, in the case of Searle himself, he can achieve a distance from the game of chess that enables him to see, in the mind's eye so to speak, the rules, the players, and the field of play simultaneously. Hence, he can say that the game of chess exists only by virtue of the rules of chess.

But now try to project this situation onto language itself. To begin with, what are the rules of chess? That question raises its ugly head again, and to maintain consistency, Searle would have to answer the rules are verbal expressions. So that, we must conclude that chess could not exist if not for the prior existence of language. But what about language itself? If rules must exist before language can exist, and if rules are verbal expressions, then we are left with the same chicken/egg dilemma that faced us when we were talking about "making a promise." How can there be verbal expressions before there is language, and how can we have language without preexistent (by definition) constitutive rules?

Let me just mention another complexity that Searle evades. When he talks about making specifications about "football" and about "sending-invitations-two-weeks-in-advance," is he really talking about football and sending-invitations, etc., or is he actually talking about the rules of making specifications, which are ultimately rules of language? For example, imagine that there are no "rules of football," but that I claim to have a "concept" of "football." Imagine, further, that I notice a group of men engaged in an activity which somehow fits my "concept," and I then make the "specification," "They played football." I do not see what is to constrain me from making such a "specification." On the other hand, if I accept a rule that "A specification is an utterance describing an activity related to a set of 'rules,' and no utterance describing any activity that is not rule-governed can in any way be considered a 'specification,' " then it is clear that I "cannot" (maybe better, I *would* not) make the specification "they played football" if there were no rules of football. But my inability to make a specification under these conditions would have nothing to do with the question of whether there can be such an activity as football without there being rules of football. My inability (or unwillingness) to make the specification would be purely a verbal matter, depending on whether I accept a certain definition of what constitutes making specifications.

Rules of games are arbitrary. Perhaps the rule of checkmate as it now exists in chess makes for the most interesting games of chess. But there is no reason that there should not have been a rule that checkmate is taking the king, or that the player with the most pieces after thirty moves is the winner, regardless of position or further possibilities for continuation. Or there seems to be no reason why a home run should not count as two runs scored if it is hit to the farthest reaches of the centerfield bleachers. Hence, I would say that to the extent that speaking a language may be a form of rule-governed behavior it is not governed by rules that create "necessary and sufficient" conditions, but by conventions that can be changed by the slightest shift in wind direction.

In one respect, moreover, language is even more arbitrary than other games. The rules of other-than-language games are calculated, by their very nature, to respect human limitations. For example, one would not make up a rule that the object used as a ball in football will be an object weighing at least eight hundred pounds. Or one would not make a rule that one is allowed to move a chessman only by grasping it between one's eyelids. The language game, however, is not only no respecter of human limitations, one of its most important functions is its capacity to inspire language users to move beyond the limitations seemingly inherent in the human condition and in language itself. Hence, it is possible to utter striking provocative sentences like, "The heavens are telling the glory of God," which, as far as I can tell, would not qualify as a speech act in Searle's system. If the philosophy of speech acts makes the claim that human lives are both shaped by, and permeated with, language, one would not want to deny that. But Searle's thesis that "speaking a language is a form of rule-governed behavior" is only partly true. Language, like human beings, can often be unruly, and for the poet, as Hart Crane put it, "Language has built towers and bridges but itself is inevitably as fluid as always."

Postmodern or Post-Auschwitz
The Case of Poe

I wish to examine that quality in Poe that enables us to think about him in so many different guises, and I would like to speculate on what it is specifically that may link Poe to "postmodern" criticism. We may think of Poe as a wholly antiquated eighteenth-century gothic writer in the Monk Lewis tradition, who somehow blundered into mid-nineteenth-century liberal, Enlightenment America. Vernon L. Parrington found that "the surprising thing is that such a man should have made his appearance in an America given over to hostile ideas"—by which Parrington meant that nineteenth-century Enlightenment America was hardly the kind of society one would expect to give rise to gothic extravagance and effete aestheticism. It is also tempting to think of Poe as a writer distinctly of his time, sharing with fellow great mid-nineteenth-century writers, like Hawthorne and Melville, leanings toward dark Romanticism and "the power of blackness." Harry Levin, of course, includes Poe in the triumvirate making up *The Power of Blackness*, and G. R. Thompson has edited a collection of essays on Poe entitled *The Gothic Imagination: Essays in Dark Romanticism*. Paradoxically, we may also consider Poe as a writer who was anachronistic not so much in looking back to eighteenth-century gothic traditions but in looking forward to French symbolism and modernism (as has been amply demonstrated by Patrick F. Quinn and Charles Feidelson, Jr.). We can also think of Poe as a writer who anticipated the post-World War II despair of the Existentialists, as I tried to demonstrate in an analysis of "The Pit and the Pendulum."[1]

And now, in an age of critical movements designated variously, and in rapid shifts, as semiotics, poststructuralism, deconstruction, and postmodernism, it is possible to look at Poe as a deconstructionist who deconstructs one of his own poems in "The Philosophy of Composition." But in the present essay, I want to think about Poe in terms of what has come to be called postmodernism, except that I should like to jettison this indeterminate, pseudohistoricist term and replace it with what I believe is the more focused and more accurately historical designation, the post-Auschwitz age. For though I cannot say what is meant by postmodern, except that it is somehow antithetically related to Modernism, I believe I can identify what I mean by post-Auschwitz. In brief, the post-Auschwitz age is one in which the nineteenth-century prophecies of Marx and Nietzsche have been realized in the Soviet gulag, on the one hand, and in the Nazi death camps on the other. As George Steiner put it in a recent issue of the *TLS*, "The doctrines or pseudo-doctrines of nineteenth and early twentieth-century chauvinism, of Marxism-Leninism, of Fascism and of National Socialism were . . . European. . . . Auschwitz and the Gulag, the systematic incineration from the air of great cities evolved from inside the politics, the technologies and the vocabularies of European culture."[2]

Whatever postmodernism may be, the post-Auschwitz age is one of total war, mass murder, and genocide; an age of the death of God and of the eclipse of Western culture and Judeo-Christian values; an age that has witnessed the end of illusions about human potential and about the indomitable goodness of the human spirit; an age of the breakdown of the Renaissance concept of the human form as that Judeo-Christian fusion of flesh and spirit so eloquently described by Hamlet in his speech to Rosencrantz and Guildenstern:

What a piece of work is a man, how noble in reason, how infinite in faculties, in form and moving; how express and admirable in action; how like an angel in apprehension, how like a god; the beauty of the world, the paragon of animals.[3]

Although Poe obviously could not have known the writings of either Marx or Nietzsche, his imagination somehow gained access to a vision of the disintegration of the human form that was enacted in the death camps and the gulag, a disintegration that we, in the latter half of the twentieth century, have been witness to. While Emerson was preaching what became the mainstream American message of the glories of the organic unity of form and the infinitude of the human spirit and of human potential, Poe had already perceived the beginnings of disintegration of the self. In fact, I cannot take credit for being the first to notice this phenomenon. Allen Tate showed himself to be not only a most penetrating New Critical close reader but a historically conscious one when he wrote, as early as 1951, without specifically making the connection to events of the Nazi era, that "Poe is . . . a man we must return to: a figure of transition, who retains a traditional insight into a disorder that has since become typical, without being able himself to control it."[4] I should like to note one more lucid insight in Tate's deservedly influential, enabling essay that I shall return to later, in discussing *The Narrative of Arthur Gordon Pym*: "Poe was a religious man," Tate wrote elsewhere in the essay, "whose Christianity, for reasons that nobody knows anything about, had got short-circuited . . ."[5] Poe, then, is postmodern because he gave us not only the earliest, but also some of the most powerful descriptions of human beings in the process of disintegration: human beings who are forced to survive *in extremis,* as of course Pym himself is required to do again and again.

D. H. Lawrence was, as far as I know, the first to perceive this strain in Poe. But as was often the case with Lawrence, his dislike of everything he thought Poe stood for led him to blame the messenger for the message. Poe, he asserted, "is absolutely concerned with the disintegration-process of his own psyche."[6] Having knowledge of the Nazi death camps and the Soviet gulag, as Lawrence did not, we can see, now, that Poe was not recording "the disintegration-process [only] of his own psyche" but of the collective psyche of Western culture. The uncanny accuracy of Poe's prophetic vision of the disintegration of the human psyche, as noted by both Lawrence and Tate, is attested to by Bruno Bettelheim, a Viennese psychologist who spent a year in Dachau and Buchenwald (before 1939). The "most dedicated followers" of the Nazi state, he wrote,

> were destroyed as persons in our sense, as may be seen from . . . the story of [Rudolph] Hoess, commander of Auschwitz. . . . While his physical death came later, he became a living corpse from the time he assumed command of Auschwitz. . . . But he had to divest himself so entirely of self respect and self love, of feeling and personality, that for all practical purposes he was little more than a machine functioning only as his superiors flicked the buttons of command.[7]

It is commonplace for European critics and men of letters to trace the beginnings of contemporary literature, and the depiction of the postmodern condition, to Baudelaire or Mallarmé. The following statement from José Ortega y Gasset's "The Dehumanization of Art" is typical:

> Poetry had to be disencumbered. Laden with human matter it was dragging along, skirting the ground and bumping into trees and housetops like a deflated balloon. Here Mallarmé was the liberator who restored to the lyrical its ethereal quality and ascending power. Perhaps he did not reach the goal himself. Yet it was he who gave the decisive order: shoot ballast.[8]

Ortega the Spaniard is still Eurocentric, though not as aggressively so as the American, Harold Bloom, who apparently accepted the labor of reviewing the Library of America volumes of Poe, edited by Patrick Quinn and G. R. Thompson, for the express purpose of trying to diminish Poe's importance as a writer and thinker in the context of world literature. Bloom writes,

> Poe's mythology, like the mythology of psychoanalysis that we cannot bear to acknowledge as primarily a mythology, is particularly appropriate to any modernism, whether you want to call it early, high, or postmodernism. The definitive judgment belongs to T. W. Adorno, certainly the most authentic theoretician of modernism, in his last book, *Aesthetic Theory.*[9]

Bloom goes on to quote Adorno at length, but I will pick up only the last two Adorno sentences: "Baudelaire marks a watershed, in that art after him seeks to discard illusion without resigning itself to being a thing among things. The harbingers of modernism, Poe and Baudelaire, were the first technocrats of art." But even this modest mention is more praise for Poe from an adored European intellectual than Bloom can stand, so he adds that "Baudelaire was more than a technocrat of art, as Adorno knew, but Poe would be only that except for his mythmaking gift." That is a very large "but," especially when one considers that Bloom did not find "mythmaking" so negligible a virtue when he wrote the book *Shelley's Mythmaking* some twenty-five years earlier. In a final burst of pique, Bloom asserts that "Poe is a great fantasist whose thoughts were commonplace and whose metaphors were dead."

In fact, one could only wish that Bloom were right about this, because if Poe's metaphors had been less alive and his thoughts not so uncannily prophetic, we would be living in a more peaceful and less threatening age. But nothing could be further from the truth. Poe's thoughts were far from commonplace for his time, and his metaphors were more alive than he could have hoped and than humanity could have feared. As has been more than amply demonstrated by Patrick Quinn, Poe's thoughts and metaphors not only were alive when Poe uttered them, but they quickly found new life in France. "In *L'Art romantique*," Quinn writes, Baudelaire

calls Poe simply "the most powerful writer of the age." . . . The sincerity underlying . . . this statement . . . may be inferred from the allusion, in *Journaux intimes*, to his morning prayers to God and to Edgar Poe as his intercessor in heaven. For Mallarmé also, Poe was a writer altogether unique, *the* poet, as we know from "Le Tombeau d'Edgar Poe." For him as for Baudelaire the stature of Poe was evidently that of a literary deity.[10]

In his powerful, authoritative account of the historical, cultural, sociological, psychological, and literary developments that led up to the Nazi death camps, Erich Kahler cites Baudelaire as having started a chain of literary events, carried on by Rimbaud, Laforgue, and Mallarmé, among others, that formed "the bridge to the *hommes absurdes et revoltes* of our own age, and in all of whom we can observe the symptoms of the same psychic disease." Of the European authors who formed the late nineteenth-century and early twentieth-century links in this chain, including Nietzsche, Ibsen, and Dostoyevsky, Kahler writes:

None of these men stood for their countries alone. What else did these great authors express, most of them with the help of a newly developed psychological perception, but the deep unrest, uneasiness and alarm at the effects of our modern middle-class civilization: the increasing hollowness and precariousness of conventional values, the derangement of human relations? What else did they voice but the rumbling of revolutionary forces, of a whole underground level of reality that burst into the open in the various crises of the twentieth century? [11]

Certainly in the cases of Baudelaire, Mallarmé, and Dostoyevsky, the "newly developed psychological perception" owed something to Poe. But the questioning of values is also a basic strain in Poe's writings: "the deep unrest, uneasiness and alarm at the effects of our modern middle-class civilization: [a sense] of the increasing hollowness and precariousness of conventional values, the derangement of human relations." And of course we can see this uneasiness in Pym. As Quinn points out, Pym keeps running away from the traditional family and from middle-class culture, as represented by his family.[12]

In addition to the new psychology and the questioning of values, Poe established for the Romantic poets a new relationship between nature and consciousness. In describing the qualities that make Mallarmé both a Romantic and a postmodern writer, Paul de Man writes that for Mallarmé

Nature, far from representing the satisfaction of a happy unproblematic sensation, evokes instead separation and distance; nature is for him the substance from which we are forever separated. . . . The symbols of failure and of negativity that play such an important role in his poetry must be understood in terms of the underlying polarity between the world of nature and the activity of consciousness.[13]

I think there can be no doubt that Poe, who in this was so different from the British Romantics, is also at the root of this particular strain in Romantic poetry, an "underlying polarity between the world of nature and the activity of consciousness" that we can translate into the term *alienation*. In fact, Gaston Bachelard makes just this point in talking about *The Narrative of Arthur Gordon Pym*, asserting that "Poe hears the call of the ocean 'because this call comes from the most dramatic of solitudes, one in which man has for his antagonist the elemental world itself. There man is alone . . . faced with a universe of monstrous forces.' " [14] I would say, further, that it is the fusion of this sense of alienation with Poe's inversion of values that results in what is perhaps Poe's most pronounced post-Auschwitz quality, his vision of the dehumanized person.

As is well known, D. H. Lawrence refused to accept the validity of Poe's vision of the dehumanized person, attributing Poe's perception to his personal sexual dysfunction and to what Lawrence took to be American Puritan attitudes toward sexuality: "All Poe's style," Lawrence observed, "has this mechanical quality, as his poetry has a mechanical rhythm. He never sees anything in terms of life, almost always in terms of matter, jewels, marble, etc. . . ." [15] But it was the nineteenth-century writer Poe who was right about the fateful path on which Western culture had embarked, and Lawrence who was rowing against the tide in trying to reassert a Romantic organicism.

Poe's vision of dehumanized man may be found even in a relatively verisimilitudinous work like *The Narrative of Arthur Gordon Pym*, a work that Poe wrote out of a multitude of both literary and documentary sources, as is definitively established in Richard Kopley's recent essay, "The Very Profound Under-current of Arthur Gordon Pym." [16] Poe's vision of dehumanization is apparent in the last two journal entries in the novel. As Grace Farrell Lee has demonstrated in "The Quest of Arthur Gordon Pym," the ending is a culmination of a descent into Hell and into the subconscious. [17] But it is also, I believe— on a less positive note than Farrell Lee—a return to chaos and a disassembling of the Judeo-Christian construct of the human form, an unravelling, so to speak, of the divine creation:

We were evidently approaching [the cataract] with a hideous velocity. At intervals there were visible in it wide, yawning, but momentary rents, and from out these rents, within which was a chaos of flitting and indistinct images, there came rushing and mighty, but soundless winds, tearing up the enkindled ocean in their course. [18]

Though Poe's novel may count among its themes a return to chaos, nevertheless *Pym* remains a work of art in which Poe scholars have traced a number of thematic and structural patterns.

These patterns, however, are often parodic. As Lee puts it, in speaking about the death and rebirth pattern, Poe's "parodic vision creates a mock communion from a scene of cannibalism by interfusing it with allusions to the last supper of Christ." [19] But it is not only that they are parodic, the patterns of conventional Judeo-Christian (which is to say the fusion of Hellenic-Roman and biblical) culture are ruptured. The conventional unifying symbols and consolidating metaphors of the culture are shattered. For example, the narrator describes his state of mind just before the four survivors are to draw lots to decide who will be cannibalized. "Even then," he writes, "I could not bring myself to arrange the splinters upon the spot, but thought over every species of finesse by which I could trick some one of my fellow sufferers to draw the short straw, as it had been agreed that whoever drew the shortest of the four splinters from my hand was to die for the preservation of the rest" (p. 134). Here the crucifixion as a symbol of God's redemptive power is returned to an absurd physicality, as the purely physical term "preservation" is used to portray the salvation of the cannibals.

It may also be of value to call attention to the parallel and disjunction between the drawing of lots here and the skill involved in playing the game of "even and odd" as it is described in "The Purloined Letter," and which has been exhaustively commented on by the two postmodern Jacques, Lacan and Derrida. [20] They have been able to convert the game itself into an eternal circle precisely because Poe knew that he was describing a game that in its purest form is infinitely circular. The schoolboy who "attracted universal admiration" for his skill in the game has converted the pure game of guessing into a test of psychological acumen. But the way in which the boy explains this acumen is itself is a mockery of the human form.

When I wish to find out how wise, or how stupid, or how good, or how wicked is any one, or what are his thoughts at the moment, I fashion the expression on my face, as accurately as possible, in accordance with the expression of his, and then wait to see what thoughts or sentiments arise in my mind or heart, as if to match or correspond with the expression. [21]

The schoolboy has mastered a guessing game by converting it into a psychological game. But in *The Narrative of Arthur Gordon Pym*, the game of lots is in earnest, and Poe knows it. James W. Gargano has reminded us that Poe's narrators are not always the same narrator and are not always Poe.[22] In this instance, we have a confirmation of Baudelaire's observation that *Arthur Gordon Pym* was "a purely human book."[23] Here the game of drawing of lots, which is a variant of the game of "even and odd" is not only in earnest but a matter of life and death. And here, as we can see, Poe takes an attitude toward the game that is quite different from that taken by Dupin in "The Purloined Letter."

Poe, of all people, recognized that death was not a game, a fact which seems to have escaped the two Jacques. Poe was, as all his readers quickly perceive, obsessed with thoughts and fears of death. And this is no less true of his "purely human book" than of his "mechanical" tales. It is not just death that Poe described, however, but violent death and murder, in *Pym*, as in many of the tales. But here again, Poe had moved into the post-Auschwitz (or postmodernist, if one prefers) consciousness, leaving his more optimistic fellow Romantics in the dust. While the British Romantics were still ephebes struggling with the shadow of their great precursor, the author of *Paradise Lost*, trying to make some sense of the heroic grandeur of evil as personified in Milton's Satan, Poe had already arrived at the post-Auschwitz recognition of what has been called (controversially) the banality of evil. In his Preface to *Prometheus Unbound*, Shelley declared, obviously with Milton in mind, that "The only imaginary being resembling in any degree Prometheus is Satan."[24] As we can see in the lot-drawing episode, Poe had passed beyond the belief that there was some epic grandeur in evil.

I cannot, therefore, agree with Walter Bezanson, who finds a "solemn rhythm" in the description of the cannibalistic act.[25] Indeed, the description, following the narrator's earlier protestations of disgust and revulsion, is all too matter-of-fact:

Let it suffice to say that, having in some measure appeased the raging thirst which consumed us by the blood of the victim, and having by common consent taken off the hands and feet, and head, throwing them together with the entrails, into the sea, we devoured the rest of the body, piecemeal, during the four ever memorable days of the seventeenth, eighteenth, nineteenth, and twentieth of the month. (p. 135)

Moreover, the very next sentence is so off-handed as to make the reader almost forget the horror that has just been described: "On the nineteenth, there coming on a smart shower which lasted fifteen or twenty minutes, we contrived to catch some water by means of a sheer which had been fished up from the cabin by our drag just after the gale."

We need not look far in the canon of Holocaust literature to find an analogue to Poe's prophetic fiction. I shall cite here two entries from the diary of Johann Kremer, doctor of medicine and philosophy, who kept part of this diary while serving as a physician in Auschwitz. The entries are dated September 5 and 6, 1942. The first entry reads:

> This noon was present at a special action in the women's camp ("moslems")—the most horrible of all horrors. Obersturmfuhrer Thilo, military surgeon, is right when he said today to me we were located here in '*anus mundi*.' In evening at about 8 P.M. another special action with a draft from Holland. Men compete to take part in such actions as they get additional rations. . . .

The editor of the diary has appended Kremer's explanation of the September 5 entry, given in a deposition to a war crimes tribunal:

> Particularly unpleasant had been the action of gassing emaciated women . . . I remember taking part in the gassing of such women in daylight. I am unable to state how numerous that group had been. When I came to the bunker they sat clothed on the ground. . . . I could deduce from the behaviour of these women that they realized what was awaiting them. They begged the SS men to be allowed to live, they wept, but all of them were driven to the gas chamber and gassed. Being an anatomist I had seen many horrors, had to do with corpses, but what I then saw was not to be compared with anything seen ever before.

In the next day's entry, Kremer writes,

> Today an excellent Sunday dinner: tomato soup, one half of chicken with potatoes and red cabbage (20 grammes of fat), dessert and magnificent vanilla ice-cream. After dinner we welcomed the new garrison doctor, Obersturmfuhrer Wirths. . . . [26]

The dissociation of sensibility and the atrophy of human conscience detectable in the Nazi Kremer's matter-of-fact depiction of the atrocity and of his own "horror" are anticipated in the narrator's description, in "The Tell-Tale Heart," of why he has murdered his victim:

Object there was none. I loved the old man. He had never wronged me. He had never given me insult. For his gold I had no desire.

The narrator's consciousness here reflects one of Tate's observations about Poe that can be applied, without missing a beat, not only to Kremer, but also to "postmodernist" criticism: "We get the third hypertrophy of a human faculty: the intellect moving in isolation from both love and moral will, whereby it declares itself independent of the human situation in the quest of essential knowledge." [27] But Poe, to do him justice, knew that his narrator was mad. Kremer, like the narrator in Poe's story, thinks he is sane.

The concluding sentences of Pym's final journal entry remain a challenge to Poe scholars, and I do not hope to resolve them here. I would, however, for my own purposes, like to point out that they embody two disfigurations of the human form, one a physical disfiguration and the other a disfiguration of color: "But there arose in our pathway a shrouded human figure, very far larger in its proportions than any dweller among men. And the hue of the skin of the figure was of the perfect whiteness of the snow" (p. 206).

The closing sentence evokes echoes of Isaiah 1:18, in particular, "Though your sins be as scarlet, They shall be as white as snow. . . ." In the biblical verse, the whiteness of snow is equated with moral purity. But in *Pym* the image of whiteness has become—not terrifying, I believe, as Melville makes it in "The Whiteness of the Whale"— but repulsive, perhaps because it is associated with the disfigured human form in the previous sentence. Poe's inversion of the symbol of purity into an image of disgust is, once again, an anticipation of the inversion of values that characterizes our post-Auschwitz age.

Deconstruction and Humanism
after Auschwitz

Auschwitz constitutes the historical context framing postmodernist antihumanism as embodied in deconstructionist literary theory and criticism. The historical uniqueness of the Nazi genocide lay not only in the totality and intensity of the cruelty that human beings inflicted on other human beings, but in the systematic dehumanization of the victims as a precondition for the slaughter. The German racist ideology that bred the death camps was, among other things, a deliberate and planned assault on the human spirit, as testimony that began to appear soon after the war ended has shown.[1] In 1947, Ramon Guthrie observed that in the concentration camp system, "Death and corruption of the body were calculated to coincide with and spread death and corruption of the spirit."[2] It is misleading to disengage contemporary antihumanism from Nazi dehumanization, for they share philosophical and cultural origins.

Thanks to Victor Farias's courage and tenacious detective work, we can no longer ignore the question of the connections between the thinking of Martin Heidegger and his long-term affiliation with, and lifetime refusal to repudiate, Nazi ideology.[3] It is now clear that Heidegger's attraction to National Socialism and his extended membership in the Nazi party were consistent with, rather than aberrant to, his thinking. By the same token, it is also becoming possible to contemplate connections between National Socialism and the post-

Auschwitz perpetuation of Heidegger-inspired antihumanist theories in the guise of what has come to be called postmodernism.[4]

The myth (perhaps "disinformation" would be a better word) persists and has been deliberately perpetuated that antihumanism not only does not suggest a rejection of humane values but actually advocates a greater humaneness than humanism itself. David Farrell Krell introduces Heidegger's "Letter on Humanism" by cautioning,

> But any opposition to humanism sounds like a rejection of humanity and of human values. Heidegger therefore discusses the meaning of "values" and of the "nihilism" that ostensibly results when such things are put in question. He finds—as Nietzsche did—that not the denial of such values but their installation in the first place is the source of nihilism. For establishment of values anticipates their disestablishment, both actions amounting to a willful self-congratulation of the representing subject.[5]

Is this not a strange logic? Stating Krell's argument in less abstract terms, he seems to be saying that the only consequence of, let us say, the "establishment of justice" as a value, is to "anticipate" the "disestablishment of justice." In other words, we should not strive to create a just society because such a society could only lead to the creation of an injust society. We should give up "humanist values" because they eventually will be corrupted. Hence, starting out with no values at all is preferable to having values that may be good in themselves, for precisely because these values may be good in themselves, they will inevitably become corrupted (disestablished). This would seem to be another way of saying that since human beings are inherently corruptible (fallen into original sin), they should avoid clinging to values that stand to be undermined by this corruptibility. Is this not, then, an argument for a leader who will determine all values and control all phases of all individual lives, thus saving his subjects from their own corruptibility? But is Krell's argument Heideggerian?

Indeed, the authority for Krell's argument and for his denial of any connection between antihumanism and inhumanity comes directly from Heidegger himself, who answered Jean Beaufret's letter requesting a clarification of Heideggerian philosophy with a response that has become the well-known and much discussed "Letter on Humanism" ("Über den Humanismus"). In spite of its title, the letter is not so much about humanism as it is an attack on humanist values. In euphemizing his antihumanist stance, Heidegger asserted:

> Because we are speaking against "humanism" people fear a defense of the inhuman [*Inhumanen*] and a glorification of barbaric brutality. For what is more "logical" than that for somebody who negates humanism nothing remains but the affirmation of inhumanity [*Unmenschlichkeit*]. . . .
> Because in all the respects mentioned we everywhere speak against all that humanity deems high and holy [it is assumed that] our philosophy teaches an irresponsible and destructive "nihilism." [6]

Written in 1946, when the ashes of Auschwitz had hardly cooled, Heidegger's claim for the harmlessness of his antihumanism warrants some further consideration. Is he, perhaps, being disingenuous? Is it wholly unjustified, in the wake of Auschwitz, for readers to suspect that one who speaks against "humanism" may indeed be glorifying the "barbaric" and affirming *Unmenschlichkeit*? And would it be only an absurd and discredited logic that would lead readers to assume that a philosophy that "speaks . . . everywhere . . . against all that humanity deems high and holy" is indeed teaching "an irresponsible and destructive " 'nihilism'?" If "all that humanity deems high and holy" consists of the sanctity of human life, of love and respect between human and human, of human dignity and love of justice, then is not a philosophy that "speaks everywhere" against these ideas glorifying the "barbaric" and affirming *Unmenschlichkeit*?

Heidegger's contemptuous dismissal of "all that humanity deems high and holy" implies that only those who are still in thrall to a discredited "logic" would insist that a denunciation of humanism is tantamount to an affirmation of the inhuman. But in fact, as a member of the Nazi party from 1933 to 1945, Heidegger certainly should have known by 1946 that one of the powerful appeals of Nazism was its assertion of primitivism and barbarism against humanism, and he should have known by that time that the Nazi assault on humanism helped to shape the mentality that implemented the death camps. In 1940, Hermann Rauschning, a former National Socialist and member of Hitler's inner circle, published an account of Hitler's table talk. Rauschning tells us that in speaking of his cultured ministerial colleagues, Hitler often mocked their pretentiousness and enjoyed shocking them:

"They regard me as an uneducated barbarian," he exclaimed jubilantly. "Yes, we are barbarians! We want to be barbarians! It is an honorable title. We shall rejuvenate the world! This world is near its end. It is our mission to cause unrest.

He then launched into a verbose exposition of what he called an "historical necessity." Barbarian forces, he claimed must break into decadent civilizations in order to snatch the torch of life from their dying fires. Then he began to speak of the treatment of Communists and Socialists.

"These people thought I would handle them with kid gloves, that I would be satisfied with speeches," he scoffed. "We are not in a position to dally with humane feelings, nor can I undertake tedious investigations into anyone's good-will or innocence. We must shake off all sentimentality and be hard. Some day, when I order war, I shall not be in a position to hesitate because of the ten million young men I shall be sending to their death. It is preposterous," he continued, growing indignant, "to expect me to look only for the real criminals among the Communists. It is just like the cowardly, inconsistent *bourgeoisie* to pacify their consciences with legal proceedings.[7]

Unlike Heidegger, Hitler did not engage in apologetics or in elaborate rationalizations of his true aims, so in his table talk he was candid about the goals and ideals of National Socialism. He proclaimed openly and clearly that National Socialism was a war against "bourgeois values," and he did not obscure the issue by claiming that one could defend the inhuman and at the same time not glorify the barbaric. Hitler also perceived that in "speak[ing] against all that humanity deems high and holy" (i.e., in speaking against bourgeois values as embodied in both Judeo-Christian ideology and in the ideology of Enlightenment liberal democracy), he was indeed calling for a return to a new barbarism. Hence, Hitler would not bother with bourgeois "legal proceedings" that hold that all are innocent till proved guilty, that those accused of committing a crime should receive a fair trial, and that only those who are actually convicted of having committed a crime should be punished. Those who are familiar with the Nietzsche-Heidegger-derived theories of Michel Foucault will have noticed that there is not much distance between Hitler's disdain for bourgeois "legal proceedings" and Foucault's attempts to discredit bourgeois ideas of justice in *Discipline and Punish*. But in Auschwitz we see where that contempt for "legal proceedings" led.

In 1933, the same year that Heidegger announced that "The Fuhrer himself and he alone is German reality and its law, today and henceforth,"[8] Lion Feuchtwanger published a devastating portrait of life in Germany during the period of Hitler's rise to power. Feuchtwanger's vision of Nazi Germany in 1933, confirms the accuracy of what Marcuse wrote to Heidegger in May of 1948: "We knew, and I myself have seen, that the beginning already harbored the end; it was the end. Nothing has been added that was not already there in the beginning."[9] Feuchtwanger saw the meaning of the beginning, and also that "the beginning . . . harbored the end. . . ."

One of the narrative strands of Feuchtwanger's *The Oppermanns* depicts the rise of National Socialism as a struggle between barbarism and humanism. Berthold Oppermann, one of the younger generation of the family and a student, is preparing a class presentation on the topic of "Humanism and the Twentieth Century" under the guidance of Dr. Heinzius, a humanist of the old school. When Dr. Heinzius is killed in an accident, his class is taken over by Bernd Vogelsang, a National Socialist, who is also a "member of the 'Young Eagles,' . . . the secret society of the youth of Germany."[10] Vogelsang disapproves Berthold's topic as too abstract, and in a conference to discuss the topic calculates that Berthold must be Jewish, and therefore must be humiliated: "There were Jewish Oppermanns and there were Christian Oppermanns. No need for a long investigation. The Jew, the despoiler, the enemy, betrays himself to the expert at a glance. Humanism and the Twentieth Century. They always hide themselves behind masks of long words" (p. 60). He eventually pressures Berthold to change his topic from "Humanism" to "What can we learn today from Arminius the German?" (p. 61).

Arminius the Cheruscan, a Germanic tribal leader who defeated Roman legions led by Varus in 9 A.D., became a cult hero to National Socialists.[11] After extensive research and soul-searching, Berthold comes to the conclusion that Arminius did not have much of an impact on world culture, and in the course of his talk, he inadvertently remarks that "The achievement of Arminius . . . remained, practically, without significance" (p. 93), prompting Vogelsang to demand that he retract his assertion. When Berthold sticks to his guns, Vogelsang subjects him to a long campaign of harrassment that finally drives him to take his own life. There is a climactic moment when the old humanist rector of the school, intimidated by Vogelsang, presents Berthold with an ultimatum: Either he recants or he will be expelled. Shocked by the ultimatum, Berthold thinks, "We are all turning into swine . . . These times are turning us all into swine and ruffians." (p. 205)

After recovering his composure, he tries to sort things out, thinking aloud to the Rector:

"When we were reading Hebbel," he finally began, slowly and deliberately, "Gyges and His Ring, Dr. Heinzius told us that throughout Hebbel there was only one theme: the wounded dignity of man. *Laesa humanitas.* . . . Dr. Heinzius explained to us very clearly just what *laesa humanitas* meant. Did only the old kings have *humanitas*? . . . Am I a bad German because Dr. Heinzius happened to get run over? He never used to interrupt our lectures. He let us speak to the end. (pp. 205–206)

Feuchtwanger understood in 1933 that Nazi ideology took its stand against humanism and "liberal democracy"; thus he dramatized the struggle between antihumanist regimentation and humanist individualism as one of the central conflicts in the novel. The latter, Feuchtwanger perceived, operates on the basis of a respect for the integral person and the conscience of the inexorable self, a caring for human dignity, and a tolerance for the speech and thought of others, while the antihumanist state seeks to destroy all of the above. After the war, Heidegger complained to Marcuse that Marcuse should not have expected him to foresee the consequences of Hitlerism because he had not been accorded the gift of prophecy. But it is more likely, as Farias insists, that Heidegger remained blind to the horrors inherent in Nazism because he was too much in tune with Hitlerist doctrines to want to know where they were leading, or after the war to know where they had led: "A genuine understanding of Heidegger's thought," Farias writes, "is impossible if one ignores [his] fidelity . . . to a whole spate of doctrines characteristic of National

Socialism: as in his radically discriminatory attitude regarding the intellectual superiority of the Germans, rooted in their language and their destiny; in his belief in the primacy of his own thought, much like Hölderlin's, taken as a paradigm and guide for the spiritual development of humanity itself; *in his radical opposition to any form of democracy*" (italics mine).[12]

Farias's indefatigable research into Heidegger's life and thinking convinced Farias that Heidegger's philosophy did not exclude a belief in racism rooted in the idea of a *Herrenvolk*, and did include a contempt for the doctrines of "liberal democracy." Heidegger's thinking also excluded the notion of the dignity of the individual human being, as was noted by Martin Buber in 1938. Discussing "the doctrine of Heidegger," Buber wrote that in Heidegger's thinking,

man reaches a condition when he can no longer stretch his hands out from his solitude to meet a divine form. That is at the basis of Nietzsche's saying, "God is dead." Apparently nothing more remains now to the solitary man but to seek an intimate communication with himself. This is the basic situation from which Heidegger's philosophy arises. . . .

There remains, however, one irrefragable fact, that one can stretch out one's hands to one's image or reflection in a mirror, but not to one's real self. Heidegger's doctrine is significant as the presentation of the relations to one another of various "beings" abstracted from human life, but it is not valid for human life itself and its anthropological understanding, however valuable its suggestions on this subject.[13]

Buber understood that one could not advocate a philosophy of antihumanism without disfiguring the human form. As a thinker and a Jew trained in German philosophy who had to leave Germany because of its racist and dehumanizing policies, how could he not be aware of the destructive element in antihumanism? He saw that Heideggerism was not only an antihumanism but a philosophy of despair that inevitably subverts the value of individual human lives. A later commentator confirms Buber's view of what was at the heart of Heideggerian philosophy. "In *Being and Time*," writes Laszlo Versenyi,

Heidegger rightly distinguished between ontic and ontological beings, between Angelus Silesius' roses and men, between the life without why and the life of care and concern. But precisely because he was right there, his present relinquishing of what alone distinguishes man from all other beings is a relinquishing of the humanity of man. In *Being and Time* Heidegger counseled facing death as a way of salvation for man. But in his last writings he goes a great deal further and advocates death pure and simple. Since merely facing death but not actually projecting ourselves into this "ultimate possibility" failed to reflect us back into authentic existence, he now advocates that we actually project ourselves into this possibility and commit (moral and intellectual, i.e. human) suicide.[14]

Within the historical context of National Socialism and the terror state, Heideggerian antihumanism becomes something more sinister than a purely abstract and physically inconsequential attack on metaphysics. In the light of the historical reality of Auschwitz, we can only perceive Heideggerian thinking as part of a culture dedicated to a complete and total negation of the value of the individual human life. Then the question becomes not whether humanism is still possible, but whether there is a real alternative to it, whether we are still willing to accept the consequences of a radical antihumanism after Auschwitz.

Framing the issue in this way, another historical phenomenon emerges more clearly. In speaking of Auschwitz we are speaking to an extent of the failure of Western culture in general, but we are also speaking more precisely of the development of a virulent strain of Western culture that achieved its most extreme form only in Germany. If it is true that any culture *might* have developed the death camp system, it is also true that only the Germans and German culture actually put a death-camp culture into practice.[15] Hitler fused age-old Christian anti-Semitism with Enlightenment racism and technology to create a culture of death.[16] Much as it may pain philosophers to admit it, Hitler and Heidegger shared a world outlook. Both sought to return German culture to pagan roots by rupturing that fusion between Hellenism and Hebraism that constitutes European humanism.[17]

No one expressed the significance of that fusion more clearly than Matthew Arnold in *Culture and Anarchy*. "The final aim of both Hellenism and Hebraism, as of all great spiritual disciplines," Arnold wrote, "is no doubt the same: man's perfection or salvation." [18] Arnold saw Hebraism and Hellenism as striving for the same sublime goal, but in his view they approached that goal from opposite perspectives. "The uppermost idea with Hellenism is to see things as they really are; the uppermost idea with Hebraism is conduct and obedience." In slightly different terms, he described the difference by asserting that "The governing idea of Hellenism is *spontaneity of consciousness;* that of Hebraism, *strictness of conscience.*[19] Although Arnold made it clear that he favored Hellenism for its moderation and "sweetness and light," he also granted that whatever it was that was civilized in Western cultures depended on the creative tension that existed between these forces. What Arnold especially did not like about Hebraism was its tendency to thwart "man's pursuit or attainment of that perfection of which Socrates talks so hopefully. . . ." Arnold felt that the Puritan (Hebraic) consciousness of "sin" tended to overshadow the Hellenic sense of sweetness and light. "It is all very well to talk of getting rid of one's ignorance," Arnold wrote, "of seeing things in their reality, seeing them in their beauty; but how is this to be done when there is something which thwarts and spoils all our efforts. This something is *sin.* . . ."[20]

In the years since the publication of *Culture and Anarchy,* our view of Hellenism has changed. Hellenic culture is no longer perceived as the exclusive embodiment of "sweetness and light." Friedrich Nietzsche underscored the dark strain in Hellenism by positing the origins of Greek tragedy as a tension between what he described as the Dionysian and the Apollonian.[21] As Nietzsche described it, the great achievement of Greek tragedy was to bring the dark forces of inspiration and the subconscious into balance with the desire for form and order. Converting Nietzsche's insight into Freudian terms, Norman O. Brown explained that Apollo is ". . . the god of sublimation." He is, further, "the god of form—of plastic form in art, of rational form in thought, of civilized form in life. But the Apollonian form is form as the negation of instinct."[22] Dionysus, on the other hand, is ". . . drunkenness; . . . life complete and immediate. . . . Dionysus does not observe the limit but overflows; for him the road of excess leads to the palace of wisdom. . . ."[23]

Writing from an American perspective that included a belief in humanist democratic principles of equality, political freedom, human and civil rights, and justice for everyone, Brown hoped it would be possible to transform the principle of civilization from an Apollonian sublimating psyche to an unshackled Dionysian spontaneity. Brown fused Jeffersonian, Madisonian, Emersonian, Nietzschean, and Freudian ideas with Christian eschatology to arrive at a vision of a nonviolent society in which humans, no longer repressing their sexual instincts, would once again (as in the prelapsarian Garden of Eden) live in perfect harmony, free from hatred, acquisitiveness, greed, frustration, and aggression. Brown's ahistorical vision, though written in the late fifties, remained oblivious to the dark side of Nietzschean Dionysianism reflected in Nazism.

Not so the vision of Thomas Mann. Feuchtwanger, in 1932–33, had tried to present an accurate portrait of what was happening in Germany under Nazi domination. In the process, he drew a prophetic picture of what would happen if the Nazis were to continue to gain power. Though he was prophetic, Feuchtwanger tended to attribute human behavior in Germany to fairly superficial motives. In *The Oppermanns*, people often commit evil acts for petty reasons. Wels, a competitor of the Oppermanns in the furniture business, hates Jews because he thinks that they have taken business from him by unfair competition. When the Nazis come to power he takes advantage of the new situation to get what he believes is coming to him. He acts out of a mixture of bigotry (dislike of the other) and opportunism. Similarly, the minor writer Gutwetter grasps at the chance to achieve fame and prominence by spouting the party line.

Mann wrote *Dr. Faustus* in the forties, when there could be no mistake about where Nazism and an ideology based on Nazi interpretations of Nietzsche were leading. Feuchtwanger had framed the rise of Nazism as a triumph of barbarism over humanism, of a xenophopic tribal culture over universal culture. Mann also perceived what was taking place in Germany in the thirties as a struggle between civilization and barbarism, but he cast the struggle in more complex terms. He presents Adrian Leverkuhn, presumably modeled in part on Nietzsche, as an artist remote from humanity and from true human intercourse, whose one sexual encounter has left him with a venereal disease that then intensifies his remoteness. Leverkuhn becomes a symbol of certain features of German culture and German society. As T. J. Reed observes, "An artist who sought to escape from the inhibitions of his conscious mind could stand for a society which sought to escape from the inhibitions men normally impose on their primitive instincts.... An intoxicated artist, an intoxicated nation." [24]

In his work-notes for the novel, written in 1943, Mann commented that "Deeper moral associations accumulated [around the Faust idea]. It is really a desire to escape from everything bourgeois, moderate, classical, . . . sober, industrious, and dependable into a world of drunken release, a life of bold Dionysiac genius, beyond society, indeed superhuman—above all subjectively, as experience and drunken intensification of the self, regardless of whether the world can go along with it. . . ." [25]

It is this artist's desire for "drunken release," and for a superhuman existence that goes beyond society—that is, beyond the long-accumulated traditional norms of socially defined good and evil—that Mann associates with excesses of Nazism. Mann himself goes on to expand on this notion that the artist's desire to escape from bourgeois social bonds has its parallel in the Nazi destruction of conventional norms of good and evil.

"The bursting of social bonds," he writes in the workbook, is also "political. Intellectual-spiritual fascism, throwing off of humane principle, recourse to violence, blood-lust, irrationalism, cruelty, Dionysiac denial of truth and justice, self-abandonment to the instincts and unrestrained 'Life,' which in fact is *death* and, insofar as it is life, only the *Devil's work*. Fascism [is] . . . a Devil-given departure from bourgeois society that leads through adventures of drunkenly intense subjective feeling and super-greatness to mental collapse and spiritual death. . . ." [26]

Mann, like Feuchtwanger, perceived that Nazism was a new barbarism, a culture of death that demanded the casting off of all moral, ethical, and religious restraints by members of what had been an advanced, sophisticated civilization. Writing as the Nazi genocide was in progress, Mann knew exactly where the barbarians of the twentieth century were to be found, and he realized that the Nazi call for a return to a primordial past was a regression to chthonic Dionysian drunkenness. Both Feuchtwanger and Mann saw Nazism as an attempt at a complete break with the historical-biblical past that had hitherto played such a significant role in civilizing Europeans. Heidegger, like the Nazi ideologues, wanted to break with Hebraism, as well as "metaphysics." But to achieve such a rupture, Christian and humanist values would have to be discarded too.

We are fond of imagining that the great thinkers are those who speak for their time yet rise above the limited ideology of their culture. But Heidegger, it is now becoming apparent, was a man of his time. From 1933 to 1945 at least, he did not dissent from the ideology of racism and positively endorsed a return to paganism.[27] On February 5, 1938, Jacques Maritain called attention to "the example and contagion of German racism . . . "[28] and went on to speak of "the somberly ardent face of pagan might which is revealing itself in men," and to point out that it is against the Jews

that racist neo-paganism first tried it strength. Its profound desire is undoubtedly, if that is possible, to drive every Jew out of the country [Germany]. But since this cannot be done, the solution has been decided upon of depriving them of political existence and of walling them up in a ghetto certainly more cruel than the ghetto of the Middle Ages, since men are now confined not because of a difference of faith and religion, against which human will and the grace of God always have recourse, but because of an irremediable difference of blood. Here we have racial anti-Semitism.[29]

How is it that the Christian Jacques Maritain in France saw what Heidegger the philosopher in Germany did not? Heidegger was blind to the ideology of "racist neo-paganism" and "racial anti-Semitism" ravaging his nation because he was too much a part of that ideology to recognize it. There were noble souls in Germany, like Martin Niemöller and Dietrich Bonhoeffer, who resisted Nazi racist ideology and paid a high price for doing so, but Heidegger was not one of that heroic and long-suffering company. At the very least, we must concede that he found nothing in his thinking that would motivate him to imitate their noble example. The primal thinker was, after all, very much a man of his time.

Through the seventies and eighties, deconstruction, a theory or methodology largely dependent on Heideggerian thinking, has become associated with issues normally associated with the menu of liberal democracy, such as equal treatment for women and minorities (racial ethnic, behavioral, or ideological), equitable distribution of wealth, and equal justice and opportunity for all. My contention in this book is that these are all worthy goals, but they are not the goals one could arrive at purely on the basis of deconstructionist ideologies; they are derived from the Enlightenment and Judeo-Christian ideologies of individualism and liberal democracy clearly set forth in the American Bill of Rights and in later constitutional amendments, especially Amendments 13, 14, 15, and 19. There is no doctrine of human rights in the literature of deconstruction. On the contrary, as Renaut and Ferry demonstrate, deconstructionist doctrine despises the ideology on which the concept of human rights is founded. Yet surely it was the ideology stated in the Declaration of Independence, the Constitution, the Bill of Rights, and the cited amendments that is responsible for the civil rights and feminist movements, which predated the appearance of deconstruction in this country.

Many academics with real or imagined grievances have seen in deconstructionism a methodology useful for attacking entrenched power and establishment thinking. But we must ask whether the same ideologies that brought us the gulag and the KZ-Lager can also provide the basis for a society of free individuals. Can literary theories based on an ideology that disdains all the institutions of democracy and disparages the individual as an inexorable self also safeguard human rights and freedom of the integral person? Is it pure coincidence that "political correctness," that is, the repression of unpopular or unapproved speech and thought, is most stringently enforced on those campuses where deconstructionism is most securely entrenched? Before accepting the program of indiscriminate destruction offered by Franco-Prussian postmodernist antihumanism it might be useful to remind ourselves of what Alexis de Tocqueville observed 150 years ago, that "In the French Revolution there were two impulses in opposite directions, which must never be confounded; the one was favorable to liberty, the other to despotism. . . . The Revolution declared itself the enemy at once of royalty and of provincial insti-

tutions; it confounded in indiscriminate hatred all that had preceded
it, despotic power [as well as] the checks to its abuses. . . ." In deconstructionist ideology augmented by Heideggerian antihumanism we
find what de Toqueville described as that "popul[ism] . . . united with
hostility to the rights of the people" in which "the professed lover
of freedom" turns out to be "the secret slave [and promulgator] of
tyranny." [30]

Notes

INTRODUCTION (pp. 1–20)

1. This attitude is supported by John M. Ellis in *Against Deconstruction* (Princeton, N.J.: Princeton University Press, 1989), 7, who writes that deconstructionist "rhetoric does not advance serious thought or inquiry but gives an impression of profundity and complexity without the effort and skill that would be required to make a substantial contribution to the understanding of the matter under discussion."

2. See J. G. Merquior, *From Prague to Paris: A Critique of Structuralist and Poststructuralist Thought* (London and New York: Verso, 1986); Luc Ferry and Alain Renaut, *French Philosophy of the Sixties: An Essay on Antihumanism*, tr. Mary H. S. Cattani (Amherst: University of Massachusetts Press, 1990); Ferry and Renaut, *Heidegger and Modernity*, tr. Franklin Philip (Chicago: University of Chicago Press, 1990).

3. J. G. Merquior presents a lucid account of the arbitrary and wholly unjustifiable attack on plain sense in the following passage. "No wonder that when structuralism was still in its prime a true scholar such as Marcel Bataillon already found it wise to call his presidential address to the Modern Humanities Research Association 'Defense et illustration du sens litteral.' Since then, how many literal meanings have been mugged, kidnapped, disfigured or openly slaughtered! Structuralism, or its progeny, has even devised a special technique to do away with it: its name is 'deconstruction,' the wilful murder of literal meaning, killed by systematic (and unwarranted) postulation of its very opposite as the secret of the text." *From Prague to Paris*, 179–180.

4. Robert Penn Warren, "A Poem of Pure Imagination: An Experiment in Reading" (originally published 1945–46), in Robert Penn Warren, *Selected Essays* (New York: Alfred A. Knopf and Random House, 1966), 201, 203–204.

5. Robert Penn Warren, *Selected Essays*, 119.

6. David H. Hirsch, "Penelope's Web," *Sewanee Review* XC, 1 (January, 1982), 119–131, and chapter 1 of this volume.

7. Although Fish has never, to my knowledge, sought support for his reader-responsism by invoking the Nietzschean idea that "there are no facts, only interpretations" in support of his reading strategies, there is certainly an echo of Nietzsche in his assumptions. It is this Nietzschean posture that leads Foucault to write, "If interpretation can never be achieved, it is simply because there is nothing to interpret . . . since after all everything is already interpretation." Michel Foucault, "Nietzsche, Freud, Marx," 189, 187. Their resounding invocation of Nietzsche is one element separating European from American reader-responsists. In his recent attack on the new academic left, Roger Kimball has presented an accurate portrait of Fish as a power-broking, calculating provocateur, who advocates outrageous positions for the sake of calling attention to himself. Kimball refers to Fish's "knack of keeping his criticism one short, provocative, step ahead of the criticism practiced by the majority of his colleagues. Looking back over his career, one sees that he early on perfected what Jean Cocteau described as the art of knowing just how far to go in going too far." Roger Kimball, *Tenured Radicals* (New York: Harper & Row, 1990), 147.

8. E. D. Hirsch, Jr., *Validity in Interpretation* (New Haven: Yale University Press, 1967), 245–264.

9. See David H. Hirsch, "Hamlet, Moby-Dick, and Passional Thinking," in *Shakespeare: Aspects of Influence*, ed. G. Blakemore Evans, Harvard English Studies, 7 (Cambridge, Mass.: Harvard University Press, 1976), 135–162.

10. Stanley E. Fish, "Literature in the Reader: Affective Stylistics," in *Reader Response Criticism*, ed. Jane Tompkins (Baltimore: Johns Hopkins University Press, 1980), 98. Originally published in *New Literary History* (Autumn, 1970). I should say here that I have seen no evidence (nor does Fish himself attempt to provide any) that Fish or his followers have established their credentials as commentators who are "more sensitized to language" than the likes of T. S. Eliot, Cleanth Brooks, Robert Penn Warren, Allen Tate, Kenneth Burke, John Crowe Ransom, or G. Wilson Knight, to name some New Critics we are being persuaded to "erase," yet whose essays on particular literary works still set a standard of linguistic sensitivity difficult to attain.

11. E. D. Hirsch, Jr., *Validity in Interpretation*, 207.

12. Frank Lentricchia, *After the New Criticism* (Chicago: University of Chicago Press, 1980), 103.

13. Ibid., 104.

14. Ibid., 106.

15. Merquior, ix.

16. F. O. Matthiessen, *American Renaissance* (London, New York: Oxford University Press, 1941) A number of books have appeared recently, some on Edgar Allan Poe, and some on the question of the "American

Romance" thesis about American fiction. These books have criticized *American Renaissance* for excluding Poe from the "canon." Matthiessen's book also excluded Harriet Beecher Stowe and Emily Dickinson. Nevertheless, I would argue that Matthiessen himself was not ideologically exclusionist, and that his book created possibilities for later inclusions.

17. A sampling of these books would include Richard Chase, *The American Novel and its Tradition* (1957), Charles Feidelson, Jr., *Symbolism and American Literature* (1953), Perry Miller, *The New England Mind: From Colony to Province* (1953) and *The Raven and the Whale* (1956), Randall Jarrell, *Poetry and the Age* (1953) [with its witty and brilliant celebration of Whitman's "Song of Myself"], William Charvat, *Literary Publishing in America, 1790–1850* (1959). In addition there were definitive critical studies of individual writers that were to have far-reaching effects, such as Stephen E. Whicher's study of Emerson, Edward H. Davidson's critical study of Poe, and Hyatt H. Waggoner's reassessment of Hawthorne; also, the groundwork was being laid for the publication of letters and new scholarly editions. And perhaps one should not fail to mention the *Literary History of the United States* (1948). The point that should not be overlooked is that in spite of a superficial conflict between scholars and critics, many of the scholars were critics and many of the critics were scholars, with the result that criticism and scholarship fed off each other at this time. I can add from personal experience that I studied with William Charvat, who though a thoroughly committed and consummate scholar, always displayed an openness toward New Critical readings, and even encouraged them in his seminars. Conversely, my senior colleague at Brown University, Hyatt Waggoner, was a brilliant critic, but he was always respectful of scholarship, and never would have dreamed of writing a critical analysis of a writer's work before familiarizing himself with whatever scholarly information was available on that writer.

18. Early interdisciplinary American studies programs usually combined the study of American history and American literature.

19. William Coleridge, *Biographia Literaria*, chapter XIV.

20. "The Poet," in *Selections from Ralph Waldo Emerson*, ed. Stephen E. Whicher (Boston: Houghton Mifflin, 1957), 225.

21. "Nature," in *Selections from Ralph Waldo Emerson*, 53.

22. "Circles," in *Selections from Ralph Waldo Emerson*, 168.

23. Some steps along the way were Ralph L. Rusk's definitive biography (1949), F. I. Carpenter's *Emerson Handbook* (1953), and Stephen E. Whicher's revisionary *Freedom and Fate* (1953).

24. As Waggoner demonstrated, the Emerson-Whitman strain had always been alive and well, even in such modernist poets as William Carlos Williams, Hart Crane, and E. E. Cummings. It was also in this postwar expansiveness that the liberating voices of Saul Bellow and J. D. Salinger were heard sounding their own barbaric yawp in fiction.

25. Cited in Norman O. Brown, *Love Against Death* (New York: Vintage Books, 1959), 305.

26. Merquior, *From Prague to Paris*, 197.

27. Ibid., 198.

28. Hyatt H. Waggoner, *American Poets* (Boston: Houghton Mifflin, 1968), xv, xvi.

29. Ibid., 162.

30. Kallen was unjustly and unconscionably maligned as a racist by Werner Sollors in his essay, "A Critique of Pure Pluralism," in *Reconstructing American Literary History*, ed. Sacvan Bercovitch (Cambridge, Mass.: Harvard University Press, 1986), 250–79.

31. Horace M. Kallen, "Of Love, Death, and Walt Whitman," *The Walt Whitman Review* XV, 3 (September 1969), 176, 177–78. Reprinted in *Norton Critical Edition of Leaves of Grass*, 979–990. I should call attention to Leo Spitzer's beautiful tribute to Whitman in his explication of Whitman's "Out of the Cradle Endlessly Rocking," in which he writes, "Whitman, unlike his two sickly European contemporary confreres [Baudelaire and Wagner], will remain for us not the poet of death . . . but the unique poet of American optimism and love of life. . . ." *English Literary History* xvi (1949), 229–49; reprinted in *Essays on English and American Literature* (Princeton: Princeton University Press, 1962), 34. Spitzer was one of the Jewish professors who was forced out of the German university system in 1933, the same year Heidegger became rector of the University of Freiburg.

32. Kallen, 179, 180.

33. It would constitute a serious oversight not to mention that Whitman became a consoling and enabling figure for gay poets. See Robert K. Martin, *The Homosexual Tradition in American Poetry* (Austin: University of Texas Press, 1979).

34. Melville to Hawthorne, June 1851, in *The Letters of Herman Melville*, eds. Merrel R. Davis and William H. Gilman (New Haven: Yale University Press, 1960), 128.

35. I am not unmindful that the early fifties were also the shameful years of red-baiting and McCarthyism, but if anything, that only underlines the continuing resiliency of the great American experiment in human freedom and possibility, as attested by the Civil Rights movement which was to follow the McCarthy era.

36. Lentricchia, 157.

37. Lentricchia, 159. See, also, John M. Ellis, *Against Deconstruction*, 21, fn. 8.

38. Merquior, 189, refers to Claude Levi-Strauss, Roland Barthes, Jacques Lacan, and Michel Foucault as a "tetrarchy," adding that the addition of Althusser would constitute a pentarchy. Merquior has the perspicacity and courage to say what many have believed but few would dare utter in the repressive atmosphere created by the poststructuralist-deconstructionist power elite: "Until 1982, when he died, there were only two persons in the world able really to understand the theories of Dr. Jacques Lacan: himself and God." (p. 149). Merquior then goes on to analyze the nonsense in two characteristically impenetrable Lacanian effusions. He later points out the obvious falsity in Derrida's oft-repeated claim that spoken language has been privileged above written language, and adds ". . . Derrida's grand 'epocal' out-

look, a direct descendant from Heidegger's equally portentous 'destruction of metaphysics' since Plato, sounds more impressive than it is" [p. 216]. And again, "Foucault and Derrida have not just transmuted the disillusionment of the structuralist world-view into nihilism—they have also directed nihilism against truth. As a result, the countercultural idea is no longer just a romantic vision—it is also an openly irrationalist *idiom of thought*" [p. 238]. See, also, John M. Ellis, *Against Deconstruction*, chapter 2, esp. 21–26, 34–37.

39. Oddly enough, this belief fuels both the hermeneutic and the reader-response (reception aesthetic) schools. Hermeneuticists see the world as a text by analogizing "interpretation." That is, if the world must be "interpreted" to be understood and if reading is the act of interpreting verbal texts, then the world is no different from a verbal text. Conversely, if the self is a fiction, then one of the fictions it might be is an empty vessel. Yet the empty vessel speaks. How can this be? It is because the emptiness has been filled by the language system, so that in speech it is not a self that speaks but language that speaks itself through the empty vessel.

40. Quoted in Farias, 287, from W. Schirmacher, *Technik und Gelassenheit* (Freiburg: 1985), 25.

41. For a balanced analysis of Nolte's views and those of other revisionist historians, see Richard J. Evans, *In Hitler's Shadow* (New York: Pantheon Books, 1989).

42. See "Like the Sound of the Sea Deep within a Shell: Paul de Man's War," *Critical Inquiry* 14 (Spring, 1988), 590–652; "Biodegradables: Seven Diary Fragments," *Critical Inquiry* 15 (Summer, 1989). As he has grown more desperate in his attempts to defend anti-Semites, collaborators, and Nazis, Derrida's attacks on those who take issue with him have grown more ad hominem and more frenzied. See Ferry and Renaut, *Heidegger*, 51, who cite an interviewer of Derrida as having commented on Derrida's ". . . somewhat acid manner of answering all [?] those who have recently attacked you in the name of 'conscience,' of 'human rights,' and criticized your deconstruction of 'humanism.' . . ."

43. Emil Fackenheim, *To Mend the World* (New York: Schocken Books, 1989; rpt 1982), 167–68, 169.

44. Hans Jonas, *The Phenomenon of Life* (New York: Harper and Row, 1966), 247.

45. Farias, 284, 285.

ONE: PENELOPE'S WEB (pp. 23–68)

1. In fact, there are those who would prohibit the asking of such questions on the grounds that "value decisions" of this kind are useless at best, and conspiratorial at worst, that they are intended only to suppress whatever is unacceptable to the "power structure."

2. Cleanth Brooks & Robert Penn Warren, *Understanding Poetry* (1938; New York, Henry Holt & Co., 1950) 44–48.

3. Stanley Fish, "Literature in the Reader: Affective Stylistics," in *Reader Response Criticism*, ed. Jane Tompkins (Baltimore: Johns Hopkins University Press, 1980), 70.

4. *The Well Wrought Urn* (1947; San Diego: Harcourt Brace Jovanovich, 1975) 194, 196, 199.

5. Stanley Fish, "Interpreting the Variorum," in *Is There a Text in This Class* (Cambridge, Mass.: Harvard University Press, 1980), 170.

6. Iser in Tompkins, ed., *Reader Response Criticism*, 50.

7. Ibid., 52.

8. Culler, *The Pursuit of Signs: Semiotics, Literature, Deconstruction* (Ithaca: Cornell University Press, 1981), 50.

9. Ibid., 96, 99.

10. Ibid., 125.

11. Steven Mailloux, *Interpretive Conventions: The Reader in the Study of American Fiction* (Ithaca: Cornell University Press, 1982), 74.

12. Ibid., 71.

13. Hyatt Waggoner, *Hawthorne: A Critical Study* (1955; Cambridge, Mass.: Harvard University Press, 1967), 118.

14. Mailloux, 75.

15. Nathaniel Hawthorne, "Rappaccini's Daughter," in *Selected Tales and Sketches*, ed. Hyatt Waggoner (New York: Holt, Rinehart, & Winston, 1950), 268–69.

16. Mailloux, 87.

17. Edward S. Casey, *Imagining: A Phenomenological Study* (Bloomington: Indiana University Press, 1976).

18. Ibid., 26.

19. Ibid.

20. James Joyce, *A Portrait of the Artist as a Young Man* (1916; New York: Viking Press, 1961) 166–67.

21. Robert Magliola, *Phenomenology and Literature: An Introduction* (West Lafayette, Ind.: Purdue University Press, 1977), 97–107.

22. Ibid., 114.

23. E. D. Hirsch, in *Validity in Interpretation* (New Haven: Yale University Press, 1967), has been the most influential American exponent of this view.

24. P. D. Juhl, *Interpretation: An Essay in the Philosophy of Literary Criticism* (Princeton, N.J.: Princeton University Press, 1980), 13, 149.

25. Ibid., 221.

26. Ibid., 70–82. Wordsworth's short lyric, "A Slumber Did My Spirit Seal," usually considered one of the "Lucy" poems, has long been a source of controversy among critics. Basically, the issue is whether the poem is Wordsworth's expression of a hopeful pantheism or a despairing resignation to the obliteration of consciousness. See, among others, E. D. Hirsch, "Objective Interpretation," *PMLA* LXXV (September, 1960), and H. S. Davies, in *Essays in Criticism*, 1965.

27. Juhl, 70.

28. Ibid., 14.

29. Ibid., 71–74.

30. Hans Robert Jauss, *Toward an Aesthetic of Reception*, tr. Timothy Bahti, with an introduction by Paul de Man (Minneapolis: University of Minnesota Press, 1982), xiv–xv.

31. Frank Lentricchia, *After the New Criticism* (Chicago: The University of Chicago Press, 1981).

32. It cannot be repeated too often that this autotelic monster is seldom to be found in the major essays of the major New Critics. To see the falsity of this allegation, one has only to read such essays, among many others, as Robert Penn Warren's "Pure and Impure Poetry"; Cleanth Brooks's "*The Waste Land*: Critique of the Myth"; or Allen Tate's essays on Poe and on Emily Dickinson. The autotelic monster is derived mainly from the Wimsatt and Beardsley essays on the intentional and affective fallacies. Contrary to current procedures in which it is assumed that the theory must precede practice, these theoretical essays were written after the fact of the practical criticism. It is also true that later minor critics did try to write essays based on the assumption of the autotelic text. But the attackers of New Criticism, and Lentricchia in writing a historical sketch of the New Criticism, do not specify the New Critical essays that contain the errors they attribute to New Critical practice.

33. Lentricchia, *After the New Criticism*, xii.

34. Ibid., 154.

35. Ibid., 190.

36. Ibid., 197.

37. Gunther S. Stent, "Prematurity and Uniqueness in Scientific Discovery," *Scientific American* 227: 11 (December 1972), 2–3.

38. Lentricchia, *After the New Criticism*, 199.

39. Ibid., 201.

40. In his *Walt Whitman and the American Reader* (Cambridge and New York: Cambridge University Press, 1990), Ezra Greenspan carefully develops Whitman's multiple, and seemingly conflicting, roles as revolutionary poet and empowered bourgeois publisher.

41. Lentricchia, *After the New Criticism*, 201.

42. See Michael R. Marrus and Robert O. Paxton, *Vichy France and the Jews* (New York: Schocken Books, 1983). Also, Ted Morgan, *The French, the Germans, the Jews, the Klaus Barbie Trial, and the City of Lyon, 1940–1945*; and Ted Morgan, "L'Affaire Topuvier: Opening Old Wounds," *New York Times Magazine*, 1 October 1989.

43. *Foucault Reader*, edited and with introduction by Paul Rabinow (New York: Pantheon Books, 1984), 85.

44. *Foucault Reader*, 78–79.

45. Ibid., 83.

46. Ibid.

47. Ibid., 170.

48. Ibid., 216.

49. *Hamlet*, act 2, sc. 2, lines 242–259.

50. William James, *The Varieties of Religious Experience* (1902; New York: Viking-Penguin, 1985). See Lectures 4–5 and 6–7, "The Religion of Healthy-Mindedness" and "The Sick Soul."

51. Joseph B. Soloveitchik, "The Lonely Man of Faith," *Tradition* VII (Summer 1965), 24.

52. Henry Thoreau, "Conclusion," *Walden and Civil Disobedience*, ed. Sherman Paul (Boston: Houghton-Mifflin, 1960), 222–23.

53. "Life Without Principle," in *The Portable Thoreau*, ed. Carl Bode (New York: Viking, 1970), 643.

54. Herman Melville, *Moby-Dick*, chapter 9, "The Sermon," 45. Norton Critical Edition, Harrison Hayford and Hershel Parker, eds. (New York: Norton, 1967).

55. Lentricchia, 351.

56. Ibid., 210.

57. This essay was written in 1982, shortly before the appearance of two books that presented conclusive evidence to show not only that Heidegger was a totally committed believer in the ideals and goals of Nazism but that he lied about his Nazism consistently from the end of the war until his death. Thus, the great philosopher of "authenticity" was in his life and in his writings a perfect model of inauthenticity. See Victor Farias, *Heidegger and Nazism* (Philadelphia: Temple University Press, 1989), and J. P. Stern, "Heil Heidegger," review of Hugo Ott, *Martin Heidegger: Unterwegs zu seiner Biographie* (Campus Verlag, 1988), *London Review of Books*, 20 April 1989. Also illuminating is Theodor W. Adorno, *The Jargon of Authenticity* (Evanston, Ill.: Northwestern University Press, 1973).

58. Martin Buber, *Between Man and Man*, tr. Ronald Gregor Smith (1947; Boston: Beacon Press, 1961), 168.

59. Lentricchia, 88–89.

60. I leave the sentence as written in 1982. But it is clear now that Heidegger was not merely ignoring the barbarism, he was part of it.

61. Martin Heidegger, *Poetry, Language, Thought*, tr. Albert Hofstadter (New York: Harper & Row, 1975), 18.

62. Lentricchia on Krieger, 232; on Hirsch, 262; on Bloom, 335; on de Man, 293, 301.

63. Ibid., 283.

64. Geoffrey Hartman, "War in Heaven," in *The Fate of Reading* (Chicago: University of Chicago Press, 1975), 41.

65. William Pritchard, "The Hermeneutical Mafia or, After Strange Gods at Yale," *Hudson Review* 28 (Winter 1975–76), 601–610. Cited in Lentricchia, 283.

66. Harold Bloom, *The Anxiety of Influence* (New York: Oxford University Press, 1973).

67. "The greatest poet in our language is excluded from the argument of this book for several reasons." Bloom, *Anxiety of Influence*, 11.

68. Harold Bloom, *Poetry & Repression* (New Haven: Yale University Press, 1976), 24.

69. Harold Bloom, *Kabbalah and Criticism* (New York: The Seabury Press, 1975), 29.

70. Ibid., 66–67.

71. Geoffrey Hartman, *The Fate of Reading*, 3.

72. Czeslaw Milosz, *The Witness of Poetry* (Cambridge, Mass.: Harvard University Press, 1983), 81.

73. It is no accident that Paul de Man's breakthrough essay was titled "The Blindness of Insight."

TWO: PAUL DE MAN AND THE POLITICS OF
DECONSTRUCTION (pp. 69–79)

1. Robert Jay Lifton, *The Nazi Doctors: Medical Killing and the Psychology of Genocide* (New York: Basic Books, 1986), 4.

2. Elie Wiesel, "In the Footsteps of Shimon Dubnov," *Modern Language Studies*, Special Holocaust Literature Issue, XVI, 1 (Winter, 1986), 105.

3. Max Weinreich, *Hitler's Professors* (New York: YIVO, 1946), 6.

4. David H. Hirsch, "Penelope's Web," *Sewanee Review* XC, 1 (Winter, 1982), 130, and chapter 1 of this volume.

5. Paul de Man, *Blindness and Insight* (1971; Minneapolis: University of Minnesota Press, 1983), 142–165.

6. Friedrich Nietzsche, "Vom Nutzen und Nachteil der Historie für das Leben," *Unzeitgemasse Betrachtung* II, in Karl Schlechta, ed., *Werke* I (Munich, 1954), 232–33, 243. Cited in de Man, 145.

7. *Blindness and Insight*, 148–49.

8. Ibid., 165.

9. Geoffrey H. Hartman, *The Fate of Reading* (Chicago: University of Chicago Press, 1975), 105.

10. Ibid., 106.

11. Joseph Jaffe, "The Battle of the Historians, *Encounter* LXIX, 1 (June, 1987), 76.

12. Paul de Man, "Heidegger's Exegeses of Holderlin," in *Blindness and Insight* (Minneapolis, 1983), 253.

13. Ibid., 15.

14. Ibid., 19.

15. Jean Amery, *At the Mind's Limits*, trans. Sidney Rosenfeld and Stella P. Rosenfeld (New York: Schocken Books, 1986), 18–19.

THREE: MARTIN HEIDEGGER AND
PAGAN GODS (pp. 80–96)

1. Those who, like Derrida, have trouble distinguishing between what constitutes resistance and what collaboration, who cannot detect the *differance* between honor and infamy, should read Jan Karski's enlightening account of his activities as a member of the Polish underground during the Nazi occupation, *Story of a Secret State*, (Boston: Houghton Mifflin, 1944). Karski was about de Man's age when the Nazis invaded Poland, but he never for a moment had any doubt that his only honorable course was to resist them and everything they stood for.

2. From a televised mock trial of Waldheim, with Ryan as prosecutor.

3. Richard Rorty, "Taking Philosophy Seriously," *The New Republic*, 11 April 1988, 31–34.

4. Primo Levi, *The Drowned and the Saved*, tr. Raymond Rosenthal (New York: Summit Books, 1988), 178–79.

5. But perhaps the dawn is beginning to break. Even Derridean acolyte Philippe Lacoue-Labarthe now acknowledges that "In the Auschwitz apocalypse, it was nothing less than the West, in its essence, that revealed itself—and that continues, ever since to reveal itself. And it is thinking that event that Heidegger failed to do." *Heidegger, Art, and Politics* (Oxford: Basil Blackwell, 1990), 35. This is fine as far as it goes. But must we not say that certain countries in the West revealed themselves more than others? It is fair to lump Great Britain and the United States, which fought Nazism at great cost, with Germany and France, the former which set up and ran the death camps and organized and conducted genocide, and the latter which, with some noble and courageous exceptions, collaborated wholeheartedly with the Germans?

6. Stephen W. Melville, *Philosophy Beside Itself: On Deconstruction and Modernism*, with a foreword by Donald Marshall (Minneapolis: University of Minnesota Press, 1986), 183, xxviii.

7. Ibid., 26, 27.

8. Ibid., 32.

9. Ibid., 33.

10. Martin Buber, *Between Man and Man*, tr. Ronald Gregor Smith (Boston: Beacon Press, 1955), 165.

11. Christopher Fynsk, *Heidegger: Thought and Historicity* (Ithaca: Cornell University Press, 1986), 175.

12. Ibid., cited on 70.

13. Ibid., cited on 160–61.

14. Ibid., 221.

15. Ibid., 222.

16. Ibid., 175.

17. Ibid., 228.

18. Stanley Corngold, *The Fate of the Self: German Writers and French Theory* (New York: Columbia University Press, 1986), 4.

19. Ibid., xiii.

20. Ibid., 13.

21. Corngold, however, shows his full awareness of what is at stake in a letter to the *TLS*, August 26–September 1, 1988, 931, where he writes, "de Man emerges as a strong philosopher of the inhuman tradition—a condition in which the important relations are necessarily inhuman." Corngold goes on to say, "I believe that de Man's critical work adheres to and reproduces, in literary theoretical masquerade, his experience as a collaborator."

22. Leon Feuchtwanger, in his 1933 novel, *The Oppermanns*, recognized the conflict as one between humanism and barbarism. Berthold Oppermann, a student in the gymnasium, is scheduled to deliver a talk on "Humanism and the Twentieth Century." When his teacher and adviser, Dr. Heinzius, is killed in a "motor-car accident," he is replaced by a National Socialist who forces Berthold to change his topic to "What can we learn from Arminius the German?" One wonders whether Feuchtwanger, in imagining this episode, which becomes the center of one strand of the narrative, was thinking of the confrontation that took place between the anti-Enlightenment, antihumanist Heidegger and the humanist, humane Ernst Cassirer at a Kant symposium at Davos in 1929, where Heidegger is reputed to have refused the hand of reconciliation offered him by Cassirer after their debate. See Hazard Adams, "Thinking Cassirer," *Criticism* XXV, 3 (Summer 1983), 193.

FOUR: PAUL DE MAN AND THE POETICS OF
PREVARICATION (pp. 97–117)

1. "Paul de Man and the Politics of Deconstruction," *The Sewanee Review* XCVI (Spring 1988), 330–338, reprinted in this volume. David Lehman, *Signs of the Times* appeared as this book was going to press.

2. Jacques Derrida, "Like the Sound of the Sea Deep within a Shell: Paul de Man's War," *Critical Inquiry* 14 (Spring 1988), 591–652.

3. Roger Kimball, "Professor Hartman Deconstructs Paul de Man," *The New Criterion*, May 1988. See also Kimball, *Tenured Radicals* (New York: Harper & Row, 1990).

4. Paul de Man, *Wartime Journalism, 1939–1943*, ed. Werner Hamacher, Neil Hertz, and Thomas Keenan (Lincoln: University of Nebraska Press, 1988); Werner Hamacher, Neil Hertz, and Thomas Keenan, eds., *Responses: On Paul de Man's Wartime Journalism* (Lincoln: University of Nebraska Press, 1989).

5. Denis Donoghue, "The Strange Case of Paul de Man," *New York Review of Books*, 29 June 1989; Leon S. Roudiez, "Searching for Achilles' Heel: Paul de Man's Disturbing Youth," *World Literature Today*, 63, 3.

6. Jan Karski, *Story of a Secret State* (Boston: Houghton Mifflin, 1944). For further testimony to the fact that there were indeed some courageous souls who acted with honor and nobility, see Wladyslaw Bartoszewski, *The Warsaw Ghetto* (Boston: Beacon Press, 1987).

7. James Atlas, "The Case of Paul de Man," *New York Times Magazine*, 28 Aug. 1988, 69.

8. *Responses on Paul de Man's Wartime Journalism*, ed. Werner Hamacher, Neil Hertz, and Thomas Keenan (Lincoln: University of Nebraska Press, 1989), 476.

9. Leon S. Roudiez, "Searching for Achilles' Heel: Paul de Man's Disturbing Youth," *World Literature Today* LXIII, 3 (Summer, 1989), 436.

10. *Responses*, 476.

11. Allan A. Ryan, Jr., *Quiet Neighbors* (San Diego: Harcourt Brace Jovanovich, 1984), 5.

12. Roudiez, 439.

13. A collection of Jauss's essays appeared as *Toward an Aesthetic of Reception*, tr. Timothy Bahti, introduction by Paul de Man (Minneapolis: University of Minnesota Press, 1982). The collection is Volume 2 of the series "Theory and History of Literature," under the general editorship of Vlad Godzich and Jochen Schulte-Sasse.

14. Ryan, 4.

15. Alexander and Margarete Mitscherlich, *The Inability to Mourn* (New York: Grove Press, 1975, 16; original German edition, Munich: 1967). Jauss advocates a theory of reading in which "meaning" emerges as a dialogue between the history-conscious reader in his own fully conscious present and the text of the historical past. But if this is an accurate description of the reading act, how does Jauss's consciousness of the historical presence of Auschwitz influence the meanings he creates in his dialogues with the text? One can read Jauss's books of literary theory and yet glean nothing of his SS past from them. Yet if his theory is valid, this historical past should leap out at us and pervade every sentence of his work. A more candid account of the Hitler past may be found in the memoir of Alfons Heck, who describes as follows his swearing-in to the *Jungvolk* on April 20, 1938, Hitler's forty-ninth birthday: "As the final act of the induction ceremony, we were handed the dagger with the Swastika inlaid in the handle and the inscription 'Blood and Honor' on its blade. On that cool, windy April afternoon, I accepted the two basic tenets of the Nazi creed: belief in the innate superiority of the Germanic-Nordic race, and the conviction that total submission to Germany and to the *Führer* was our first duty." Alfons Heck, *The Burden of Hitler's Legacy* (Frederick, Colo.: Renaissance House, 1988), 57.

16. See Hans Koop, *The Menten Affair* (New York: Macmillan, 1978), and Malcolm G. MacPherson, *The Blood of His Servants* (New York: Times Books, 1984).

17. Donoghue, "The Strange Case of Paul de Man." Quotations here and below are from pp. 36–37.

18. Frank Leutricchia, *After the New Criticism* (Chicago: University of Chicago Press, 1980), 283–84.

19. The earliest and perhaps most cynical and insensitive deployment of this tactic is Jacques Derrida's assertion: "To judge, to condemn the work of the man on the basis of what was a brief episode . . . is to reproduce

the exterminating gesture which one accuses de Man of not having armed himself against sooner." This is Derrida's circumlocutory way of repeating the revisionist historians' attempt to put the murderers on an equal footing with those murdered. Hence, Derrida portrays a person who collaborated with the actual "exterminators" as the "victim" while anybody who takes exception to de Man's collaborationist activities "reproduces," by Derridean logic, "the exterminating gesture." By Derridean deconstructionist logic, the Nazi sympathizer becomes the victim and those who probe the implications of his having been one become Nazis.

20. Aleksander Kulisiewicz, "Polish Camp Songs, 1939–1945," tr. Roslyn Hirsch, *Modern Language Studies* XVI (Winter 1986), 3–9. Originally in *Regiony Kwartalnik Spoleczno-Kulturalny* I (1976), 5–11.

21. Hans Georg Gadamer, *Truth and Method* (New York: Crossroad, 1982; first English edition, Sheed & Ward, 1975; first German edition, 1960), 150.

FIVE: FRENCH SHAME AND THE NEW
THEORY (pp. 118–132)

1. See J. G. Merquior, *From Prague to Paris: A Critique of Structuralist and Poststructuralist Thought.* London & New York: Verso, 1986; Luc Ferry and Alain Renaut, *French Philosophy of the Sixties: An Essay on Antihumanism*, trans. Mary H.S. Cattani. Amherst, Mass: The University of Massachusetts Press, 1990; and by the same authors, *Heidegger and Modernity*, trans. Franklin Philip. Chicago & London: The University of Chicago Press, 1990.

2. A useful bibliography of these works (there are more than two hundred listed) may be found in Cynthia Haft, *The Theme of Nazi Concentration Camps in French Literature* (The Hague and Paris: Mouton, 1973), 213–225. David Rousset's powerful narrative of concentration camp life, *L'Univers concentrationnaire*, was published in Paris in 1946. French narratives and poems of the Holocaust period were published as early as 1945 and appeared, one might say regularly, for the rest of the decade.

3. Frank Lentricchia, *After the New Criticism* (Chicago: University of Chicago Press, 1980), 145.

4. Ted Morgan, *An Uncertain Hour* (New York: Arbor House/William Morrow, 1990), 198–199. One of the still unrecognized Nazi crimes was their imposition of criminality on people who, in spite of weaknesses and prejudices and petty hatreds, might have lived decent lives had not the Nazis encouraged and even required acts of cruelty in the name of an ideology derived from German metaphysics.

5. Vladimir Jankelevitch, *L'Imprescriptible* (Paris: Editions de Seuil, 1986), 84–85, 86.

6. See Ellen S. Fine, *Legacy of Night: The Literary Universe of Elie*

Wiesel (Albany: SUNY Press, 1982), 10–30 and the selected bibliography, 188. Ms. Fine is a thorough and responsible scholar who works out of the French tradition, but she cites not a single French source in her discussion of *Night*.

7. Jankelevitch describes the behavior of the elites during the war as follows: "Everything that happened happened because the 'elites' were not equal to the challenge: writers put their stylistic virtuosity and special literary brilliance . . . at the service of the best offer, whether it was collaboration, a new Europe, or an anti-Bolshevik crusade; artists accepted shameful invitations and dishonorable trips in return for some childish flattery; functionaries profited from the ease with which they could build careers on unnamable evictions and from despicable laws! They missed even the most trivial occasion to behave with courage and honor. They remained mute in the country of Jules Simon, of Michelet and of Victor Hugo, when a word of protest, even the humblest gesture, might have proved that there were still some free men, and not only talkers and clowns; when the desperation of the situation should have aroused the moral conscience, the critical acumen, and the civic spirit of the "intellectual," no one showed up but the vain man of letters. When they should have been reacting to events as citizens, the writers were preoccupied above all else with getting their pieces published or with founding reviews. They were incapable of anything but literary reflections" (100–101). In the light of this shameful past, is it surprising that French intellectuals should arrive at the position that language is not referential and the writing of history impossible?

8. Micheline Maurel, *An Ordinary Camp*, tr. Margaret S. Summers (New York: Simon & Schuster, 1958), 11. For a historical confirmation of this phenomenon, see Michael M. Marrus and Robert Paxton, *Vichy France and the Jews* (New York: Basic Books, 1981; Schocken, 1983).

9. Ernst Nolte, *"Vergangenheit, die nicht vergehen will. . . ." Frankfurter Allgemeine Zeitung*, 6 June 1986.

10. Tom Bower provides a plausible explanation of why this business remained unfinished. "Emotions in . . . France were very high in the immediate aftermath of the war. Old scores were settled with little ceremony. Known collaborators were not likely to be given even the semblance of a trial. Some committed suicide after a visit from the survivors of a betrayed local Resistance group. Others were just shot in the street. Even more, however, escaped any punishment. Their victims had disappeared into the concentration camps and never survived. Those who did return were often too exhausted, sick and bewildered to seek out their denouncers. After the initial blood-letting and feuds, collaborators and resistants alike just wanted to resume a normal life." Tom Bower, *Klaus Barbie: The Butcher of Lyons* (New York: Pantheon Books, 1984), 50.

11. Charles S. Maier summarizes this unreconciled past as follows: "The historian Henry Rousso has traced four phases in French society's confrontation of the memory of Vichy: a decade of incomplete mourning from war's end to the mid-1950s; a Gaullist insistence on France as a country of Resisters

united behind the general; a 'return of the repressed,' signalled by Marcel Ophuls's film . . . *The Sorrow and the Pity*; and finally, since 1974 an episode of 'obsession,' marked on the one hand by the awaking of Jewish memory and on the other by anti-Semitic revivals." *The Unmasterable Past* (Cambridge, Mass.: Harvard University Press, 1988), 162. Maier cites his source as Henry Rousso, *Le Syndrome de Vichy 1944–81* (Paris, 1987).

12. It has been argued that poststructuralism and deconstruction cannot be traced to Nazi roots because Derrida, sometimes considered the founder of deconstruction, is Jewish. First of all, one must reject such racist and essentialist arguments out of hand. Would not such an argument echo the Nazi ideology, that So-and-so must act in such and such a way because of his race? Secondly, one must point out that there is very little Jewish substance in Derrida's writings. He has chosen to be a French intellectual, rather than a Jewish intellectual, just as Hannah Arendt, for example, chose to be a German intellectual. Moreover, in choosing as his guiding light a German philosopher who remained a loyal Nazi as long as it was safe to do so, and in defending Paul de Man's anti-Semitism and Heidegger's Nazism, Derrida has told us exactly how sensitive he is on "the Jewish question."

13. Michel Foucault, "Panopticism," in *Discipline and Punish*, tr. Alan Sheridan, (New York: Pantheon Books, 1977).

14. Michel Foucault, *Politics, Philosophy, Culture: Interviews and Other Writings, 1977–1984,* edited and with an introduction by Lawrence D. Kritzman (London: Routledge & Kegan Paul, 1988), 3–7.

15. Ferry and Renaut, *French Philosophy of the Sixties: An Essay on Antihumanism*, tr. Mary H. S. Cattani (Amherst: University of Massachusetts Press, 1990), 77. Citations from Foucault, *Histoire de la folie a l'age classique* (Paris: Gallimard, 1972), 552–53, 554. It is instructive to compare Foucault's violent and sadistic Nietzschean Dionysianism with the more benign (and perhaps more naive) Emersonian Dionysianism of Norman O. Brown. For Brown, the Dionysian ego would not have reinstituted "a power to annihilate," but would have removed the root causes of human violence by eliminating sexual repression.

16. Jorge Semprun, *The Long Voyage*, tr. Richard Seaver (New York: Grove Press, 1964), 36. Originally published as *Le Grand Voyage* (Paris: Libraire Gallimard, 1963).

17. Foucault, *Politics, Philosophy, Culture*, 3–4.

18. Ibid.

19. Charlotte Delbo, *None of Us Will Return* (New York: Grove Press, 1968), 39. Originally published as *Aucun de nous ne reviendra* (Geneva: Editions Gontheir, 1965).

20. *The Long Voyage*, 170.

21. Jankelevitch, p. 88.

22. Ibid., 89. Compare Charles C. Maier: "In France, notes Rousso, borrowing the term from Pascal Ory, a *mode retro* of the 1970s tried to conjure up the lived experience of Vichy, including a fascination with its inversion of values and even its anti-Semitic *chic*" (*The Unanswerable Past*, 162).

23. Compare Merquior: "Derrida, who has no discernible positive programme, harnesses the ontology of absence to a quite different task [than Heidegger]. His leitmotiv is not the appeal to an uncanny salvation but the relentless undermining of the western code of values. Hence the paradoxically parasitical status of deconstruction: it feeds on the text of tradition, from Plato and Rousseau to Freud, Husserl and Saussure. Yet it has no theory other than the systematic reversal of western thought. . . ." (*From Prague to Paris*, 227).

24. See Ferry and Renaut, *Heidegger and Modernity*, 2, 52, 95, *et passim*. It may be objected that humanists have also tended to avoid dealing with the Holocaust. While such an objection is justified to some extent, those few who have been willing to engage Holocaust issues were humanists. The humanist François Mauriac, it should be remembered, wrote a touching foreword to Elie Wiesel's *Night* (1958). Erich Kahler, whose *The Tower and the Abyss* (1957) has yet to be superseded as an analysis of the significance of the Holocaust for Western culture, was surely one of the great humanists of the century. *The Survivor: An Anatomy of Life in The Death Camps* (1976), a major study of Holocaust literature, was written by an American, Terrence Des Pres, who was not only a humanist but was trained as a New Critic. Among those to whom he expresses "an endless debt" in his acknowledgments is Reuben Brower, who schooled at least two generations of Harvard students in New Critical reading techniques. Lawrence Langer's *The Literature of Atrocity* (1975), an important book-length study of Holocaust writings, relies heavily on New Critical methods of close reading. Writing about the Holocaust has become an insuperable problem for deconstructionists because their belief that "human dignity" is nothing but a "humanist" fiction deprives them of a viable point of view.

25. For an analysis of the reactionary strain in Heideggerism, see "Heidegger, Nazism, and Modernity," in Ferry and Renaut, *French Philosophy of the Sixties* and *Heidegger and Modernity*, tr. Franklin Philip (Chicago: University of Chicago Press, 1990). See their introductory chapter and their chapter on Foucault for an analysis of the way in which Heidegger and Marx were violently yoked together. One must say this much for the deconstructionist movement: in spite of its authoritarian origins and tendencies, it led American literary critics to reexamine the alleged inviolability of literary works now referred to as "the canon." Merquior writes that "Poststructuralism has been the seat of theorrhea in the humanities—ambitious 'theory' as a pretext for sloppy thinking and little analysis, fraught with anathemas against modern civilization" (*From Prague to Paris* 253).

26. Semprun, 43.

27. There are many survivor narratives, but only a small percentage are written from this perspective. Primo Levi, in *Survival in Auschwitz* (first Italian edition, 1958), writes from the perspective of a scientist trained in empirical observation. Jean Amery, an intellectual and a humanist, in *At the Mind's Limits* (first German edition, 1966), writes from a perspective closer to Semprun's. He, too, was a resistance fighter captured by the Gestapo, tor-

tured, and sent to a concentration camp. Unlike Semprun, however, Amery had a Jewish parent, which made him a killable Jew under the race laws of Heidegger's Nazi Germany.

28. Semprun, 45.

SIX: COLLABORATORS AND DECONSTRUCTORS (pp. 133–142)

1. Paul de Man, "The Jews in Contemporary Literature," *Le Soir* 4 March 1941; cited in Stanley Corngold, "On Paul de Man's Collaborationist Writings," in *Responses on Paul de Man's Wartime Journalism*, ed. Werner Hamacher, Neil Hertz, and Thomas Keenan (Lincoln: University of Nebraska Press, 1989), 80–81. Also see, by the same editors, *Wartime Journalism, 1939–1943: Paul de Man* (Lincoln: University of Nebraska Press, 1988), 45. It is relevant to call attention to the fact that de Man was older than Semprun because Jacques Derrida and others who seem to know very little about the Holocaust have defended de Man by implying that his tender age might serve to exonerate his having chosen to engage in collaborationist and anti-Semitic writings. Derrida, for example, writes, "But in the several months to follow, the very young journalist that he [de Man] will have been during less than two years [1940–1942] will be read more intensely than the theoretician, the thinker, the writer, the professor, the author of great books that he was for forty years" "Like the Sound of the Sea Deep within a Shell: Paul de Man's War," *Critical Inquiry* 14 (Spring 1989), 591). Reading Derrida, one might conclude that the journalist in his twenties had no more choice in becoming a collaborator than the ten-year-old boy portrayed by Semprun had in becoming a stone-throwing Nazi, or than the German sentinel had in coming to France to murder Semprun and others.

2. Frank Lentriccia, *After the New Criticism* (Chicago: University of Chicago Press, 1980), p. 159.

3. Lentricchia, 301.

4. J. G. Merquior also comments on this inconsistency in Lentricchia, an inconsistency that extends to his admiration for Foucault as an antidote to Derrida. Merquior writes, "de Man's preposterous reduction of history to a textual puzzle did not go unchallenged. The main challenger, Frank Lentricchia, earned prominence as a historian of criticism for whom . . . both structuralism and deconstruction originally contained radical promises belied and betrayed by their transatlantic acclimatization. Yet on close inspection the 'radical' structuralism Lentricchia seems to have in mind is chiefly the work of Barthes in the *Mythologies* phase, still basically pre-structuralist . . . and his claim that Derrida's dismantling of meaning is far more rigorous than its American counterparts cries out for substantiation. . . . Much as I share Lentricchia's impatience with the ritualistic puzzle-mongering of deconstruction, I fail to see how post-structuralism qua geneaology (Foucault)

can kill the virus of poststructuralism qua exegesis (Derrida)" (*From Prague to Paris*, 250).

5. Paul de Man, *Blindness and Insight: Essays in the Rhetoric of Contemporary Criticism*, 2d Ed. with an introduction by Wlad Godzich (Minneapolis: University of Minnesota Press, 1983), 8–9.

6. De Man, 11. The syntax of the last part of this sentence is puzzling. In keeping with de Man's theme, it seems the clause should read, "the other is always free to make what he says he wants differ from what he [actually] wants." Of course, stated in this way de Man's assertion is merely a repetition of what we all know, that some people are liars or hypocrites.

7. For an analysis of the deconstructionist rejection of human essence, see Ferry and Renaut, *French Philosophy of the Sixties: An Essay on Antihumanism*, tr. Mary H. S. Cattan (Amherst: University of Massachusetts Press, 1990), 15–32 *et passim*.

8. De Man, 11. One cannot help being struck by the sinister image that ends the last sentence: "we hide rage or hatred behind a smile." Stanley Corngold has called attention to the fact that de Man's "late work is marked by a recurrent and major tone of arbitrary violence," which leads Corngold to conclude that this pattern of violence in the writing "represents a fascination or even complicity with violence." Corngold, "On Paul de Man's Collaborationist Writings," 81, 82.

9. There is an unfortunate tendency for deconstructionists to play fast and loose with Saussure. Merquior observes that "Saussure's 'difference,' which in the *Course in General Linguistics* humbly denotes the diacritical nature of linguistic signs, was converted [by Derrida] into a portent of ever-delayed meaning based on a pun on *difference* (differance, a mix of differing and deferring): a modest scientific conceptual tool became burdened with an unexpected metaphysical load, quite alien to the original empirical analysis of semiotic phenomena." (*From Prague to Paris*, 223). In the present instance, de Man's formulation seems somewhat sloppy. What is "an actual expression?" and what does he mean by "what it signifies?" Is he saying only that words are not identical to referents? Or is he saying an expression never means what it means?

10. David Hirsch, "Paul de Man and the Politics of Deconstruction," *The Sewanee Review*, XCVI (Spring 1988), 333 (reprinted in this volume).

11. *Blindness and Insight*, 2d ed., 165.

12. I wrote the essay in which I first drew this parallel between deconstruction and revisionist historiography in January 1988. Charles S. Maier puts a finer point on it in his 1988 book: "How, it will be asked, do revisionist accounts of Auschwitz or apologias for the German army represent any historiographic postmodernism? This is not the claim. They are not cited as postmodern works, but as products of a diffused postmodern historical sensibility" (*The Unanswerable Past*, 170).

13. See Paul de Man's introduction to Hans Robert Jauss, *Toward an Aesthetic of Reception*, tr. Timothy Bahti (Minneapolis: University of Minnesota Press, 1982), viii, x: "The methodology of the Konstanz school [of which

Jauss is a major participant] is mostly referred to as Rezeptionasthetik. . . .
Jauss's relationship to the hermeneutic tradition is itself by no means simple
or uncritical."

14. De Man, introduction to Jauss, *Toward an Aesthetic of Reception*,
xi–xii.

15. One assumes that de Man goes through the ridiculous acrobatics of
using the phrases "work of the past" and "time of its elaboration" in order to
preserve the dogma that we are not to "privilege" certain verbal constructs
by designating them as literature. So when he says "a work of the past,"
maybe he is referring to anything produced in the past. Nevertheless, we will
assume he means a literary work.

16. De Man, introduction to Jauss, xii.

17. Hans Robert Jauss, "Response to Paul de Man," tr. Andreas Michel,
in *Reading de Man Reading* ed. Lindsay Waters and Wlad Godzich (Minneapolis: University of Minnesota Press, 1989), 203, 204.

18. De Man, introduction to Jauss, xii.

19. The ubiquity of Heidegger's contribution to antihumanist thinking
is stressed by Stephen Holmes in his essay "The Permanent Structure of
Antiliberal Thought." Holmes writes, "Martin Heidegger's influence on contemporary American antiliberals, though subterranean and indirect, is all-
pervasive. Hannah Arendt and [Leo] Strauss made a decisive contribution
here, adapting Heidegger's harsh diagnosis of modernity to the mental horizon of their new American audience. . . . They could not plausibly say that the
'decline' of modern times resulted from a forgetfulness of Being. That would
have been wholly unintelligible to their culturally backward readers. They
responded to this marketing problem by Americanizing Heidegger's basic
idea. Decadent modernity, they said, resulted from a forgetfulness of x—of
the Greek polis, on the one hand, of classical natural law, on the other." In
Liberalism and the Moral Life, ed. Nancy L. Rosenblum (Cambridge, Mass.:
Harvard University Press, 1989), p. 246.

20. Ernst Nolte, "Vergangenheit, die nicht vergehen will . . ." (The
Past that Will Not Pass), *Frankfurter Allgemeine Zeitung*, 6 June 1986. See
Richard J. Evans, *In Hitler's Shadow: West German Historians and the Attempt to Escape from the Nazi Past* (New York: Pantheon Books, 1989),
28; also see 34–46 and chapter IV, where Evans demolishes Nolte's flimsy
arguments.

21. Evans, 33–34.

22. *Frankfurter Allgemeine Zeirung*, 6 June 1986. The "tasteless slip"
was a comment by the mayor of Grefenbroich in the Rhineland that the local
government finances could be brought into balance by "beating to death a
couple of rich Jews." It is only in the context of the obliteration of the memory of Auschwitz that such a comment can be described as nothing more
ominous than a "tasteless slip." To say that *Shoah* depicts SS guards in the
death camps as victims is a travesty of interpretation.

23. "Like the Sound of the Sea. . . ," *Critical Inquiry* 14 (Spring, 1989), 651.

SEVEN: DECONSTRUCTION AND THE SS
CONNECTION (pp. 143–165)

1. Jon Wiener, *The Nation*, 9 January 1988, 22.

2. *The Nation*, 4 June 1988. Later in this letter, Jauss states that "My friendship with Paul de Man . . . was not based on any kind of ideological sympathy but on our mutual interest in our work as scholars and theoreticians. . . . De Man's former sympathy with and advocacy of Nazi ideology was as unknown to me as—I imagine—my former service in the Waffen-SS was to him." Perhaps. But one wonders, then, why de Man went out of his way, in the introduction to Jauss's collection of essays, to point out that though certain "study groups . . . in the field of literary theory . . . are, at times centered on a single, dominating personality and take on all the exalted exclusiveness of a secret society, with its rituals of initiation, exclusion and hero-worship . . . nothing could be more remote from the spirit of the group of which Jauss is a prominent member" (vii). Doth not de Man protest too much? Does not this talk of a "dominating personality" and of "a secret society, with its rituals of initiation, exclusion, and hero-worship" sound very much like the SS? And who had accused the Constance school of having these qualities, thus requring de Man's denial?

3. Heinz Höhne, "There's Butcher Mentality," in *Bitburg and Beyond*, ed. Ilya Levkov (New York: Shapolsky Publishers, 1987), 239, 240, 241. Reprinted from *Der Spiegel* 29 April 1985. Late in the war the Waffen SS became a rather motely crew, but in 1939 it was still an elite corps, and the organization Jauss joined was one that had already committed some heinous crimes, including the murder of the Federal Chancellor of Austria, Dr. Engelbert Dollfuss, on July 25, 1934, a crime publicly celebrated four years later. We must also bear in mind that Waffen-SS training included, "three times a week, . . . a lecture on the inspiring life of the Fuehrer, the ideology of National Socialism or the philosophy of racial selection. . . ." Gerald Reitlinger, *The SS: Alibi of a Nation, 1922–1945* (New York: Da Capo Press, 1957), 77. Also see Heinz Höhne, *The Order of the Death's Head* (New York: Coward-McCann, 1969), chapter 16, "The Waffen-SS."]. Reitlinger writes that SS atrocities "were common during the eighteen days' war [September, 1939] but the organised reign of terror began after the fighting was over. . . . [Ulrich] Von Hassell called it the "SS reign of terror in Poland.' "

4. James J. Weingartner, *Crossroads of Death* (Berkeley: University of California Press, 1979), who reexamines the conduct of the trial from a German perspective.

5. Charles W. Sydnor, Jr., *Soldiers of Destruction: The SS Death's Head Division, 1933–1945* (Princeton, N.J.: Princeton University Press, 1977), 3.

6. Ibid., 27.

7. Robert Lewis Koehl, *The Black Corps* (Madison: University of Wisconsin Press, 1983), 163, 164. Martin Gilbert adds that "The mass killings of September and October 1939 in German-occupied Poland left five thou-

sand Jewish dead." *The Holocaust* (New York: Holt, Rinehart, & Winston, 1985), 99.

8. According to Sydnor, "In the harsh crucible of Poland, the grim heritage of the concentration camps was violently transformed into an ethos of war that became and remained a key element in the Waffen SS character of Eicke's Totenkopf formations. . . . Their military capabilities were employed . . . in terrorizing the civilian population through acts that included hunting down straggling Polish soldiers, confiscating agricultural produce and livestock, and torturing and murdering large numbers of Polish leaders, aristocrats, businessmen, priests, intellectuals, and Jews." *Soldiers of Destruction*, p. 37.

9. Hannah Arendt, *Eichmann in Jerusalem* (New York: Viking Press, 1963), 52.

10. Primo Levi, *The Drowned and the Saved* (New York: Summit Books, 1986), 30.

11. I use the term "silenced" advisedly. American graduate students who can cite chapter and verse on Paul de Man and Jacques Derrida have never heard of Jorge Semprun, and are not likely to be assigned any of his works as part of their graduate reading.

12. Jorge Semprun, *The Long Voyage*, tr. Richard Seaver (New York: Grove Press, 1964, 70, 71. Originally published as *Le Grand Voyage* (Paris: Libraire Gallimard, 1963).

13. The literature on the arguments for uniqueness is too extensive to be listed here. But the argument is elegantly expressed in chapter 4 of *In Hitler's Shadow*, and in Saul Friedlander, "The Historical Significance of the Holocaust," *Jerusalem Quarterly* I (Fall 1976), 36–59. The most brilliant and most comprehensive analysis of the uniqueness of the Holocaust remains Erich Kahler's *The Tower and the Abyss* (New York: George Brazillier, 1957). For an analysis of the uniqueness of the Holocaust from a philosophical and theological point of view, see Emil Fackenheim, *Quest for the Past and Future* (Boston: Beacon Press, 1968), and *To Mend the World* (New York: Schocken, 1982, 1989); and Steven T. Katz, "The 'Unique' Intentionality of the Holocaust," in *Post-Holocaust Dialogues* (New York: New York University Press, 1985).

14. Kahler, 66, 68, 75.

15. Jadwiga Bezwińska & Danuta Czech, eds. *KL Auschwitz Seen by the SS: Höss, Broad, Kremer* (Auschwitz: Publications of Państwowe Muzeum w Oświęcimiu, 1972), 37, and 22 in the foreword by Jerzy Rawicz. Of course, this is the inverse of the Eichmann defense that "I was just obeying orders." Here we have a commandant who pleads that human slaughter was committed in Auschwitz because his underlings refused to obey orders.

16. Ibid., 18.

17. Ibid., 220.

18. Ibid., "Foreword," 8.

19. Arendt, 135.

20. Kahler, 88.

21. Jauss, "Response to Paul de Man," 205. By a strange coincidence, Eichmann claimed that "he had lived his whole life according to Kant's moral precepts, and especially according to the Kantian definition of duty" (Arendt, 135–6).

22. See chapter 11 in Victor Farias, *Heidegger and Nazism* (Philadelphia: Temple University Press, 1989), where he provides an account of how the leading professors of philosophy, including Heidegger, clambered over each other in pursuit of academic advancement and other venal ambitions in Nazi Germany.

23. See chapters 8 and 9 in Farias, where he documents Heidegger's infatuation with the ideology of the Ernst Roehm faction of the Nazis. As Farias clearly demonstrates, Heidegger, ever mindful of his own skin, became a more cautious Nazi after the Night of the Long Knives, June 30, 1934, when Roehm and his followers were purged. See also Weinreich, *Hitler's Professors*.

24. See Terrence Des Pres's brilliant chapter, "The Excremental Assault," in *The Survivor: An Anatomy of Life in the Death Camps* (New York: Oxford University Press, 1976).

25. For example, if the SS had behaved in accordance with accepted "rules of war," they would have executed Russian officers by firing squad, permitting them to die with honor in uniform.

26. "The essence of the camp indoctrination [for recruits to Theodor Eicke's Waffen SS] was threefold. The SS recruit was drilled to obey without question every order, no matter how harsh. He learned to hate absolutely the 'enemies behind the wire' as sub-humans who were a lethal political and racial threat to the security of the Reich. And finally, from his superiors and from the example set by Eicke, he acquired a sense of esprit and camaraderie built around the theme that the Totenkopfverbände, with the responsibility of guarding the most dangerous enemies of the state and the racial community constituted an elite within the SS." Sydnor, *Soldiers of Destruction*, 315.

27. Arendt, 64.

28. In a more or less Marxist mode, Richard Rubenstein offers a theory of the Holocaust warmly embraced by William Styron. "We are more likely to understand the Holocaust," he writes in *The Cunning of History*, "if we regard it as the expression of some of the most profound tendencies of Western civilization in the twentieth century. . . . In the moral universe of the twentieth century, the most 'rational' and least costly 'solution' of the problem of disposing of a surplus population is unfortunately extermination. Properly executed, extermination is the problem-solving strategy least likely to entail unanticipated feedback hazzards for its planners" (New York: Harper & Row, 1975), 21. But this theory overlooks the ideology of hate and the cruelty toward the victims. It also fails to explain why the SS had to dehumanize the victims before exterminating them. It also does not explain why the Jews should have been singled out as a "surplus population." Moreover, the process of extermination was not clean and efficient. It was very

messy, efficient only in the sense that it permitted the extermination of large numbers of people in a relatively short time. Finally we must ask, in some amazement, whether Rubenstein really believes it is true that the extermination of human beings carried few "unanticipated feedback hazzards for its planners." Is mass murder, then, so insignificant an activity that the perpetrators remain untouched and uncontaminated? Was there no "hazzard" in turning the population of a nation into mass murderers and accomplices to mass murder?

29. Tadeusz Borowski, *This Way for the Gas, Ladies and Gentlemen*, selected and tr. by Barbara Vedder, with an introduction by Jan Kott (Harmonscourt, England: Penguin Books, 1967), 29.

30. Charlotte Delbo, *None of Us Will Return* (New York: Grove Press, 1968), 99.

31. *King Lear*, act 4, sc. 1, ll. 36–37.

32. From Berdyaev's book on Dostoyevsky, as reprinted in The Norton Critical Edition of *Crime and Punishment*, ed. George Gibian (New York: Norton & Co., 1964), 621–622.

33. *Auschwitz: True Tales from a Grotesque Land*, tr. Roslyn Hirsch (Chapel Hill: University of North Carolina Press, 1985), 69.

34. Aleksander Kulisiewicz, "*Kolysanka Dla Birkenau*" ("Lullaby from Birkenau"), from the recording, *Songs of the Concentration Camps*, translated from the Polish record album, *Piesni Obozowe* (Polskie Nagrania: Muza, 1979), #SX1715, by Roslyn Hirsch. According to the program note on the album jacket, the song "was written in Sachsenhausen, 1943, for the four-year-old son of Tomasz Kotarbinski, Andrzejek. The father received it for keepsake when he was sent with a death transport to KL Auschwitz, where his wife and three children had already been sent. Kotarbinski, a music teacher, memorized the song hoping he would be able to sing it to his son in Birkenau." The song was collected and performed by Kulisiewicz. Permission to use the material has kindly been granted by Krzystof Kulisiewicz, Aleksander's son.

35. Charles W. Sydnor, Jr., points out that "The problem of understanding the institutional complexity of the SS, and the role and functions of the Waffen SS within it, has been compounded by the efforts of the postwar apologists for the Waffen SS to portray it as an army of anti-Communist idealists who belonged to an organization separate, independent, and distinct from the SS. The apologists have further claimed, and have secured wide public credence for the thesis, that the men who served in the Waffen SS as frontline soldiers were in no way involved in or responsible for crimes committed by other SS agencies during the Second World War" (*Soldiers of Destruction*, xv, n. 5.)

36. Robin Mackness, *Massacre at Oradour* (New York: Random House, 1988), 70–71. Also see Sydnor, who writes, "like other crack formations of the Waffen SS, the wartime experience of the Totenkopfdivision was characterized by its ability to retain both its fighting spirit and combat effectiveness

in defeat as well as victory, and by its utterly ruthless behavior in the execution of political and military tasks against enemy civilians and soldiers" (276–297). Also see Sydnor, 320–321.

37. Arendt, 52.

38. A. M. Rosenthal, *New York Times*, Sunday, 29 July 1990, Op Ed page, 19.

39. Saul Friedlander, "The *Shoah* Between Memory and History," *Jerusalem Quarterly* 53 (Winter 1990), 122.

40. Ibid., 123.

41. Kahler, 76.

42. *KL Auschwitz as Seen by the SS*, 221, 279.

43. Kahler, 77.

44. Farias, Part II and Part III, 79–278.

45. Lentricchia, *After the New Criticism*, (Chicago: University of Chicago Press, 1980), p. 159.

46. Charles A. Maier, *The Unanswerable Past*, 170.

47. Jacques Derrida, "Like the Sound of the Sea . . . ," *Critical Inquiry*, Spring, 1988, p. 593. With characteristic self-effacement and consistency, Derrida, the unyielding foe of the Logos and all transcendentalisms, borrows the words and transcendentalist Faith of the Apostle Paul in 2 Corinthians, 13: 3–4 (King James Version), "Since ye seek a proof of Christ speaking in me, which to you-ward is not weak, but mighty in you. For though he was crucified through weakness, yet he liveth by the power of God. For we also are weak in him, but we shall live with him by the power of God toward you." Thus does Paul de Man speak in Derrida, and thus de Man shall live in us and we shall all live in the collaborator de Man who, like Jesus, was crucified in his weakness.

48. This antihumanism, according to Ferry and Renaut, "was always based on a line of argumentation according to which the humanism of modern philosophy, although apparently the liberator and defender of human dignity, actually succeeded only in becoming its opposite; the accomplice, if not the cause, of oppression" (*French Philosophy of the Sixties*, xxv). Merquior writes, "Nietzsche's posterity among the *Kulturkritiker* reproduces this bifurcation. Foucault . . . took the first path—of sceptical, openly irrational history; Heidegger, and nowadays Derrida, represent the second—the way of antimetaphysical philosophy" (*From Prague to Paris*, 259).

49. Richard Evans attributes to Ernst Nolte an attempt "to imply that the historiography of the Third Reich has been written *from the perspective* of the victors, under the inspiration of the surviving victims. This suspicion is strengthened in *The European Civil War*, where Nolte goes out of the way to say that 'the literature on the "Final Solution" comes to an overwhelming degree from Jewish authors,' which has given it a simple 'perpetrator-victim pattern.' " (*In Hitler's Shadow*, 32–33).

50. Even enlightened Marxists tend to fall back on the old clichés. Consider the rhetorical blow Terry Eagleton imagines he is delivering when he asks "Who is concerned with the uniqueness of the individual, the im-

perishable truths of the human condition or the sensuous textures of lived experience in the Foreign Office or the boardroom of Standard Oil?" *Literary Theory: An Introduction* (Minneapolis: University of Minnesota Press, 1983), 199–200. This Americaphobia is the link that makes cozy bedfellows of the reactionary Heidegger and the revolutionary Marx. Marxists hate America, of course, as the embodiment of conservative capitalism, while Heideggerians detest America as the agent of progress and advanced technology.

51. *French Philosophy of the Sixties*, xv–xvi.

52. Amos Funkenstein, "Theological Interpretations of the Holocaust: A Balance," in *Unanswered Questions: Nazi Germany and the Genocide of the Jews*, ed. François Furet (New York: Schocken Books, 1989), 298–99.

53. Ibid., 299, 301. I do not want to go into the issue here of the differences between writers on Auschwitz itself. The best known witness narrative remains Elie Wiesel's *Night*, and Wiesel provides a powerful countercurrent to both Heideggerianism and to Levi. Wiesel, as Funkenstein says of Levi, never loses sight of "the concrete man," but this concrete man is always perceived "over-against" God. The clearest and most comprehensive nontheological and nontranscendental exposition of the relationship between Heidegger's philosophy and Nazism, and between Heidegger's Nazism and his French defenders, is Tom Rockmore, "Heidegger After Farias," *History of Philosophy Quarterly*, 8, no. 1 (January 1991), 81–102. I highly recommend this essay to anyone interested in the topic. I did not have the benefit of reading this outstanding and thoroughly convincing essay until my book was in press, but Rockmore presents the important ethical and philosophical issues in a clear chronological context and with precise analysis. His evaluations of the arguments of Heidegger's French defenders are also of great value.

EIGHT: MARXISM, HUMANISM, AND LITERATURE IN THE UNIVERSITY (pp. 169–178)

1. See especially, Karl Marx and Frederick Engels, *The German Ideology*, edited and with an introduction by C. J. Arthur (New York, International Publishers, 1984). The French wife-killer is Louis Althusser, who develops his notions of ideology, the repressive state apparatus (coercive systems), and the ideological state apparatus (educational systems) in *Lenin and Philosophy and Other Essays*, tr. Ben Brewster (New York: Monthly Review Press, 1971). Deconstructionists and Marxists, who now have more skeletons rattling in their closets than an orthopedic bone bank, understandably seek to minimize connections between a writer's life and work, as though what a person does were not a truer indication of what he or she believes than what he or she says. For example, can a man murder his wife without believing that he enjoys the right to exercise unlimited power over her person? For a thorough analysis of the uses of the term *ideology*, see Onesimo T. Almeida, "The Concept of Ideology: A Critical Analysis" (Ph.D. diss., Brown Uni-

versity, 1980). The well-paid Marxist is a member of the Duke University faculty.

2. James H. Kavanagh, "That Hive of Subtlety: 'Benito Cereno' and the Liberal Hero," in *Ideology and Classic American Literature*, ed. Sacvan Bercovitch and Myra Jehlen (Cambridge: Cambridge University Press, 1986), 353.

3. Aleksander Wat, *My Century*, tr. Richard Lourie, with a foreword by Czeslaw Milosz (Berkeley: University of California Press, 1988; first Polish ed., London: 1977. See also Czeslaw Milosz, *The Witness of Poetry* (Cambridge, Mass.: Harvard University Press, 1983), 92.

4. Adam Michnik, *Letters from Prison*, tr. Maya Latynski, foreword by Czeslaw Milosz (Berkeley: University of California Press, 1987; first English ed., 1985; the original Polish essays were published underground in London and Poland), 3.

5. Ibid., 7.

6. Terry Eagleton, *Literary Theory: An Introduction* (Minneapolis: University of Minnesota Press, 1983), 94.

NINE: AND WHAT ARE YOU, READER (pp. 179–192)

1. George Dekker, *The American Historical Romance*, Cambridge Studies in American Literature and Culture (Cambridge and New York: Cambridge University Press, 1987); Robert Shulman, *Social Criticism and Nineteenth-Century American Fictions* (Columbia: University of Missouri Press, 1987).

TEN: METAPHORS AND STRUCTURES (pp. 193–218)

1. See Gordon M. Messing, "The Impact of Transformational Grammar," *Linguistics* 66 (1971), 56–74. Ohmann's analysis has also been challenged by John Russel, "From Style to Meaning in 'Araby,'" *College English* 28 (1966), 170–71. Ohmann replies, 171–173.

2. The full sentence reads: "gazing up into the darkness I saw myself as a creature driven and derided by vanity; and my eyes burned with anguish and anger." Russel comments perceptively on the final clause and its relation to the previous one.

3. Richard Ohmann, "Literature as Sentences," *College English* 27 (1966), 62. Reprinted in *Essays on the Language of Literature*, ed. Seymour Chatman and Samuel R. Levin (Boston: 1967), 231–38, and in *Readings in Applied Transformational Grammar*, ed. Mark Lester (New York: 1970), 137–48.

4. Messing, 67.

5. The question of meaning in relation to transformational grammar remains open. J. C. Nyiri has reviewed the problem with admirable succinctness and lucidity, underlining Chomsky's early hostility to semantic considerations, and concluding that the solution to the problem is to bring semantics and grammar onto a single descriptive plane through the device of subcategorization, a concept introduced by Chomsky in his paper "Some Methodological Remarks on Generative Grammar," *Word* 17, (1961) 219–39. In theory, the weakness of the concept seems to be that in order to refine descriptive technique sufficiently so that a syntactic analysis will also provide precise information, it will eventually be necessary to provide a subcategory for every word in the language. In this same article, Nyiri discusses the semantic theory advocated by J. J. Katz. He demonstrates that the two basic assumptions made with regard to this theory, that "it is (1) compatible with Chomskyan grammar and (2) philosophically adequate" are not valid. J. C. Nyiri, "No place for Semantics," *Foundations of Language* 7 (1979), 56–69.

6. Messing, 67.

7. Max Black, *Models and Metaphors* (1962; Ithaca: Cornell University Press, 1972), 36.

8. Ibid., 39.

9. "More about Metaphor," in *Metaphor and Thought*, ed. Andrew Ortony (New York: Cambridge University Press, 1979), 28.

10. *Models and Metaphors*, 44.

11. "More about Metaphor," 28.

12. *Models and Metaphors*, 39–41.

13. John Searle, "Standard Approaches to Metaphor and a Proposal for Literary Metaphor," in *Metaphor and Thought*, 93.

14. Ibid., 114.

15. Ibid.

16. Ibid.

17. Ibid., 115.

18. See Donald A. Schon, "Generative Metaphor: A Perspective on Problem-Setting in Social Policy," in *Metaphor and Thought*, 254–283.

19. Bruce Fraser, "The Interpretation of Novel Metaphors," in *Metaphor and Thought*, 172–185.

20. Paul Ricoeur addresses the problem in *The Rule of Metaphor*, trans. Robert Czerny (Toronto: University of Toronto Press, 1977), 389–395 et. passim.

21. Michael J. Reddy, "The Conduit Metaphor—A Case of Frame Conflict in Our Language about Language," in *Metaphor and Thought*, 286.

22. Ibid., 286–87.

23. Zenon W. Pylyshyn, "Metaphorical Imprecision and the 'Top-Down' Research Strategy," in *Metaphor and Thought*, 434.

24. Max Black, in *Models and Metaphors*, 27–28.

25. *The Poems of Emily Dickinson*, ed. Thomas H. Johnson, 3 vol. (1951; Cambridge: 1977) II, 506 (poem, no. 657).

26. Reddy, 296.

27. Paul Ricoeur, *The Rule of Metaphor*, 305. See also Ricouer, "The Metaphorical Process as Cognition, Imagination, and Feeling," *Critical Inquiry* V, 1 (Autumn, 1978), 153: "I suggest that we take the expression 'split reference' as our leading line in our discussion of the referential function of the metaphorical statement." Ricouer discusses the questions of dead and living metaphors and of the entropy of metaphors on pp. 280–295 of *The Rule of Metaphor*.

28. *The Rule of Metaphor*, 310.

29. Ibid., 306.

30. Ibid., 313.

31. Ibid., 319.

32. Ibid., 312.

33. Jean Amery, *At the Mind's Limits*, trans. Sidney Rosenfeld and Stella P. Rosenfeld (New York, Schocken Books, 1986), 19. Compare Emil L. Fackenheim's pinpointing of the "internal nemesis" in Heidegger's "ontic-ontological circle": "The ontic-ontological circle exists because the ontological analysis (which must claim universal valitidy) rests on an ontic fore-knowledge (which is radically particular); and it is said to be nonvicious because the ontic foreknowledge *itself* rises to universality. . . . However, Heidegger becomes less acceptable, not to say ominous, when his circle is considered in terms of the 'more concrete' historicity. In so doing we add such characteristics as *Mitsein*-in-fate (a community or, possibly, a *Volk*) and the 'recovery of inherited possibilities,' or 'tradition.' The ontological analysis of these too must claim universality; it too rests on an ontic foreknowledge: but can the 'more concrete' ontic foreknowledge too rise to universality?" Emil L. Fackenheim, *To Mend the World* (1982; New York: Schocken Books, 1989) 165.

ELEVEN: SPEECH ACTS AND THE LANGUAGE OF LITERATURE (pp. 219–243)

1. John Searle, *Speech Acts: An Essay in the Philosophy of Language* (New York: Cambridge University Press, 1969).

2. William P. Alston, *The Philosophical Quarterly* XX (April 1970), 172–179, finds "difficulties in Searle's way of drawing" the distinction between linguistic conventions and underlying rules, and between regulative rules and constitutive rules. He asserts that the distinction "collapses" in its application to promising and adds in a footnote: "I think it collapses everywhere . . ." (179).

3. Some confusion stems from Searle's indeterminacy on the question of whether rules are verbal formulations describing and/or prescribing, or whether rules are the patterns of behavior themselves. The ambiguity is apparent in the question that Searle asks: "Can one follow a rule without knowing the rule?" Or is he asking, "Can one follow a rule without knowing that

he is following a rule?" I would say that in either case the answer is, "No."
But Searle argues for an affirmative answer by citing the example of people
who speak his dialect of English. These speakers pronounce words ending in
"ng" and "nger" according to certain patterns which can then be formulated
into the rule: "Wherever the word is formed from a verb the g phoneme
does not occur; where it is not so formed the g is separately pronounced." I
would not say that Searle has "discovered a rule," but that he has managed
to give an abstract description of a certain pattern of behavior on the basis
of careful observation of many individual instances of such behavior. I will
present a counterexample. Suppose that our hypothetical chess player who
has learned to play chess without ever having the rules formulated knows
that a pawn moves in such and such a way and no other. In this instance,
does not knowing that the pawn moves in this way constitute knowing the
rule that the pawn moves in this way? Or is "knowing a rule" only "being
able to express the rule verbally?"

4. I would like to register my surprise, however, at the fact that Searle
does not include, as one of the necessary conditions of promising, some kind
of temporal commitment. Consider the following example:

A says to B: I promise to marry you.
B answers: Good. Let's get married, right now.
A replies: No, not now. Let's wait.

Five years later, with A and B still unmarried, the same dialogue is repeated.
Ten years later, B is killed in an accident, still not married to A. A will never
get the opportunity to keep his or her promise. How will we ever know
whether A intended to keep the promise or not? In other words, a promise is
meaningless when there is no indication of a time at which or before which
the promise is to be fulfilled.

5. David Holcroft, "Performatives and Statements," *Mind* LXXXIII, 329
(January 1974), makes a similar argument in drawing a contrast between
explicit and implicit performatives. "I promise to be there is an explicit performative, while "I shall be there" has been erroneously called an implicit
performative. The difference is that the former "contains a device which
makes explicit what act is being attempted by a serious literal utterance of
itself." In making this distinction, Holcroft eliminates the problem of implicit
performatives, and he is able to arrive at a very clear definition of performative itself: "Certainly, if a performative is taken to be a sentence which
contains a device which makes explicit what act is being attempted by a serious and literal utterance of itself, then much that has seemed perplexing no
longer is. In particular, there is no need to fear that every sentence will turn
out to be a performative, thus rendering futile any attempt to treat performatives as a distinctive class of sentences" (17). But while this definition is
clear, it does not solve the problem that any utterance made in the first person
and in the future tense, that is "serious and literal," amounts to a "promise," and therefore is not only an "implicit" performative, but may as well
be called an explicit one. The narrowness of Holcroft's definition minimizes

the possibility of ambiguity, but it also makes the concept thus defined relatively uninteresting. It is analogous, for example, to defining a poem as any utterance presented in iambic pentameter lines with end rhymes following a pattern of AA, BB, CC, etc. Such a definition would do away with much controversy, but also much poetry. I shall continue to take the position that the key problem is the imputation of intention. So long as we accept the concept of "serious and literal utterance," there seems to me no satisfactory way of squeezing out of the dilemma that any first person future serious literal utterance is the equivalent of a promise. We could, of course, define any linguistic act in such a way as to insist that it is only the kind of act it declares itself to be through use of "act indicator devices," so that a vow is any utterance declaring itself to be a vow, and a threat is any utterance declaring itself to be a threat, etc. But such a method of defining is obviously arbitrary and would have very little usefulness in helping us to deal with natural language as it is spoken by human beings.

6. I must emphasize, at this point, that I am in no way playing down the actual power of language. I just do not think that such power derives from "constitutive rules" of the kind we have been talking about here. The power I am thinking of, however, is the kind exercised by such utterances as the biblical Commandments, which are not so much a case of "how to do things with words," but of "how words do things to us." I cannot explain just what this power is, and I do not want to be falsely mystical or obscurantist about the matter. But it is clear that for certain people such words have had the power to penetrate to the marrow of their souls and transform them into completely different beings. That is the power that impresses me, and it does not come from a rule like "The utterance of Pr counts as the undertaking of an obligation to do A."

7. In "The Commitment Fallacy," *Noûs* V, 4 (Nov. 1971), 385–394, Les Holborow states the belief that the sincerity condition is adequate if the promisor knows "that others will hold that he is in fact obliged," revising the condition "to mean that the speaker intends that his utterance will make him responsible *in the eyes of others* for intending to do A . . . ." I believe that Holborow improves on Searle, but he still does not explain how "the eyes of others can oblige a man to keep his promise" (387–388). Holborow goes on to develop a position with which I am in substantial agreement, viz, that empirical evidence (usage) suggests that promises are not invariably considered binding by promisors. He then becomes involved in what I believe to be the false issue of "intention." Finally, Holborow states the utilitarian position "that if everyone took undue advantage of the fact that insincere promises are possible, the whole practice of making promises would collapse, and if a given man takes undue advantage, he soon loses the right to use the practice. Practices such as this, like the parity of sterling, require general public confidence" (389). I would only add to this that empirical evidence seems to indicate that the practice of making promises, like the parity of sterling, ain't what it used to be.

TWELVE: POSTMODERN OR POST-AUSCHWITZ
(pp. 244–254)

1. Vernon L. Parrington, *Main Currents of American Thought* vol. 2, *1800–1860: The Romantic Revolution in America* (1927; reprint, New York: Harcourt, Brace, & Co., 1954), 56; Harry Levin, *The Power of Darkness* (1958; New York: Knopf, 1960); G. R. Thompson, *The Gothic Imagination: Essays in Dark Romanticism* (Washington State University Press, 1974); Patrick F. Quinn, *The French Face of Edgar Poe* (Carbondale: Southern Illinois University Press, 1957); Charles Feidelson, Jr., *Symbolism and American Literature* (Chicago: University of Chicago Press, 1953); David H. Hirsch, "The Pit and the Apocalypse," *Sewanee Review* LXXVI (Autumn 1968), 632–652.

2. George Steiner, "New Movements in European Culture," *Times Literary Supplement*, Jan. 1–7, 1988, 10.

3. *Hamlet*, act 2, sc. 2, lines 292–95.

4. Allen Tate, "The Angelic Imagination," in *Essays of Four Decades* (Chicago: Swallow Press, 1959), 405.

5. Ibid., 402.

6. D. H. Lawrence, *Studies in Classic American Literature* (1923; reprint, New York: Doubleday & Company, 1953), p. 73.

7. Bruno Bettelheim, *The Informed Heart: Autonomy in a Mass Age* (Glenco, Ill.: Free Press, 1960), 238.

8. José Ortega y Gassett, *The Dehumanization of Art* (Garden City, N.Y.: Doubleday Anchor Books, n.d.), 28.

9. Harold Bloom, *New York Review of Books*, 11 Oct. 1984, 34–35.

10. Quinn, *The French Face of Edgar Poe*, 12.

11. Eric Kahler, *The Tower and the Abyss* (New York: George Braziller, 1957), 145.

12. *The French Face of Edgar Poe*, 175 ff.

13. Paul de Man, *Blindness and Insight* (New York: Oxford University Press, 1971), 70.

14. Cited in *The French Face of Edgar Poe*, 191.

15. Lawrence, *Studies*, 78.

16. *Studies in The American Renaissance*, ed. Joel Myerson (Charlottesville: The University Press of Virginia, 1987), 143–175.

17. Grace Farrell Lee, "The Quest of Arthur Gordon Pym," *Southern Literary Journal* 4 (Spring 1972), 22–33.

18. *The Narrative of Arthur Gordon Pym*, in *The Imaginary Voyages*, vol. 1, *Collected Writings of Edgar Allan Poe*, ed. Burton R. Pollin (Boston: Twayne, 1981), 205. Hereafter references to this work will appear in the text.

19. Lee, 28. Also see John Irwin, *American Hieroglyphics* (New Haven: Yale University Press, 1980), 136–140 *et passim*.

20. For both essays and details of original publication, see John P. Muller & William J. Richardson, eds., *The Purloined Poe* (Baltimore, Md.: Johns Hopkins Press, 1988).

21. "The Purloined Letter," *The Collected Works of Edgar Allan Poe*, ed. Thomas Ollive Mabbott (Cambridge, Mass.: The Belknap Press of Harvard University Press, 1978), III, 984. In a footnote, Mabbott attributes this idea to Tommaso Campanella (994–995).

22. James W. Gargano, "The Question of Poe's Narrators," (1963; reprinted in *Poe: A Collection of Critical Essays*, ed. Robert Regan (Englewood Cliffs, N.J.: Prentice Hall, 1967), 164–171.

23. Quoted in Quinn, 173.

24. *Shelley's Poetry and Prose*, ed. Donald H. Reiman (New York: W.W. Norton & Company, 1977), 133.

25. Walter Bezanson, "The Troubled Sleep of Arthur Gordon Pym," *Essays in Literary History*, ed. Rudolph Kirk and C. F. Main (New York, 1965).

26. "Diary of Johann Paul Kremer," in Jadwiga Bezwińska and Danuta Czech, eds., *KZ Auschwitz Seen by the SS* (Auschwitz: Publications of Panstwowe Muzeum w Oświęcimiu, 1972), 215–217.

27. Tate, p. 404.

CONCLUSION (pp. 255–268)

1. There were, of course, witness accounts that told of Nazi atrocities even before the war ended, such as Jan Karski's *Story of a Secret State* (Boston: Houghton Mifflin, 1944). A French translation was published in Paris in 1948 under the title *Mon Temoignage devant le monde*.

2. David Rousset, *The Other Kingdom*, trans., with an introduction, by Ramon Guthrie (New York: Reynal & Hitchcock, 1947), 13.

3. Victor Farias, *Heidegger and Nazism*, ed., with a foreword, by Joseph Margolis and Tom Rockmore; trans., Paul Burrell with the advice of Dominic Di Bernardi; German materials trans., Gabriel R. Ricci (Philadelphia: Temple University Press, 1989). Ignored by Heideggerians is the second volume of Walter Kaufmann's three-volume work, *Discovering the Mind: Nietzsche, Heidegger, and Buber* (New York: McGraw-Hill, 1980), in which Kaufmann also makes clear that the connections between Heidegger's thinking and his allegiance to Nazism are not incidental. For a discussion of the impact of Farias's book on German and French intellectuals, see the excellent foreword to the English edition.

4. For a thorough discussion of the Heideggerian antihumanist grounding of postmodernism, see Luc Ferry and Alain Renaut, *French Philosophy of the Sixties: An Essay on Antihumanism*, trans. Mary H. S. Cattani (Amherst, Mass: University of Massachusetts Press, 1990); by the same authors, *Heidegger and Modernity*, trans. Franklin Philip (Chicago: University of Chicago Press, 1990).

5. David Farrell Krell, ed., *Martin Heidegger: Basic Writings* (New York: Harper & Row, 1977), 191.

6. Ibid., 225, 226. See also bilingual French/German edition: *Lettre sur L'Humanisme*, trans., with an introduction, by Roger Munier (Paris: Aubier, Editions Montaigne, 1964), 120, 122. This edition also provides useful bibliographical background.

7. Hermann Rauschning, *The Voice of Destruction* (New York: Putnam, 1940), 80.

8. Speech to students, printed in the *Freiburger Studentenzeitung* [. . .] VIII. Semester (XV), Nr. 1, 3 November 1933, p. 1, cited in Guido Schneeberger, *Nachlese zu Heidegger*, Bern, 1962, p. 136.

9. Farias, p. 285.

10. Lion Feuchtwanger, *The Oppermanns* (New York: Carroll & Graf, 1983), 55. Subsequent page numbers of citations from this novel given in text.

11. Reporting his prison conversations with Jurgen Stroop, the SS General who supervised the suppression the Warsaw Ghetto uprising, Kazimierz Moczarski tells of Stroop's veneration for Arminius: " 'Think of it, Herr Moczarski, the Cherusci, the bravest German tribe, were my ancestors.' . . . The statue of Hermann [Arminius] the Cheruscus, which towered over the principality, was a constant reminder to Lippe's Herrenvolk [super race] of their glorious Germanic past." *Conversations With an Executioner* (Englewood Cliffs, N.J.: Prentice-Hall, 1981), 14–15.

12. Farias, 7–8.

13. Martin Buber, *Between Man and Man* (1947, first English ed.; (Beacon Press, Boston: 1961) 167.

14. Laszlo Versenyi, *Heidegger, Being, and Truth* (New Haven: Yale University Press, 1965), 193.

15. To assert the uniqueness of Hitler's death camps is not to minimize the brutality, cruelty, and barbarism of the Communist gulag. But cruel as they were, the Soviet camps were different in degree and purpose from the *KZ-Lager* system. One need only read Aleksander Wat's *My Century* alongside any Auschwitz narrative to see the differences.

16. For an analysis of the inherent racism in Enlightenment thought, see George L. Mosse, *Toward the Final Solution: A History of European Racism* (New York: Howard Fertig, 1978), 1–62.

17. Of course, this is a complex issue that has defied experts. What seems to me still the best explanation of the causes leading to Auschwitz is Erich Kahler's *The Tower and the Abyss*. For varying points of view, see George L. Mosse, *Nazism: Toward the Final Solution* (New York: Howard Fertig, 1978); Arno Mayer, *And the Heavens Did not Weep*; Raoul Hilberg, *The Destruction of the Jews*; Lucy Dawidowicz, *The War Against the Jews*; Yehuda Bauer, *A History of the Holocaust* (New York: Franklin Watts, 1982). For bibliography and discussions of German revisionist historians, see Richard J. Evans, *In Hitler's Shadow* (New York: Pantheon Books, 1989).

18. Matthew Arnold, *Culture and Anarchy* (Indianapolis & New York: The Bobbs-Merrill Company, Inc., 1971; orig. published in 1869), 108.

19. Ibid., 109.

20. Ibid., 112.

21. Friedrich Nietzsche, *The Birth of Tragedy*, trans. Francis Golffing (Garden City, N.Y.: Doubleday, 1956), 19–42 et passim.

22. Norman O. Brown, *Life Against Death: The Psychoanalytic Meaning of History* (New York: Vintage, 1961; rpt. Wesleyan Press, 1959), 174.

23. Ibid., 174, 175.

24. T. J. Reed, *Thomas Mann: The Uses of Tradition* (Oxford: Clarendon Press, 1974), 364.

25. Ibid.

26. Ibid., 365.

27. Hans Jonas expressed this in the clearest terms in his address to the Second Consultation on Hermeneutics in 1964: "My theological friends, my Christian friends—don't you see what you are dealing with? Don't you sense, if not see, the profoundly pagan character of Heidegger's thought?" *The Phenomenon of Life* (New York: Harper & Row, 1966), 248.

28. Jacques Maritain, *A Christian Looks at the Jewish Question* (New York: Longmans, Green, and Co., 1939), 12–13.

29. Ibid., 12, 18, 19.

30. Alexis de Tocqueville, *Democracy in America*, trans. Phillips Bradley (New York: Vintage Books, Random House, 1945; orig. published in 1835), I, 100.

Index

UNIVERSITY PRESS OF NEW ENGLAND publishes books under its own imprint and is the publisher for Brandeis University Press, Brown University Press, Clark University Press, University of Connecticut, Dartmouth College, Middlebury College Press, University of New Hampshire, University of Rhode Island, Tufts University, University of Vermont, and Wesleyan University Press.

Library of Congress Cataloging-in-Publication Data

Hirsch, David H.
The deconstruction of literature : criticism after Auschwitz /
David H. Hirsch.
  p.   cm.
  Includes bibliographical references (p.) and index.
  ISBN 0-87451-535-1 (cl). — ISBN 0-87451-566-1 (pa)
    1. Deconstruction.   2. Criticism.   3. Literature—History and criticism.   I. Title.
PN98.D43H57   1991
801'.95—dc20   91-50367
∞